A MONEY MANAGEMENT GUIDE FOR THE

CONTEMPORARY
*W*OMAN

MONEY,

PROPERTY

&

WEALTH

MARGARET B. SCHULMAN

PROBUS PUBLISHING COMPANY
Chicago, Illinois

Library of Congress Cataloging in Publication Data Available

ISBN 1-55738-241-7

Printed in the United States of America

BB

1   2   3   4   5   6   7   8   9   0

Contents

Preface

This is a book about ownership of assets. It covers ownership of all kinds, and it deals with assets of all kinds — securities, bank accounts, real estate, and every conceivable form of wealth, including the earnings derived from these assets. The book is intended for a wide readership. It may appeal mostly to women because, frankly, I believe ownership has not been presented to women readers in this manner. However, it will be more valuable if the men in their lives also look between the covers of the book. The premise is put forth that men and women who live together, either in or out of marriage, and who own assets should consider retaining some separate ownership (instead of joint). This is not a blanket edict, merely a proposal. Reasons are given, pro and con, for the act of *considering* such ownership as a part of overall financial and personal planning. Ownership labels are explained, and the reader is urged to give some thought to the significance of these labels before buying a home, making an investment decision, getting married, getting divorced, giving a gift, or making a will.

The book also is intended to appeal to the single woman (or man), one who is either divorced, widowed, or for any other reason unmarried. The consequences of co-ownership with an adult child, or any other adult, are discussed. Almost anyone who has accepted the popular belief that joint ownership is desirable because it avoids probate, or that all married people should hold property jointly, or that a living trust saves taxes may benefit from the exposure to a wider viewpoint that is presented in the book.

It is doubtful that everyone will accept this idea. I am merely suggesting that the reader have an open mind. My experience, particularly in connection with adult education courses I have conducted, has convinced me that women want this information. Anyone is free to look into the subject and, hopefully, will find it useful — perhaps even eye-opening.

Appendix 1 contains a brief summary of certain state laws that might be of interest to readers of this book, just to provide a quick look. If you think anything applies to you, you should see an attorney.

Appendix 2 contains samples of documents that might be used in different life situations. They are **not** intended to be taken from the text and used as such. The reader is cautioned not to feel a particular sample might be useful and to remember that any document relevant to a particular situation must be tailored specifically by one's own lawyer.

This is not a legal reference book and should not be treated as such. It is, rather, the author's point of view. The reader may find it useful as a guide to understanding ways of owning assets and as a new look at one's ownership decisions.

A word of caution to be applied throughout: a number of tremendously complex subjects are tackled in a necessarily summary fashion. To do otherwise would require many volumes. Nevertheless, the author believes the individual who is, after all, the potential user of information on these various subjects would prefer an **introduction** rather than remain naive. The presumption is that a reader interested in a particular topic will utilize the background supplied here to pursue further knowledge and will also become a better informed client when seeking professional advice.

The valuable critiques and suggestions of the following individuals are gratefully acknowledged: Stanley Kamerow, Attorney at Law, Washington, D.C.; Michael Schuster, Director of Litigation, Legal Counsel for the Elderly, AARP; David Weaver, Professor Emeritus of Law, George Washington University; Kenneth Fleishman, Certified Public Accountant, Bethesda, Maryland; Edwin Hanger, Bank Loan Officer, Washington, D.C.; William Kramer, President of Sidney Kramer Books, Inc.; and Pamela van Giessen, Editor, Probus Publishing. These individuals very kindly reviewed certain portions of the book. Any errors, of course, are my own responsibility.

Margaret B. Schulman
Washington, D.C.

Introduction

Women's Choices

Women today, at any stage of life, have *choices* about asset ownership. They may not know it. If they do know, they may not exercise their right to specify *how* they want to own their assets. Sound ridiculous? It's not. Most women simply go from Stage One — living alone for the first time away from the family home — to Stage Two — living with a friend (of either sex) and sharing an apartment — to Stage Three — *buying* the apartment with the friend — to that stage when you suddenly become aware that you have to make a decision that you did not consciously have to make before: **How do you want to take title?**

That is a phrase that might be thrust at you for the first time when you apply for a mortgage and certainly will be asked when you sit down before the settlement officer.

Let us consider the career woman who is just starting to acquire some savings. She first accumulates a small sum in an interest-bearing bank account, a certificate of deposit, or shares of a money market fund. At first, there is no problem saying, "It's mine! I own it. I can deal with it as I wish. I can use it to buy something I want, or I can save it until I have enough to make a bigger investment, maybe to buy stocks, or even save up enough to make a down payment on — yes! — a condominium apartment!" As assets grow and, maybe simultaneously, life's complications grow, the need to make *ownership decisions* grows. **Each and every woman can make those decisions** whether she is an unmarried career woman living alone, living with a friend, getting married, becoming a mother, becoming a "non-working" housewife, getting divorced, becoming a widow, getting remarried, growing old, taking care of parents or an ill husband, planning her estate, establishing a business, helping adult children, giving gifts to grand-children, and so on. It was not always so.

In the past, women were hampered by state laws that restricted their ownership rights. In addition, they were brain-washed into believing in their business acumen inadequacy, were brought up on a "father knows best" mentality, and followed a path of least resistance. Many even were guilty of the sin of inertia.

Laws have changed, and attitudes have changed, but tradition still provides guidelines that many follow. Time-worn paths seem safer. Women (as well as that other sex) want to feel comfortable with the investment decisions they make. *How* to own assets should be just as much an object of thoughtful decision as to *what* the assets should be in the first place. Knowing how to own and deal with assets eventually requires knowing what ownership labels mean.

The very idea of separate ownership also involves understanding how women acquired their insecurity. Like a psychiatrist delving into hidden paths of behavior from childhood to try and find how the adult is affected, let us go on a journey into a murky past to find out why women (some women, maybe even *most* women) are ownership-insecure. Unlike the psychiatrist's journey which only goes back to a person's early years, these travels will take us into the distant past — perhaps centuries ago.

Background

As would-be property owners, the search for our roots will take us back to Biblical days.

When land was apportioned among the tribes on the plains of the desert, women were not allowed to inherit until a claim was presented by the daughters of a patriarch who had died in the wilderness, and their claim was accepted. They only "won" this right if there were no sons. "When a man dies leaving no son, his patrimony shall pass to his daughter" (Numbers 27, *New English Bible,* 1972, Oxford University Press, New York. p. 183).

Laws in this country evolved largely from the Common Law of England, laid down by judges and early statutes. It solidified practices and concepts that remained in effect for centuries. English law provided for land (the symbol of family wealth just as it was in Biblical days) to be bequeathed to the eldest son and to his male heirs. It was a common practice in England up to the 18th and 19th centuries to restrict inheritances to "the male heirs of my body." This was called a "fee tail male," meaning that the lord who owned the estate could see that it stayed in the family by limiting its descendance to males.

Suppose there were no male heirs, only females? Then it was possible for the female to inherit. What if she did inherit a thousand acres and a castle, and then she got married? Alas, during the marriage she lost control over her wealth. Her husband took over. He took over not necessarily because he was a bully, but because the law gave him that right. The law gave husbands what was called a "life estate." He was entitled to the rents and profits of the property. He could sell his wife's interests, use them to pay his debts, or convey his life estate without the consent of his wife. Having married a wealthy woman, he also acquired, along with the wife, a legal "estate by marital right." When a woman married (with or without a great amount of wealth), she gave up her property rights. These rights were suspended during the marriage. She could look forward to widowhood to recover what had not been dissipated by her husband during the marriage.

These ancient laws and concepts were perhaps the result of a misplaced benevolence based upon the assumed male superiority in such matters. Conceived in what are now outmoded behavior patterns designed to protect women, the restrictions on inheritance by women and the restrictions on property-holding by married women have been abolished in all states. However, the attitude restraints linger. The same attitude restraints affect some unmarried women and often are still in force during the marriage.

Henrik Ibsen's Nora emerged from the doll house in which her wealthy husband had placed her with these words:

"When I was at home with father, he told me his opinion about everything, and so I had the same opinions; and if I differed from him I concealed the fact, because he would not have liked it. He called me his doll-child, and he played with me just as I used to play with my dolls. And when I came to live with you . . . I was simply transferred from father's hands into yours . . . I believe that before all else I am a reasonable human being, just as you are—or, at all events, that I must try and become one." (Henrik Ibsen, "A Doll's House" Act III. Published in 1879).

Unlike Nora, women of today not only have the choice of working and owning assets they acquired through their labors in the workplace but in many cases *must* work in order to achieve the desired living standard. In Nora's day, work was for the very poor or hard-pressed women who labored as servants or as factory workers. Very few careers were open to them. How did women acquire wealth? The answer is: with great difficulty. Restrictions on inheritance, male dominance in the household, and the impermissibility of learning a profession or having a job status equal to a man's kept women where husbands wanted them — in the house, where the services of a devoted child-bearing, hard-working housewife by his side was every man's due, or else she was an ornament to be dressed up and shown off, like Nora. Sharing wealth during marriage was unthinkable. At least, it was in England and in the U.S. states that adopted the English Common Law as the basis of their marital property laws.

In certain western states of this country, however, there was a glimmer of fairness when it came to sharing during a marriage. Those are the community property states, where laws were influenced by French and Spanish settlers. The theory of community property is that each spouse has an equal interest in the property and earnings acquired during the marriage. For example, in a community property state, even tips given to a married waitperson (as they are called today) are community property.

Napoleon was famous for having established a very enlightened civil code in France. This was brought to Louisiana by French settlers.

There are seven other states that have adopted versions of the community property law inherited from the Spanish and French. These states are: Arizona, California, Idaho, Nevada, New Mexico, Texas, and Washington; the jurisdiction of Puerto Rico also follows community property law, and Wisconsin recently adopted a system of community property.

Although the Spanish antecedents of community property states appeared to be forward-thinking as early as the Middle Ages by establishing community sharing for marital property, this custom was later changed by a system of rules established for classifying separate and community property. "Separate" meant property brought into a marriage. These rules were designed for the only Spaniards who had substantial property — the landed gentry. The noble family lived on the land and obtained wealth from the land, usually by the labor of others or by rental to others. The Spanish marital property system was designed to keep the wealthy family estate intact so that it would remain in the family and pass along from generation to generation by means of the male bloodline. (Sound familiar?) The family wealth and estate was bequeathed to the first-born son. If that son died childless, half of the estate would go to a brother, half to other male relatives. There was an elaborate system of succession — through the sons. Noblemen who did not have land often *acquired wealth* by means of "booty," which was in the form of gifts from the king to the officer in appreciation of his services. Strict community property concepts would have classified these gifts (payments), like today's tips, as belonging to the married couple. However, such gifts were classified as separate, enabling the officer to buy real estate which could then remain in his bloodline.

One similarity between the French/Spanish community property concepts and the English common law concepts was that both systems designated the husband as the manager of marital property. He was in charge! If you think this is an antiquated idea, think again.

The old presumption that the husband was the operator of a family business owned by a married couple led to an unfair result that the Social Security Administration finally took steps to correct in 1982 because of a California lawsuit. A wife had worked for years in the family business but received no credit toward Social Security records of earnings. After all, he was presumed to be the operator, and he received all the credits toward his Social Security account. The new rule was brought to the attention of recipients by means of an enclosure with Social Security checks that were issued March 1982. This was a red alert to wives who had worked side by side with husbands in a family business but received no Social Security credits because he was presumed to be the operator!

The reader is cautioned that much of the above discussion is subject to the valid criticism that it is greatly oversimplified. Of course, it is not possible to compress thousands of years of history into a few paragraphs and there is a hazard of rushing to a desired conclusion without establishing a proper background. It is safe to say, though, that the presumptions of male dominance and control over family wealth no longer exist in a legal sense. However, customary behavior in a family setting still seems to lean toward reliance on the father/husband as the authoritative member. The wife who does not establish habits of separating earnings from **her** investment property but customarily puts such earnings into **their** joint account may find that this method of accruing earnings will merit another look.

There is supposedly is a "rethinking" from time to time. Some contemporary writers worry that women are throwing in the towel and going back to their shrinking violet days. In writing about the feminism movement, columnist Richard Cohen had this to say:

"What's supposed to be shocking about the alleged counterrevolution is that the faded-away feminists are not the followers of Phyllis Schlafly but younger women—beneficiaries of everything feminism has to offer. They are the ones who are reportedly rejecting feminism, finding it ideologically strident—threatening both to themselves and to the men who mean so much to them. Some of these younger women say they simply prefer more traditional life styles. They want men to pay for dates, want to opt out of careers and raise kids—want some of the things their mothers had.

"But this is no defeat for feminism. After all, what these women are really saying is that now they have the freedom to make those choices. This is a luxury their mothers did not have. When younger women either question or reject feminism, they are simply acknowledging what it has done for them. They can choose to have a career or not, work full time or part time, take their husband's last name or keep their own . . . These choices were simply unavailable until quite recently . . ." (©*The Washington Post*), Oct. 26, 1982).

What we are dealing with here is a very complex subject. There is more to understanding property ownership than the effect of psychological attitudes and behavior patterns. **Who** owns **what** covers the whole gamut of wealth and wealth-building, human behavior, family relationships, and progression through life's stages. Learning what different types of ownership mean is a necessary prerequisite to making decisions as to ownership of your assets.

We've heard a lot about **choices** women have (or do not have) in today's world. There is one **pro-choice** movement we can all support; "making choices about property ownership" is its name.

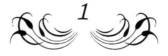

Credit

Women and Credit

It is all very good and well to talk about choices, separate ownership, confidence in your business ability, and all the rest. Unfortunately, a quick deflation can occur if you go to the bank to apply for a mortgage on a small condominium and your application is denied. How can that be? You have a good job, and the loan will be secured by the real estate, so the bank is protected. Why can't you borrow? You cannot be discriminated against in the granting of credit just because you are a woman. (The answer is, however, you may be discriminated against in the granting of credit just because you are a woman.)

Of course, legally, the bank cannot refuse you credit for any of the "wrong" reasons. The bank cannot inquire about your childbearing or birth control practices or throw into the hopper its fears that you might stop working to have a child; a creditor cannot refuse to consider alimony as income (because of its fears that the payments might stop); the creditor cannot refuse to grant credit because you have retained your maiden name after marriage; a creditor cannot refuse credit because your income is part-time if paid to you regularly; and so on. The proscriptions against discrimination have been spelled out in the Equal Credit Opportunity Act, enacted in 1975. How can it happen, then, that your application for credit is denied?

Lenders may not deny credit for reasons that would leave them open to a claim of discrimination, but they can deny credit for the "right" reason: your credit-worthiness, regardless of sex. Subtly, within that camouflage, it is possible that your sex is a factor. Only if you could show that you were denied at the same time credit was granted to *your exact counterpart* as to job, reliability, income, etc. *but male*, could you claim discrimination. It is best to see what will make you credit-worthy in the eyes of the lender.

How to Establish a Credit History

The first thing is to have had and **paid promptly** charge credit cards. If you have a regular income, you should be able to acquire one or two charge accounts — either at your local favorite department store, or for oil and gas, or from one of the majors: American Express, Visa, Mastercard, etc. The important point is to establish a credit history for a period of time, perhaps a year or more, showing prompt payment of each month's required amount. The credit issuer is happy to continue to extend credit on that charge, meanwhile piling up interest charges on the unpaid balance, but do not let unpaid balances become a mountain of debt.

Let a car be your first big credit purchase. With the price of cars today, very few people can buy without financing the purchase. If you go to a bank for a consumer credit loan on the car, you will have made a beginning. Pay the monthly amount promptly. It should be easier to get a car loan than a mortgage on real estate because the sum involved is less, and it is easier for the bank to get back the money loaned if you default (because, of course, the amount loaned is less than the value of the car, even used). The other way to finance the purchase is through the dealer's own financing program. With a proper record of employment, this is probably the easiest and quickest way to get credit for the purchase of the car. After all, automobile sales staff and dealers are anxious to sell cars and no doubt have the cost of possible repossessing factored into the price or the interest charges on the loan.

As a neophyte borrower, you must start somewhere. That first application is a little like your first job application: "State your experience." You haven't any. Every first-time applicant has faced that Catch-22 and wondered if her years as a baby-sitter in high school or a volunteer activities coordinator in college would qualify as "experience." Later in life, other problems are faced: you are married and want to establish credit in your own name (because you read somewhere it would be a good idea); you are divorced and have a bad credit history because you purchased property jointly with your ex-husband, and he defaulted on the mortgage payments; you recently returned to the work-force after taking time out for child-raising, and you want to establish your own credit; you want to go into business as a caterer (you did this in your own kitchen and now want to branch out); or you want to borrow on your own, not just your husband's, reliability as a good credit risk.

Beware of pitfalls. Knowledge of local and state laws also is important, as in this scenario. Emily had been married for 39 years in a stable marriage with no thought of divorce or separation. Thoughts did occur to the couple, however, of separating their property ownership because the lawyer they consulted recently advised it in order to do some proper estate planning (with tax saving techniques). Along with the idea of separate property owned by her (with which she was delighted), she decided to try her wings in the investment real estate market. With assets of her own on her "net worth" statement and income from those assets, she applied for a mortgage after paying a 20 percent down payment on a rental condominium. Amount of the mortgage she requested: $40,000. Amount of her assets: $300,000. Why, then, was her mortgage application denied? It was denied because in the state where the real estate was located, dower laws are on the statute books.

The doctrine of dower is a holdover from our ancient legal past. As observed today in the states that have not abolished dower altogether, it is a protection for either husband or wife with regard to real estate. A married woman or man has the right to own property in her or his own name, but lenders always require the other spouse to sign the mortgage. By signing the mortgage loan agreement, the spouse who is not buying the property and is not going to own it agrees to give up his or her dower right. Without the signature of both spouses, the mortgage lender would be unable to sell the property if it became necessary (if Emily defaults on the mortgage).

Dower will be discussed more fully in the ensuing pages of this book. For now, rest assured that this mysterious linking of Emily with her husband is not a form of discrimination against her as a woman, housewife, or whatever. She can still be the sole owner. If she sells the condominium at a later date, she can convey good title provided her spouse, if alive, signs the deed also to the new owner. If Emily is a widow at that time, she can convey the title alone because her husband's dower right has been extinguished with his death.

There is a method of financing a real estate purchase that is open to anyone and that might appeal to the buyer in the shoes of the first-time young woman or the more mature long-time wife — or anyone. That method is to finance through your seller. There are advantages in this; you do not have to apply to a bank for a mortgage. Your seller, if that person is a careful business person, will still require a financial statement from you and all the legal documents that the bank would require. If you are married, the seller will still want your husband's name on the mortgage loan, but the seller as part of the deal may agree to forego "points." Points are the usual percentages charged by a mortgage lender for making the loan, typically one, two, or three percentage points of the amount of the loan.

A Co-Signer

It is possible that your mortgage lender, either bank, investment company, or private individual, will want additional assurance that the loan will be paid — and will not consider your financial statement to be strong enough. The lender wants your parent (if you are young and on your first buying venture) to co-sign the note. That should not disturb you. It is the same kind of assurance the lender might ask if the applicant is a male instead of a female. Someone who has had a background of paying a mortgage note (as an older person might have) gives the bank a more secure feeling. No one can deny that banks need a "secure feeling" in today's climate. One day you will be that older person who will co-sign for your child. The fact remains that if you make the mortgage payments as they come due and meet your obligations, you, not your parent, will be establishing a credit record.

Sharing the Debt

What about buying the property with your roommate? Suppose you can't swing the down payment alone, but by teaming up with a roommate, together you can convince the bank that you are reliable mortgagors. That's a whole new ballgame, and you will want to know more of what this involves. It may be that after peeking into the next chapter you will realize that this step should be reserved for a more permanent move in your life — perhaps teaming up with a future spouse — or planning to live together indefinitely.

Buying the condominium alone is a straight-forward move. Establish credit alone, take title alone, and life will be much simpler. Joining forces with someone for economic reasons only may lead to complications you never contemplated. It can be done, of course, but first learn the hows and whys and, perhaps, the why-nots.

Title

Title and Ownership

"Ah, at last," you are saying, "Now we are getting to the 'nitty-gritty.' That's why I bought this book!" Well, hopefully, what follows will help (and not confuse you). Frankly, though, if you are confused, you have lots of company — even among attorneys, other than real estate and tax specialists. Ask a married couple how they own their home, and they usually will reply, "Jointly." What does that mean? "It means," they answer, "if one of us dies, the other inherits the home. That is what we both want." Don't drop it there. Ask them, "What does the deed say?" They probably will be stumped and will not have the slightest idea what the language is in the deed. Here are some samples of types of language in a deed:

(1) To Frank Adams and Freda Adams, husband and wife, as Tenants by the Entireties.

(2) To Jane and John Black, husband and wife, as Joint Tenants with Right of Survivorship.

(3) To Mary Cheese and Melvin Domino, husband and wife, as Joint Tenants.

(4) To Lana Edam and Lennie Fox, as Tenants in Common.

Here are some explanations:

(I) To Frank Adams and Freda Adams, *husband and wife,* as *Tenants by the Entireties.* In this deed, Frank and Freda have taken title as tenants by the entireties, a form of ownership that applies only to a husband and wife legally married. Not every state still recognizes tenancies by the entireties. If your state does recognize this form of ownership, you may "take title" in this fashion. You do not have to use this form of ownership. There are special characteristics with this type of ownership. If you own property in this manner, it cannot be owned separately unless you agree to sever the tenancy by the entireties. The other methods of severance are by divorce or by death of one of the spouses.

If you and your husband own your home (or any other property) in this manner, a creditor cannot come waiving a judgment and try to collect by attaching your property. (Of course, you are both liable for a joint debt.) Suppose your husband has been sued in a civil suit, and the plaintiff won. While you are alive, the creditor cannot collect by placing a lien on that jointly held property, because the only methods of severance are agreement of the spouses, divorce, or death. If your husband dies while the judgment is outstanding, the creditor is out of luck. At the moment of your husband's death, *you* became the owner of the entire property. The creditor cannot now attach the property because it is yours and the debt was your husband's. *Your* property is not liable for *his* debt. Many married people like this aspect of ownership. Caveat: some states have abolished this form of property ownership for the very reason that it is a deterrent to satisfaction of debts and restricts creditors' rights.

(2) To Jane and John Black, *husband and wife*, as *Joint Tenants with Right of Survivorship.* In this form of property holding by husband and wife, the ability of creditors to reach the property is not avoided. Jane and John are in the same position as any two people who hold property jointly, whether married or not. The property can be severed by a creditor even against the wishes of the spouses, just as property jointly held by non-married people can be severed. The legal effect of such a severance (by a court action) is that the two former joint tenants now become tenants in common, and each one is responsible for his or her debts.

There is, however, a major difference between Jane and John, and non-marrieds who hold property jointly. It has to do with taxes. The estate tax effect (if estate taxes apply) is that Jane or John will owe no federal estate taxes on the death of one of them. There is also an income tax effect having to do with the basis either would take in case of inheritance. This will be covered later under tax discussions. As to estate taxes, when any two (or more) people own property jointly and they are not married, the Treasury levies an estate tax (if the amount of the total estate requires such a tax) as if the first joint owner to die was the owner of the entire property so held. Then it is up to the surviving joint owner to come forward and prove that he/she helped pay for the property and that it did not belong wholly to the joint owner who died first.

(3) To Mary Cheese and Melvin Domino, *husband and wife*, as *Joint Tenants*. Mary Cheese and Melvin Domino are married but do not have the same last name because she chose to retain her unmarried (or professional name). Deeds these days have to be very specific in naming husband and wife because spouses no longer routinely have the same last name. Mary and Melvin also have listed themselves just as "joint tenants." In some states, joint tenancy between husband and wife automatically means the same thing as "tenants by the entireties." In such case, Mary and Melvin will own the property in exactly the same way as Frank and Freda in (1) and Jane and John Black in (2). If the state law does not still recognize the "tenancy by the entirety" type of ownership, Mary and Melvin will be like any other joint tenants who are not married to each other. The one thing common to ownership by any of these couples is that there is a "right of survivorship" built in to the deed. If one owner dies, the other becomes the owner of the property "by right of survivorship."

(4) To Lana Edam and Lennie Fox, as *Tenants in Common*. Lana and Lennie are not married but have bought a condominium together, and have chosen to take title as "tenants in common," which is entirely different from other forms of cotenancy. Confused? Are you wondering, "Is that 'joint' ownership, too?"

The answer is that it is a type of co-ownership. It is a way for two (or more) people to own real estate (which is not easily divisible into slices like a pizza) to own property jointly but as tenants in common. This means that each owns an undivided share of the whole. Of course, they could have bought small individual pizzas (pizza restaurants are very accommodating), and each then would have been the owner of a small whole pizza. Splitting a big pizza between two buyers (eaters) means that each gets one half. Undeniably, when gobbled up, each has consumed one half.

Real estate is less clear cut. Lennie and Lana are looking at a condominium consisting of one bedroom, living room, dining area, kitchen, and bathroom. When Lana and Lennie buy it, they will not each own separate rooms but one half of the whole apartment. If they go their separate ways after a period of living together, they will have to come to an agreement as to how to handle the split of the ownership. This will be discussed more fully in Chapter 4. You can see, though, that two women who *rent* together might be better off not to *buy* together. In fact, it might be simpler if Lana and Lennie had not bought the condo together. In their case, however, we can assume that they had intended it to be a permanent relationship or eventual marriage — a different ballgame altogether.

As a practical matter, you don't really have to worry about labeling the ownership as "tenants in common." The reason is in most states where owners are listed by name only, there is a presumption that they are owners as tenants in common. Any other type of ownership should be spelled out specifically. The deed always should state that the grantees (buyers) are *joint tenants and not tenants in common*. If the buyers are married and want to take title as joint tenants, the deed should state specifically that the grantees are *joint tenants and not tenants in common or by the entireties*. This avoids uncertainty as to what the buyers really wish.

Because there is difference of opinion as to the legal effect of a deed to a husband and wife that describes the grantees merely as joint tenants, it clarifies their ownership status if they state whether or not they wish to own as tenants by the entireties, not merely as joint tenants. Caveat: in a state that automatically gives *"entireties"* status to a joint tenancy by husband and wife, it would take a real estate attorney to advise the couple on the law of that state. The significant feature of tenancy in common ownership is that there is *no built-in survivorship*.

What about property that is transferred to new owners by will? Sally and Betty, sisters, inherited a share of the condominium their grandmother had lived in until her death. Grandmother had executed a will giving all of her estate to her children and any grandchildren who survived their parent. Sally and Betty take the share of their late mother. There were five other owners who were Grandmother's children. Therefore, Sally and Betty became owners of a one-sixth share of the whole. Sally and Betty and all of the other takers under Grandmother's will are tenants in common with each other. This happens. Things sometimes get pretty sticky if all of these heirs do not get along with one another, or if there is merely disagreement about management or sale of the property. They become forced partners in a real estate venture that they might not have undertaken except for the inheritance. There are ways to handle this. They might enter into a formal agreement as partners; one might buy the share of another; or there might be a partition action filed in a court.

Does all of this title designation just relate to real estate? Unfortunately for your state of mind, the answer is "No." Although we are used to thinking that the term "property" means "real property," that is just common usage. "Property" means everything we own. The significant feature of property is ownership. You may own property outright, or you may own an "interest" in a piece of property. For example, joint owners each own a "survivorship interest" in the whole property. During the period of joint ownership, there are many pro and con features (right to some income, for example, but inability to control the whole property). Tenants in common each own an outright share of the whole property. Furthermore, the term "property" includes real property and personal property. Real property generally refers to land and buildings and things permanently attached to them. In a legal sense, personal property is everything else, essentially. Even investment assets are considered personal property, such as your stock certificate. To complicate things further, you should know that personal property may be "tangible" (as your car) or "intangible" (your pension rights).

Of course, you don't have to "title" all of your possessions, but you do "title" your stock certificate. The way you list the ownership indicates the way you *choose* to own it. Every state has laws spelling out that state's attitude toward ownership designations. Some states, for example, do not recognize tenancies by the entirety in personal property, just in real property. In other states, tenancies by the entirety are recognized in personal as well as in real property. In almost all states, there is statutory language that makes it incumbent on the individuals involved to specify joint ownership of either real or personal property. If not specified, the ownership is as tenants in common. For example, you may have seen this label on a bond: "Joan Johnson and James Johnson, JTRS, Joint Tenants with Right of Survivorship and not as Tenants in Common." Maybe it puzzled you. Now you know what it means.

What about community property states? In some of these states, a husband and wife may hold property as joint tenants or tenants in common or as community property. Also, either a husband or wife (or both) may have separate property. In California, for example, an inventory of the separate *personal* property of either spouse may be recorded in the office of the county recorder in the county where the parties reside, and such a record is evidence of the title of such property. The real property ownership would be evidenced by the deed, which usually is recorded anyway in order to protect third parties in relying on record title. A discussion of the evidence of ownership by people who are not married to each other is not applicable here because community property only refers to a property-holding system for marrieds.

Ownership of Securities

What would you do with an inheritance of $10,000, $20,000, or $100,000? Depending on your degree of investment expertise and your pre-inheritance wealth, you probably would discuss your sudden windfall with a broker and get that person's advice about how to invest the money. Don and Mary did just that. Mary inherited $100,000 from an aged, childless aunt, her mother's beloved oldest sister who had been a wealthy lady and had never married. Mary and Don are not married but are planning to get married in six months. Don is active in his family's business and is making a good salary. Mary is a clinical psychologist in private practice. They decide to go to the broker's office together. Both are interested in learning how to invest and realize having a nest-egg this big at the beginning of their marriage is unusual for a young couple. They are determined to invest it wisely.

The broker, more correctly called "investment adviser," is John Smart. He is a former professor of economics at Middletown University, they learn, and is president of an investment and economic consulting firm, Smart Associates. He tells Don and Mary that he is an "asset allocator." He believes a portfolio should be split equally among stocks and bonds, Treasury notes, cash, and real estate. He recommends that the money be split into five equal segments, 20 percent (in this case, $20,000) into domestic stocks, and additional equal $20,000 amounts in bonds of utility companies, three-year Treasury notes, money market funds, and real estate. Of course, "real estate" is meant to imply ownership of shares in real estate investment trusts or limited partnership interests or real estate-related stocks. Don and Mary try to digest all of this and decide to mull it over before making a decision.

Look for a moment at another couple planning their first investment. Armed with $10,000 in savings made up of a small inheritance and a bank certificate of deposit, Jane and Joe visit a firm and are channeled to a broker who handles investors with smaller amounts to invest. Jane and Joe are married. The inherited money, $5,000, is Joe's. The certificate of deposit is in their joint bank account and is made up of earnings from their respective jobs. Investor adviser No. 2, Mr. Too, recommends putting $3,000 into a bond fund, $2,000 into a growth stock fund, $2,000 into a money market fund, and $3,000 into a real estate investment trust. Mr. Too does not rely on economic and political forecasts. Instead, he uses a computer to collect fundamental earnings and dividends forecasts from analysts. Jane and Joe open a joint brokerage account and apply all of the $10,000 as recommended by Mr. Too.

Jane's mother, a recent widow, with a nest egg of $20,000 to invest, seeks out a broker recommended by her friend, a widow who has had a bit more experience investing on her own. Mr. Playit Safe prefers putting his "widows and orphans" into long-term Treasuries and government funds. Mrs. Jane's mom wants to share her account with Jane, and opens a joint brokerage account. She has all the securities listed: JTRS. Mr. Safe doesn't argue. In fact, he does not say one word about how the account and securities in the account should be owned. Neither did Mr. Smart or Mr. Too.

These knowledgeable advisers use their technical expertise in advising clients about the best investments for certain life situations. Their advice may be excellent and appropriate. Very often, however, the financial planner or investment adviser fails to deal with the subject of naming the *ownership* of the investments. In each of the situations described, **how** these investors label the ownership of their assets may have an effect they had not considered on their overall planning. It is desirable for everyone, experienced investor or neophyte, to know the significance of ownership of assets.

It is all too easy to rely on the "expertise" of a professional adviser and assume that he or she, in advising *what* to purchase as an investment, is also an "expert" on *how* to acquire the investment. Unfortunately, you must make your own decision. Here are some guidelines.

When two people buy securities as joint owners, each loses control over the whole asset. If you are married, for example, you can have an understanding with your broker (while, of course, adhering to rules of the brokerage firm) that one of the two spouses can place orders to buy or sell with the broker in the joint account. There also should be an understanding between the spouses that this is an acceptable way to manage that particular asset or group of assets. If they do not agree, there could be conflict. Whether or not there is compatibility and cooperation in that management is up to the married couple.

In a joint husband and wife account, there is no question of gift taxes even if only one puts up the money because there is no such transfer tax between spouses. When one person establishes a joint account with a broker but titles the account joint with another and buys securities in that account, a gift occurs at the moment of purchase. This happens quite often between an elderly parent and adult child, because the parent wants to avoid probate and feels this is a simple way to transfer assets on death. What people do not consider, however, and *what the broker won't tell them*, is that it is possible that a gift tax return should be filed documenting this gift. Some brokers perhaps are keyed into gift tax consequences but not all. So, what should the investor do? Ask. If the amount being invested in the joint account would result in a gift over $10,000 to the other joint name on the security, either the broker, your accountant, or your lawyer should know of the need to file such a tax return. Outside professional advice might cost something. You could say you read about it here. Of course, if it suits you to just keep your securities in your own name, do so. You always can make a gift separately to your beloved son or daughter or daughter-in-law or to anyone. If the value of the gift is over $10,000, a gift tax return must be filed. The same thing is true if the co-owners are an adult and a minor child. If you are burning to give away money and can't wait to learn about $10,000 gifts, you can peek ahead to gift-giving, p. 60.

What about an account in "street" name? A "street" name usually is used to deal on margin or to facilitate trading. If you establish such an account with your funds but label the account "joint" for yourself and another person, and the securities are still registered in the name of the broker, you have not made a gift to the other person. The gift will occur when the other person sells a security and withdraws the funds. An account in a street name is like a joint bank account set up by one person.

Bank Accounts

First of all, you should know something about the effect of your state's laws on joint ownership. In some states, for example, laws spell out the legal consequences of joint bank accounts. Other states allow the deposit agreement with the bank to define the rights of the joint holders of the account. In most instances, the account will provide for payment to and allow withdrawals by any of the joint owners of the account. Upon the death of one of the joint owners (proof by means of a death certificate), the bank usually will reregister the account in the names of the survivor or survivors.

In some instances, a joint account may be a "convenience account." In such cases, one person deposits all the funds and has the sole right to them while alive. The other joint owner acts only as "agent" for the depositor of the funds. Some elderly people engage in this type of "agency" with another adult or with an adult child, reasoning that this is a simple way to satisfy that gnawing question, "Who will take the money out and pay bills if I am incapacitated?" The unintended consequence may be that if the deposit agreement and local law unrelentingly provide that the survivor (a son, for example) is the owner upon the death of the depositor (a parent), a less conveniently located daughter living across the country will be left out in the cold. An equally effective way to provide for an agent to act in case of emergency is to execute a "power of attorney." Most banks have a simple form for this, but it will be restricted to use with a specific bank account.

There is an unexpected result of establishing a joint bank account with another if you put **all** of the money into the account. You are leaving the possibility open for the other signor on the account to withdraw some or all of the funds. When a noncontributing joint owner withdraws funds, a gift occurs at that point in time. If you allow the co-signor to withdraw funds, it can be held that you legally made a gift at that time. Of course, you can come forward and prove that you never *intended* to make such a gift. You might argue that you created the joint bank account for convenience only or to avoid probate on that particular asset. The latter estate planning action often occurs when a grandmother, for example, establishes a joint bank account (or, let's say, a certificate of deposit at her bank) in her name and that of grandson Michael. She wants Michael to get the account automatically on her death. Meanwhile she keeps the income and duly reports it on her income tax return. True, it will go to Michael without the hassle of probate if Grandmother dies while co-owning the account, but if Grandmother has a taxable estate, the account's value will be included among her assets. The reason for this result is that it was not a present gift of the asset *during her lifetime* but a *testamentary gift* only (one that occurs at the death of the donor).

Intent as a Factor

There are traps for the unwary. A recent court decision involved a set of facts in which a resident of state Y asked his landlady if she would mind being a co-tenant with him on his bank account for the sole purpose of withdrawing money for him if he became ill or incapacitated, since he had no relatives or close friends. (Obviously, he trusted the landlady.) After he had changed the bank account to read "Joe Smith and Mary Bell, JTRS," Mary Bell, the landlady, had the temerity and lack of consideration to contract an illness and die. The state Y inheritance tax law demanded a tax on assets passing to a survivor of joint tenancy, regardless of which of the prior joint tenants had put up the money. Alas, Joe Smith had to pay a tax on his own money when he became the surviving joint tenant. Federal law also would have required that he pay federal estate taxes (if any were incurred) because of its rule that the first joint owner to die is presumed to be the owner. In the latter situation, Joe easily could have proved that he provided the total "contribution" to the bank account monies. At the local level, however, Joe's attorney must have earned a pretty penny while helping him prove that he *did not intend* to give Mary Bell a real survivorship interest.

There are situations in which what one "intended" can be the decisive factor, but in such situations, as in the case above, it might take a lawsuit to prove a certain intent, or lack of intent. The Superior Court of D.C., Tax Division, was more sympathetic to the cause of the tax payer in a case decided in 1979 on similar facts to the fictitious one described. That court held that proof of lack of intention to make a gift of the survivorship interest would be controlling. (*Novak* v. *D.C.,* CCH Inheritance, Estate and Gift Tax Reporter, 21027, Feb. 13, 1979).

In most states, there is a way in which one co-tenant acting alone can sever the joint tenancy. Assume that Bill and Sam, brothers, own property as joint tenants with right of survivorship. Bill decides that this is a poor arrangement and that he no longer wants his co-tenant to "inherit" from him. Furthermore, he wants to sell his share, which, as was pointed out earlier, merely represents a "survivorship interest." The only way this can be done amicably is to have Sam join in the transfer. Sam refuses. Bill files an action in court requesting partition. In order to avoid having a new potential "heir" step into Bill's shoes, the court action and sale to buyer X by one JTRS owner (Bill) immediately *severs* the joint tenancy and turns it into a *tenancy in common.*

Tenancy in common essentially removes the *survivorship feature* from joint ownership. Each of two tenants in common owns a separate portion, and each may will, convey, give, and exercise unrestricted control over his portion, just as in sole ownership. Where state law allows one joint tenant to sever the joint tenancy by acting alone, a creditor with a judgment against one joint tenant *may* attach that joint tenant's interest to satisfy the judgment. The theory behind this seemingly impossible act is that since the joint tenant can sell and convey away his interest because such a sale and transfer will convert the joint tenancy into a tenancy in common, then *so can his judgment creditor.*

Javier was here! Sorry about writing in this Book) I'm Just trying But, to leave my mark. Because I'm Just very cool, Super cool 1994

3

Creditor's Rights

Title and Lawsuits

What in the world could be the connection between how you hold title to property and the hazard of potential litigation? Unfortunately, there are many lawsuits filed in this litigious society. Not all are meritorious, nor are the demands for damage awards always reasonable. It is possible that the way in which a potential defendant holds title to property could be a deterrent to a lawsuit. The message could go out to a prospective plaintiff that it would do no good to sue because the defendant's property is unreachable in the event of a verdict for the plaintiff. An empty judgment with no assets to attach does not reward the plaintiff. How would this work?

The Married Defendant

In general, a creditor may obtain a court judgment and endeavor to place a lien or attachment on the property of a married person if he or she holds it as a joint tenant with a spouse in a state that recognizes tenancies by the entireties. However, the creditor may have to wait and hope that the spouse who is liable on the debt outlives the spouse who is not liable. If the judgment debtor dies before the spouse, the judgment creditor can forget about collecting. Suppose that Dr. and Mrs. A live in a state recognizing tenancies by the entireties, and suppose that all of their property is held in this manner (see Figure 3.1). Dr. A has been the defendant in a malpractice lawsuit attempting to claim damages of $10 million. The judgment against him is for $3 million, but Dr. A's liability insurance stops at $2 million. He still owes $1 million on the judgment, but all of his property is tied up with his wife's in tenancies by the entireties. If the wife dies, Dr. A becomes the sole owner of their joint tenancy property. The creditor can then attach the property to satisfy his claim. Alas, poor Dr. A. However, if Dr. A dies and his wife is the survivor, the creditor's claim is extinguished as to that property. Mrs. A takes possession and control of the property free of the lien and the claim. Poor judgment creditor.

This is not a fictitious scenario. Doctors today are plagued with astronomical malpractice claims. Some potential malpractice plaintiffs or some claimants' appetites for million-dollar-plus damage claims might, just might, be deterred by an awareness that the form of ownership of the defendant's property will present an obstacle to collection.

Suppose that a doctor faces a malpractice lawsuit and then suddenly decides to transfer his separately owned property into joint ownership with his wife or into her separate ownership. That would be an action to defraud potential creditors and would be voidable. Suppose instead that the couple always has retained assets in separate ownership. Here is how that might be useful in thwarting would-be litigants; if the doctor's creditors try to take possession of his jointly owned property, as we have seen, they probably would be unsuccessful so long as the doctor's wife is alive. The creditors gamble that one day she will predecease the doctor and that he then will become owner of the entire property (by his survivorship interest) so that it will all be reachable to satisfy the judgment lien. The patience of the creditors would be rewarded. In some states, a judgment lien may remain viable for as long as twenty years. How, then, would separate ownership work? Because no one knows how the gamble on survivorship will be resolved (until it is), owning property separately enables the husband and wife to assure themselves that at least some of their assets (those owned by the non-sued party) are insulated totally from attack by a judgment creditor.

High-income professionals are indeed targets. In fact, this is the motivating force behind their purchase of "umbrella" liability insurance policies and behind the promotion of such policies by insurance companies. The argument is unassailable: "You, Dr. (lawyer, corporate president, big-name athlete, actor, etc.), are a target. Let your car touch another's; let your teen-age driver have an altercation with another driver; let your dog bite a passerby; let a passenger on your boat fall into the water and get hurt, and you might be slapped with a huge lawsuit. Protect

Figure 3.1   Status of State Laws as to Common Law Marriages, Dower, Curtesy, Recognition of Tenancy by the Entireties, and Community Property

	Common Law Marriages Recognized	Curtesy Abolished	Dower Abolished	Tenancies by the Entireties Recognized	Community Property State
Alabama	X	X	X		
Alaska		X	X	X^1	
Arizona		X	X		X
Arkansas		X^2		X	
California		X	X		X
Colorado	X	X	X		
Connecticut		X	X		
Delaware		X	X	X	
Florida		X	X	X	
Georgia	X	X	X		
Hawaii				X	
Idaho	X	X	X		X
Illinois		X	X		
Indiana		X	X	X	
Iowa	X	X	X		
Kansas	X	X	X		
Kentucky				X	
Louisiana		X	X		X
Maine		X	X		
Maryland		X	X	X	
Massachusetts		X^2		X	
Michigan		X		X	
Minnesota		X	X		
Mississippi		X	X	X	
Missouri		X	X	X	
Montana	X	X	X		
Nebraska		X	X		
Nevada		X	X		X

(table continues)

Figure 3.1   Status of State Laws as to Common Law Marriages, Dower, Curtesy, Recognition of Tenancy by the Entireties, and Community Property (continued)

	Common Law Marriages Recognized	Curtesy Abolished	Dower Abolished	Tenancies by the Entireties Recognized	Community Property State
New Hampshire		X	X		
New Jersey		X	X	X	
New Mexico		X	X		X
New York		X	X	X^1	
North Carolina		X	X	X^1	
North Dakota		X	X		
Ohio	X	X^2		X^1	
Oklahoma		X	X	X	
Oregon		X	X	X^1	
Pennsylvania	X			X	
Rhode Island	X	X	X	X	
South Carolina	X	X	X		
South Dakota		X	X		
Tennessee		X	X	X	
Texas	X	X	X		X
Utah	X	X	X		
Vermont				X	
Virginia		X	X	X	
Washington		X	X	X	X
West Virginia		X^2			
Wisconsin		X	X		
Wyoming		X	X	X	
Dist. of Columbia	X	X^2		X	
Puerto Rico		X	X		X
Virgin Islands		X	X	X^1	

1. In real property.
2. Dower applies to both spouses.

yourself with this dandy policy with lots of coverage." These arguments make sense. At the same time, attending to your form of property ownership also makes sense and is a type of preventive planning in which you can engage. A word of caution: large transfers of property from one form of ownership to another should be undertaken only with the advice and assistance of your legal adviser. In some states, property transfer from one spouse to joint ownership or the reverse requires a middleman or a "straw." It is not a do-it-yourself activity.

One more disquieting word should be added with regard to lawsuits or potential lawsuits against wealthy defendants. One of the modern concepts of litigation is the pretrial use of "discovery" techniques. A trial is supposed to represent a test of legal issues and a determination of the facts in a controversy. Elements of "surprise" are for movie and television versions of a trial. Therefore, facts that are "discoverable" prior to trial encompass a wide area. In many states, when the claim for damages is based on the defendant's alleged negligence and a case can be made for "punitive" damages, the defendant's net worth is discoverable. Here is what one writer said about punitive damages:

"The defendant's wealth is irrelevant if punitive damages are viewed solely as compensatory. Since almost all jurisdictions use punitive damages to punish and deter, however, any award of punitive damages must be measured relative to the defendant's net worth in order to ensure that the judgment is large enough effectively to achieve these goals." (Debra Dison, "Pretrial Discovery of Net Worth in Punitive Damages Cases," 54 So. Ca. Law Review, July, 1981).

The significance of this type of thinking is a chilling recognition that if you face the potential hazard of being a defendant and whether or not a charge of gross negligence against you is proved at trial, in some jurisdictions a lawyer can ascertain your net worth in advance of the trial by means of written questions called "interrogatories" or by taking your deposition. True, the lawyer has to show some basis for an allegation of gross negligence, but the allegation sometimes can be made with relative ease.

What can a potential defendant do? Of course, insurance purveyors want you to insure, insure, insure against potential liabilities. Nevertheless, claims made in the millions cannot, in all practicality, be covered by buying more liability or malpractice insurance. In fact, today there is a reversal of the trend to urge purchase of more insurance. Insurers are limiting the sale. Here is one possible answer for the married high-risk individual. Share the wealth. Transfer wealth to your spouse. Split your assets down the middle, or even transfer a greater proportion to the spouse who is not at such high risk of a lawsuit. As stated before, this cannot be done after the occurrence of the events that might give rise to a claim. It has to be a customary way of life. It's something to consider.

The Unmarried Defendant

Mrs. Smith, a widow, established a joint tenancy in a piece of investment real estate and paid all of the money for the purchase herself but listed her adult son, Richard, as JTRS co-owner. She figured that Richard would inherit the property anyway and that with this survivorship interest, the property would avoid probate and go to him directly after her death. Something unexpected happened.

Richard was driving his Cadillac one day, and there was an automobile accident. A mother and infant child in the other car were injured severely. Witnesses were on hand to testify that Richard went through a red light and was at fault. The plaintiff secured a judgment far in excess of Richard's insurance coverage. A lawyer discovered that the only thing of real value that Richard had (since the Cadillac was financed up to the hilt) was his joint tenancy interest in his mother's investment real estate. Can that interest be attached? Law in that state provides that during a joint tenant's life, his undivided interest can be reached by his creditors on the theory that each joint tenant can sell or transfer his interest during life, thus substituting a tenancy in common. Therefore, Richard's interest may also be reachable by a judgment creditor who can step into Richard's shoes and sell that interest to satisfy the judgment.

Mrs. Smith cried, "Wait! It is my property, not Richard's. I only wanted him to get it on my death. It is his inheritance. I never intended to give him a present interest in the property." The admirable plan to enjoy the property today and let Richard receive it tomorrow without probate and its attendant delays and costs has gone awry. Hindsight says: "I should have kept the property in my name and avoided this entanglement. Now I will lose part of my property to pay Richard's debt."

What should Mrs. Smith have done to avoid this debacle? She had a choice. She should have kept her property. Sound selfish? It isn't really. She would have made her life less complicated. Richard will get her estate eventually. At present, she retains control over her property. Furthermore, if the property is income-producing, Richard should be receiving part of the income and reporting it on his income tax return. Also, don't forget, Internal Revenue Service rules require that Mrs. Smith file a gift tax return when she placed the property in joint ownership with Richard. Review: any gift over the value of $10,000 must be reported to the IRS on a gift tax return. We will see later that no gift tax would be due at that time, but the return is due. There are two reasons for giving the gift at the present time:

(1) All appreciation after the date of the gift belongs to the donee (in this case, Richard); and, (2) the jointly owned property goes "by operation of law" to the surviving joint owner (Richard) upon Mrs. Smith's death. It avoids probate, the process everyone regards (rightly or wrongly) as a legal hassle to be avoided, if possible. There are also some other considerations to be thrown into the hopper. The value of the jointly owned asset will be included in Mrs. Smith's estate on her death (because Richard did not contribute to it, remember). If she really meant it as a *present* gift, she should have gone through with it — filing the gift tax return, giving him part of the income, etc.. Most of all, she has given up *control*. Think it over, Mrs. Smith. Do you really want Richard to have a say in handling this property? You have a **choice**. There is another possible hazard to consider when you are contemplating placing your property in joint tenancy with another. Suppose your co-tenant files for personal bankruptcy.

Bankruptcy

Let's change the facts in the scenario of Mrs. Smith and her son Richard. After Mrs. Smith purchased real estate and listed her son Richard as her joint tenant even though he contributed nothing to the purchase price, Richard's debts in his shop, Popcorn-at-the-Beach, began to increase. Popcorn-at-the-Beach lost customers because a new shop, Popcorn-on-the-Road, was more accessible and attractive. The merchants who sold Richard the corn for popping and the butter and the lessor of the popcorn-making machine demanded payment on bills Richard could not pay. Alas, his only solution was to declare personal bankruptcy. How did this affect Mrs. Smith?

When a person is in bankruptcy proceedings, his or her property becomes the property of the "trustee" in bankruptcy. This court-appointed trustee may sell property of the bankrupt individual to satisfy claims of creditors. Does that include property he "owns" as joint tenant with another? Yes. Under the federal Bankruptcy Code, an interest as a joint tenant or tenant in common may be reachable. Mrs. Smith, who really owns the joint tenancy realty she shares with Richard, had better be pretty quick (and her lawyer very savvy) in order to prove to the court that she is the owner of such jointly held property and that it should not be subject to the bankruptcy proceedings.

Suppose the co-owners are spouses. Would this make a difference? Apparently not if the spouses own merely as joint tenants (and not as tenants by the entireties). What could spouses caught in this situation do? One way to avoid such liability might be to own property separately. In that case, at least the assets owned by the nonbankrupt spouse would be unreachable to satisfy the debts of the bankrupt spouse. Caveat: A transfer of property *after* threat of bankruptcy looms would be an unlawful act to thwart rights of creditors and should be avoided strictly.

We have discussed some of the ways in which your property ownership can deter lawsuits or minimize the attractiveness of your assets as a target in the eyes of creditors to whom you don't feel you owe anything. There is another type of lawsuit which is keeping lawyers busy today, and that is the lawsuit between two formerly compatible people, in fact *loving* people, who now want to sue each other over splitting up property following the split-up of their former loving relationship. This discussion can begin with the nonmarital relationship and what happens when it ends.

Cohabitation

Cohabitation and Ownership

Because this book is about *property* and *assets* and *ownership*, not much time will be spent on budgets and day-to-day living, or on how to resolve disagreements when one partner adores Chinese food and the other goes for French. We are talking about something that can outlast the relationship: the condominium apartment or the investment assets you each own.

Most couples who live together give little thought to the possible legal consequences of their actions. Today, because social acceptance of such arrangements has become commonplace, there is a growing tendency to engage in dissolution planning. This process spreads out a formula (of sorts) in advance as to what the economic consequences should be if a split becomes a reality. Such planning sometimes even takes place in contemplation of marriage.

Courts that formerly frowned on dissolution planning in marriage because it was deemed to be against public policy now accept such planning as a prelude to a more "peaceful" divorce, if that occurs. Will such a type of planning threaten the relationship or lead to the actuality of an event (dissolution) the prospective cohabitants or the bride and groom entering into a marriage believe will never happen to them? Surely, blissful partners-in-love don't need to agree on how to disagree. Unthinkable! Perhaps, but for the moment let's explore this new phenomenon.

Written Nonmarital Partnership Agreements

The chief reason for entering into a written nonmarital agreement is to negate any inference that an oral agreement exists or that you even have an "understanding." Let's be adult and realistic about this. If you are the owner of property that you wish to *retain* as your property, you will want to assure that a claim is not made against it or you at some future date. Possibly your about-to-be partner will not like the idea of a written agreement. If there is any under-the-surface mistrust or doubt about the purpose to be served by entering into a written agreement setting forth the parties' respective property rights, or if either party doesn't like the idea of disclosing too much about her or his wealth, maybe the idea of cohabitation will require a second look.

Who will write the agreement? You could, or you could go to an attorney and have an agreement written for you. You could use the bare-bones agreement found in Appendix 2 of this book, or you could use a combination of all three. Perhaps the best technique would be to draft your own agreement somewhat along the lines of the sample Nonmarital Agreement found in Appendix 2. Then show it to an attorney (perhaps a friend?), and see if there is anything more you should include. Caveat: the agreement in Appendix 2 is a creative document that might be compared with the poetic marriage "ceremonies" that some young brides and grooms devise today when they write their own script for the wedding. The *legal* marriage is the one evidenced by the contract entered into in accordance with the laws of the state. There isn't any *"legal" nonmarriage.* You're on your own. If a controversy over who owns what later arises when the blissful life together ends, the very terms of the agreement might provide the basis for a solution.

If such an agreement is entered into, it should not be taken lightly, even though it is not the sort of contract to be found in a legal form book. It is a new area of law. A lawyer experienced in family law should be consulted, especially if you are talking about a sizeable amount of property owned by either of the parties or if you are thinking about buying real estate together. Furthermore, even if you don't own all that much property right now, you might acquire investment assets in the future. How will you deal with this? If you want your separate assets to remain separate, say so. Your agreement will protect your property ownership just as the laws of all the states spell out the legal consequences of marital ownership.

What goes into the agreement? One of the crucial parts of the agreement may be a recital in some form of your present financial position. Are you prepared to disclose financial facts about your net worth? An alternative might be a waiver by both parties of this disclosure. A woman entering into such an agreement should be wary of such a waiver. Your partner may be reluctant to disclose his wealth. It might be his objective to be less than candid on this subject, fearing a later "palimony" claim after a period of living together. Some courts have opened their doors to such a claim, and in more and more cases have granted "palimony."

In the famous case of *Marvin* v. *Marvin,* which had wide publicity in the press, actress Michele Marvin tried to prove that she and Lee Marvin had entered into an *oral* agreement to "combine their efforts and earnings and to share equally any and all property accumulated as a result of their efforts whether individual or combined." Although she further claimed that she had agreed to give up her career as a singer and devote herself to providing companionship and housekeeping services, she eventually lost after a long journey through the courts of California.

The significant feature of the Marvin case is that the parties lived in California, a community property state, and Michele's attorney tried to reason that California cohabitants were similar in law to California married couples. The fact that the state courts accepted the plaintiff's case and agreed to try it was a first. Prior to *Marvin,* courts were open only to married litigants seeking court-ordered property distribution in divorce. The idea that cohabitants could plan privately for the economic consequences of their relationship's dissolution received an approving nod only after *Marvin.* One wonders if Michele would have been more successful if she had insisted on a written agreement.

The Unwritten Agreement

Actually, it is probably unrealistic to expect a couple to sit down, pen and pencil (or computer) in hand, and write out an agreement in advance of their decision to live together. They probably just move in together. If there is a later dispute over financial arrangements or distribution of assets, sometimes a court can infer an implied agreement from the actions of the parties. What can be implied, if the facts warrant it, is that the parties acted as partners, so that earnings or property can be allocated without regard to sex or marital-nonmarital status. Another theory, which has been put forward by disappointed plaintiffs (who are almost always women), is that the evidence shows that the parties intended property to be held by one of them (the, usually male, defendant) in trust for the other, thus establishing a "resulting" or "implied-in-fact" trust. This simplified statement overlooks the complex legal arguments that must be made. For example, the plaintiff must have provided *value* for use by the defendant in acquiring the property. If the household services *contributed* by the plaintiff eliminated the defendant's need to purchase those services, so the argument goes, then the wealth of the defendant was enhanced, thus enabling him to acquire the property. More often, though, both parties work, and one does not stay at home filling the shoes of a "traditional" housewife. One way of urging a court to divide assets on the basis that the relationship was like a marriage is to claim that a common-law marriage existed. This is, however, one more evidence of our rapidly changing laws and customs since most jurisdictions do not now recognize common-law marriages.

Common-Law Marriage

In states that recognize common-law marriages (see Figure 3.1), either by state law or in court decisions establishing precedents, one may attempt to prove that either or both of the parties regarded (or did not regard) a particular relationship as a common-law marriage. A common-law marriage is one in which the parties agree to live together in a marriage-like relationship but do not solemnize the marriage in a legal manner.

If a common-law marriage is proved (by various types of evidence, such as using "Mr. and Mrs.," having joint bank accounts, and "holding out to the public as a married couple"), then the question of rights in property that one or the other of the party's claims is decided on the same legal principles on which the rights of legally married people are decided. If one of the parties in a cohabiting relationship can convince a court that he or she *believed* a marriage existed, and if the relationship is found to be a marriage, a conflict between the parties might in some states be decided on traditional principles relating to settling property conflicts between partners to a marriage, as in divorce. However, most jurisdictions do not now recognize common-law marriage. (See the State Law Summaries in Appendix 1.)

One idea accepted in the United States is that human beings have fundamental rights and liberties to enter into agreements and privately order an arrangement of their assets during a particular period of time or living arrangement or in contemplation of a future event. This is an argument that has been used to justify pre-marital agreements and, likewise, pre-nonmarital agreements. The logic is: adults can do what they please, if not illegal or disturbing to the peace. Caveat: do not include in your agreement a provision regarding sexual services. That would be an unenforceable clause and might make the whole agreement unenforceable.

As to the desirability of a written agreement and even its *requirement* (as has been proposed) to provide court access in the event of a conflict, one writer states:

> ". . . the requirement of a writing may pose an undue disadvantage for women. The problem is that frequently, although not always, the party with

the greater bargaining power in intimate relationships is the man. He can simply refuse to enter into a written agreement that would not be to his advantage were the relationship to end. This places the woman in the position of either entering into or remaining in a long-term living-together arrangement without a written agreement to protect her economic interests or risking the loss of the relationship. To some, this may not be disturbing but only a matter of individual choice that raises no social policy or social justice considerations. Yet in light of the practical reality that more and more couples will be cohabiting without marriage, there is justifiable concern about a rule that would have the effect of providing no remedy especially in the case of a long-term relationship." [Perry, Twila L., "Dissolution Planning," *Family Law Quarterly,* Spring 1990, p. 118. American Bar Assn., Chicago, Ill.]

Statute of Frauds

There is a legalistic consideration with regard to oral agreements between cohabitants. It has an awesome name: "Statute of Frauds." The English Statute of Frauds, passed in 1677, has been adopted in some form in nearly all of the states in this country. The requirement in these statutes is that certain transactions are unenforceable if they are not in writing. Among these transactions are contracts that cannot be performed within one year and agreements affecting ownership of real property.

The argument has been made that this technical requirement of contracts applies to the commercial world and should not be applied strictly to oral or implied agreements between parties in noncommercial living-together arrangements. Difficulties of proof (because of no writing) should not prevent or interfere with enforcement on some equitable grounds.

Some states still apply these statutes to living-together agreements. In a New York case, for example, a New York appeals court held that a woman could not recover against a man's estate for work, labor, and services in his bar and grill and for her services in domestic ways over a period of seven years. The *oral* promise the man had made to her to compensate and care for her was held void under New York's statute of frauds, which required such agreements to be in writing (in re Gordon's Estate, 202 N.Y.S. 2d 1; 1960). In *Marvin* v. *Marvin*, the court simply held the statute inapplicable to cohabitants Lee and Michele because there was no marriage (557F. 2d 106; Col 1976). In a 1982 Wyoming case, an oral contract claimed by one of the parties relating to property was held violative of the statute of frauds (*Bereman* v. *Bereman,* 645 p. 2d 1155; Wyo. 1982), although in another Wyoming case (*Kinnison* v. *Kinnison,* 627 p. 2d 594; Wyo. 1981), an oral contract was upheld because both parties stipulated that such an oral contract existed.

Buying Real Estate

What should you and your cohabitant do if you plan to buy real estate together? Do it; don't just talk about it. If you think it is something you may do in the future and want to pin down the plan, then write it down. Review Chapter 2 on title. If you take title as joint tenants with right of survivorship and one partner dies, that survivor becomes the instant owner of the property. Do you want that to happen? Think about it. You might have other relatives who have closer ties to you than the person you lived with but did not marry. It might be better to consider owning as tenants in common. Then you will each own an undivided share. If you want to execute a will giving your live-together partner your share, you can do that. If you execute a will (as you should as a property-owner), the property will go to whomever you have named in your will.

Suppose when you go to apply for a mortgage, the lender insists on your owning as joint tenants with right of survivorship. If you don't like the idea, try another lender. If it has to do with your credit rating, go back to square one. Have you paid attention up to this point to acquiring a good credit rating? That was Lesson One. Each applicant for the mortgage should have a satisfactory credit rating in order to qualify for a mortgage issued to both of you. Furthermore, you should each know something (know a good deal, in fact) about the credit-worthiness of the other. You are partners in a real estate purchase, and an agreement here is all-important. In addition to a non-marital partnership agreement, you should have an agreement for tenants in common to own real estate together. See Appendix 2 for a suggested form of agreement.

If only one person applies for the mortgage in order to get the thing started and later plans to convey the condo to the two of you as tenants in common or joint tenants, stop right there. There will be a gift tax problem. What if the owner keeps it in his name? You will owe him rent. He has to report it as income. He takes a deduction on his tax return for the mortgage interest and real estate taxes. If your "rent" goes to pay off the mortgage, you are just helping him pay his debt, and you are getting no credit for it. Sound complicated? It is. See a real estate lawyer. If you get married, though, your problems might be solved because there is no gift tax for transfers between spouses.

If you are contemplating an investment acquisition that does not require financial cooperation as real estate might, there is nothing wrong with buying it and owning it separately. There is nothing wrong with married people owning investments separately, either. There is a whole new look at property ownership today, less intermingling of assets and more independence. Try it. You might like it.

Here is a bit of wisdom: The largest investment ever made by the average *married* or *non-married* couple is the purchase of their home. Yet, a large majority of couples sign complex contracts to purchase without *first* consulting an attorney. Avoid this big mistake!

Marriage

Traditional Marriage

This chapter will be brief. Why? Because so much more attention is being paid today to *dissolution* of marriage than to the long traditional marriage, "for better or worse, 'til death do us part."

In the past, the young bride worked for a year or two after marriage and then disappeared into the house, had babies, and emerged from time to time to attend parent-teacher meetings until the children went to college. Then, maybe, she timorously dusted off her shorthand and went back to work but only to fill the void left in her empty house. Has anyone today ever heard of the "empty-nest syndrome?" (It hardly exists.)

Property Ownership in Marriage

The young couple also typically pooled their assets, perhaps money given to them as wedding presents, and put everything into a joint account, even though the bride's Aunt Helen had given them $10,000 and all of the groom's relatives together had managed to scare up about $800. These two people love each other and want to do everything *together*, so why worry? To suggest at the outset of the marriage that they might not always want to do everything together is to be a doomsayer and killjoy. "Joint" is the way their parents did things, and "joint" is the way they intend to go.

Babies start to enter the picture. Wife Doris stays home to become a traditional mother and housewife. Hubby Dan, meanwhile, is piling up a reserve fund but, lovingly, labels it "joint." Eventually they have enough to make a down payment on a first home (house, mobile home, condominium). How will they take title? Step One, of course, is to apply for a mortgage. Then they learn they do not have a lot of choice in certain circumstances. If the state where the property is located has laws of dower on its statute books, the bank will want both spouses to sign the mortgage agreement. Let's review the subject of dower.

Dower

As we have seen in the introduction, a husband under the old English common law (adopted in most American states) could use up his wife's property legally because he had that "estate by marital right." Therefore, in order to avoid becoming liable for the support of indigent widows whose husbands had squandered their fortunes, states also adopted the English concept of dower. This was an interest in the real estate of a deceased husband that state law gave to a widow to provide her with a means of support after her husband's death. It was originally a *life estate* (meaning an *income interest only* for her life) and stemmed from the reality that crops or rents from the land typically would provide this income. Therefore, it pertained to real property. Usually it was a life interest in one-third of the real estate owned by the husband at any time during the marriage. This meant a husband could not disinherit a wife totally. She had a lien on his real estate, and if he attempted to sell his real estate while his wife was alive, it was necessary for her to join in the conveyance by signing the deed, thus signifying that she gave up her dower right in that piece of property.

This is not dead law. Certain states still have dower provisions in their statutes (see Figure 3.1), and in those states it is essential that both spouses join in any conveyance of real estate that either spouse owns in order to give the buyer good title. A look at Appendix 1 will tell you whether or not your state still retains dower (and "curtsy," which is the husband's form of dower) provisions on its lawbooks. Now you can see why the bank wants both husband and wife to sign the deed of trust or mortgage agreement. If Doris and Dan were unable to make the mortgage payments and the bank had to foreclose, the bank would stand in the shoes of the mortgagors (Doris and Dan) and could not convey the property to a buyer with "good and marketable title" unless both had signed the deed.

Statutory Share

What about the states that have abolished dower? Some states considered the dower laws too restrictive to free transfer of real estate and abolished this antiquated law. However, in practically every state a surviving wife who has been left out of her husband's will may "elect to take [her 'statutory share'] against the will." The statutory share evolved from the dower protection for a widow. It is no longer merely a *life income interest* in the lands or real property of the husband but is usually an *outright ownership* of the prescribed share (such as one third) of all of her late husband's wealth. Statutory election to take against the will applies to both spouses.

The right of either spouse to "take against the will" is a safeguard existing, in some form, on the statute books of all states. It prevents disinheritance of one spouse by the other unless they agree to be disinherited. Such agreement can be in the form of an oral or (preferably) written agreement not to elect a statutory share if the will of the first spouse to die provided that all the wealth of that spouse (or most of it) would go to that spouse's children (by a prior marriage). This type of antenuptial agreement often has been used by mature individuals who have separate assets derived from a former marriage that ended in the death of a former spouse. Example: widow meets widower, each having separate estates. They decide to get married, but prior to the marriage they enter into an antenuptial agreement agreeing to forego this very statutory right of election. Each is then free to execute a will leaving his/her wealth to his/her children. A sample of an antenuptial agreement can be found in Appendix 2.

Taking Title

Now follow Doris and Dan to the great event known as the "closing." This is the ceremony that occurs usually in the office of a title company or an attorney who also functions as a title officer. The question arises, "Do you want the deed to read: 'To Doris Doolittle and Dan Doolittle, husband and wife, as *Tenants by the Entirety?*" Let's review this form of ownership. A good legal description:

"A tenancy by the entirety is a form of concurrent ownership which resembles a joint tenancy but exists only between husband and wife. This form of concurrent ownership is a product of the common law doctrine that a *husband and wife are one person* and are each seized of the entire estate. The most significant incidents of this concurrent estate are the unilaterally indestructible right of survivorship; the inability of either spouse, acting alone, to alienate his interest in the property; and the broad immunity from the claims of separate creditors . . . As long as the parties are united in marriage, neither spouse can effectively convey an interest in the estate nor compel a partition of the property without the other's consent . . . The entry of a final divorce decree dissolves the tenancy by the entirety and converts it into a tenancy in common. The court is then authorized to apportion the property among the parties to the divorce as it sees fit . . .." [*Travis* v. *Benson*, 360 A. 2d 506, July 14, 1976, District of Columbia Court of Appeals.] (Italics added.)

In some states, joint tenancy with right of survivorship between husband and wife automatically means "tenancy by the entireties." In others, the less restrictive joint tenancy with right of survivorship (JTRS) is allowed to mean just that, as it would if applied to ownership by partners other than spouses.

The Doolittles will have to look to their attorney to inform them as to the law in their state (or see Appendix 1 of this book for a preview). Then the decision will be up to them: JTRS or tenancy by the entireties? In either case, a divorce will sever the joint ownership. "Entireties" ownership does provide a protection from unsecured creditors, and this might appeal to some married property owners — especially with regard to the family home. Caveat: some states have abolished the tenancy by the entireties form of property holding for the same reason that dower has been abolished in certain states, feeling that both tenancy by the entireties ownership and dower concepts restrict rights of creditors and limit free transferability of real estate.

Can a married woman own real estate alone? Yes, of course, but if the property is located in a state that still has dower on its statute books, her husband must join in a conveyance of the property when she sells it by signing the deed to the buyer, thus signifying his giving up of his rights of dower (or "curtsy"), so that the buyer can receive "good and marketable title."

Do the court's words in *Travis* v. *Benson* "husband and wife are one person" bother you? Here is a definition:

"By marriage, the husband and wife are one person in law . . . The very being or legal existence of the woman is suspended during the marriage, or at least is incorporated and consolidated into that of the husband, under whose wing, protection and cover she performs everything." [Blackstone's Commentaries on English Law, published in 1765]

Perhaps you want to throw Blackstone against the wall, but this was the common law definition and is illustrative of the kind of thinking that related to property rights of married women. As a matter of fact, changes began to take place over a century ago. State legislatures began to pass laws known as "Married Women's Property Acts." These laws gave married women the right to own separate property. This reform was completed by the early 1900s, but many married women remain timid about owning separate property. Outdated customs even linger in our very documents. In certain states, a deed of real estate to a married woman might contain this language: "To Jane Brown, as feme sole, to acquire, hold, use, control, and dispose of said property *as if she were unmarried.*" Are women free and unfettered if they wish to exercise their right to own separate property? Not exactly. It takes two members of the marital team to throw off the shackles of the past. You may be ready, but your husband may find he likes the old ways best.

Let's recognize that the typical marriage today consists of husband and wife and one or more children, and that the wife returns to work after having a child because: she is a professional and does not wish to lose ground in her profession; she has to work to contribute to the family budget; she wants to work to contribute to the joint savings to put the children through college; she wants to buy her own investment assets. Let's face it; she also has to be the primary juggler of work time, mothering time, household time, wife time, and (more and more, today) daughter (or daughter-in-law) time (see *Newsweek,* July 16, 1990, "The Daughter Track"). All of these demands on her time can cut into the earning capability of the wife. Two-career families do not necessarily mean equal earning opportunities. If there is strict adherence to "separate ownership means investment acquisitions separately earned in the marketplace," the career wife is perhaps no better off than her stay-at-home sister. How does she acquire separate assets? Ah, that is the question! The answer is, by *planned separation* of assets owned by husband and wife. We will see in Chapter 6 on estates that this is the very activity urged on spouses by their attorneys when they engage in estate planning in order to conserve the family assets. It will take an enlightened husband to understand or accept this arrangement if he earned most of the money.

Pre-Marital Agreements

The possibilities of second, third, etc. marriages are so commonplace today that we wonder whether there will be very many couples in the future celebrating their 30-, 40-, or 50-year anniversaries. In practice, it is more acceptable to the parties to enter into premarital agreements in second marriages than in first. As seen earlier, entering into a pre-marital agreement is one recommended form of planning to arrange for the eventual transfer of assets earned during a prior marriage while contemplating entrance into a new marriage.

There is another possible use of a premarital agreement perhaps not even in the minds of the prospective bride and groom but very much in the minds of the original earners of the family wealth — the parents of one or the other of the potential newlyweds. It is often likely that the future in-laws of one of the bridal pair (or in-laws on both sides) will want to have a say as to how the family assets are to be protected and preserved for heirs of the family that earned the wealth. This is especially true where the family assets consist largely of a family business. There is a desire to protect and preserve these assets as they follow a trail down through the generations. Grandmother and Grandfather want the family business, the securities, etc., to end up in the hands of their grandchildren. Parents and grandparents of the bride or bridegroom may not be the only ones interested in asset protection. The business partners of the prospective spouse might be very concerned when the new spouse of their business associate gains a toehold in the business.

The acceptance of divorce today as an all-too-common way of life and, in fact, the changing attitude toward prenuptial agreements both on the part of the participants and the courts has opened the doors to a new group, edging out the caterers and florists in setting the scene for the wedding. The question becomes, just how far can these interested non prospective spouses go in forcing their wishes on the bridal pair?

More is being written by advice-purveyors today about preparing for divorce than about preparing for a lasting marriage. First, we learn that courts in many states have held that prenuptial agreements relating to property rights and even potential alimony in the event the current marriage ends in divorce are not void per se as they once were because they were considered against public policy. Of course, such agreements usually have been upheld in the past for property arrangements in the event of a spouse's death if they met certain criteria relating to fairness, disclosure, etc., but an agreement contemplating divorce was unthinkable. Not so any more.

The same criteria in general have been followed in scrutinizing pre-divorce prenuptial agreements. Of course, the inclusion of possible clauses reflecting the wishes or conditions imposed by third parties may muddy the marital waters without really creating legal enforceability. One authority says he has "found no comprehensive discussion in legal literature of the rights of third persons in prenuptial agreements," and goes on to say:

> "This is no insubstantial matter. Take, for example, this case: A grandparent smiles happily at the wedding of his granddaughter, having reviewed and

seen her and his new grandson-in-law sign a prenuptial agreement prepared by his eminent counsel. What he does not see is the secret [later] revocation of the agreement by the couple which would cause him to turn over in his grave. By then, it is too late for him to change the will he made in reliance on the existence of the agreement." [Zabel, William and Frunzi, Susan C., "Ménage à Trois in Premarital Agreements," *Trusts and Estates,* June, 1987, p. 35]

There have been various attempts to insert clauses to assure enforceability of the desired conditions imposed by parents, grandparents, business partners, or others having a stake in the dispersal or perceived improper disposition of family assets or shares in a business. However, it is an unsettled area of law. In the case of an actual divorce, a court may order distributions of a share of business profits but is likely to be inhibited in so doing if the interests of other participants are affected adversely. In fact, the contingency of divorce and provision for it may be a natural part of business documents. An agreement specifying in advance whether the husband or wife will retain the business and how any interest of the divorcing spouse will be paid for may be just what the other business partners want. Such a document could anticipate and solve difficult questions without disrupting the business. However, enforceability of such a contract and the state's attitude toward such documents (if precedents are available) should be studied before relying on it as unbreakable.

Consider this: in some equitable distribution states, a spouse's contribution to the success of the business owned by the family of the other spouse might be a factor considered by a court, and this might apply regardless of which spouse held title to the shares. A suggested way to preempt a court-ordered distribution of shares is to have the shareholders execute a buy-sell agreement, which is a normal business agreement anyway but specify that in case of a court-ordered distribution to a non-shareholder spouse, the other shareholders have a right of first refusal. As a further precaution, the current spouses also sign the buy-sell but with separate legal representation. The conclusion drawn from this discussion is almost no conclusion, but it is useful to have these considerations in mind when planning to preserve family property and attempting to control its future disposition.

6

Estates

Estate Planning and Joint Ownership

Let us go back for a while to Doris and Dan Doolittle, our loving married couple introduced earlier. They have been married for forty years. All of their children are married. There are darling little grandchildren. Doris and Dan have kept all of their assets (and now there are quite a few) in joint ownership. Years ago, they had wills executed when the children were young.

They now decide to visit an attorney to draw up new wills. The attorney asks for a list of their property and asks how it is owned. They proudly show him a list: stocks, bonds, two investment condominiums, a beach house, Treasury notes, Dan's vested pension amount. All except the pension is jointly owned: their brokerage account, safety deposit box at the bank — everything. The value of their holdings is more than $1.5 million. Although they lovingly labeled their investments "joint," Dan earned all the money (except for the wedding present money, spent long ago). Doris stayed at home and took care of the children and the house (and, later, Dan's elderly parents and Doris' elderly parents). The lawyer says, "Dan, you should transfer some of these jointly owned assets into separate ownership, some for you and some in Doris' name." Dan is aghast. He is on the verge of refusing to do anything so foolish and so foreign to his behavior over the years and in fact considers walking out of the lawyer's office. Doris says, "Calm down, Dan. Listen to our lawyer's explanation." Briefly, here it is:

The reason for separate ownership of assets in the case of Doris and Dan who have accumulated a sizeable estate over the years has to do with planning to save federal estate taxes when one of the spouses dies. Unless the tax laws are changed after these words are published (and beware, tax laws are *always* subject to change) **an estate valued at $600,000 will not be taxed when it passes to heirs.** There is also no limit on the amount that can pass to a spouse without federal estate taxes being levied. This is known as the 100 percent marital deduction, and it was made part of our tax laws in 1981. Prior to that time, only 50 percent of an estate could go to a surviving spouse tax-free. The 100 percent marital deduction also applies to lifetime transfers between spouses. This gave transactions between spouses a new look, because prior to 1981 lifetime gifts to spouses also were subject to only a 50 percent deduction from taxes. It is impossible to over-emphasize the significance of this enactment for married people. It spells "freedom" in their planning, in their ability to transfer assets and money from one to the other, in the ordering of their assets as it suits them, and not according to a formula imposed by a tax code that eyed a couple as something other than an economic partnership. Furthermore, couples are relieved of the burden of filing gift or estate tax returns for property that is transferred from one spouse to the other.

The $600,000 Exemption

This is also known as "exemption equivalent," just to complicate things. However, "exemption" and "exemption equivalent" mean the same thing. The language is based on the fact that when enacted, the law provided for a phase-in of something called the "unified credit" over a period of time until the amount of the unified credit equaled $192,800. When applied to a transfer of assets either during life or at death, a tax is computed based on a tax table for such transfers and from that tax (known as the "tentative tax") $192,800 is subtracted. The result of all this arithmetic is that $600,000 ends up being free of transfer taxes (gift or estate taxes). Here is how it would work:

By virtue of the 1981 legislation, a husband or wife can transfer free of federal tax any amount to a spouse plus up to $600,000 to anyone else who is the object of his bounty. A wealthy widow or widower also can transfer $600,000 estate tax-free. What is taxed is the amount over $600,000.

Figure 6.1 is a schedule showing the federal gift and estate tax rates.

Hazarding over-simplification, it is probably safe to say that if you wish to estimate roughly your estate tax, you would list your assets (including jointly

---

Figure 6.1   Unified Gift and Estate Tax Rates

If taxable amount is —		The tax is —		
Over	But not over	This	Plus %	Over
$ 0	$ 10,000	$ 0	18	$ 0
10,000	20,000	1,800	20	10,000
20,000	40,000	3,800	22	20,000
40,000	60,000	8,200	24	40,000
60,000	80,000	13,000	26	60,000
80,000	100,000	18,200	28	80,000
100,000	150,000	23,800	30	100,000
150,000	250,000	38,800	32	150,000
250,000	500,000	70,800	34	250,000
500,000	750,000	155,800	37	500,000
750,000	1,000,000	248,300	39	750,000
1,000,000	1,250,000	345,800	41	1,000,000
1,250,000	1,500,000	448,300	43	1,250,000
1,500,000	2,000,000	555,800	45	1,500,000
2,000,000	2,500,000	780,800	49	2,000,000
2,500,000	3,000,000	1,025,800	53	2,500,000
3,000,000		1,290,800	55*	3,000,000

SOURCE: *J.K. Lasser's Your Income Tax* © *1991*, J.K. Lasser Institute (New York: Simon & Schuster, 1990).

---

owned assets, but only one-half if you own the assets jointly with your spouse), deduct an estimated amount (such as 10 percent) for estate administration and expenses, and deduct your debts and liabilities. Then, from the figure you've calculated, find the tax (tentative tax) in the tax rate table. From the latter figure, deduct the unified credit amount. The resulting figure would be your payable tax. If you are married, you do not need to be overly concerned, because there is no tax on property passing from you to your spouse. What may interest you at this point is the bite that will be taken out of the inheritance of your (and your spouse's) eventual heirs (your children) in order to pay federal estate taxes on the remaining assets from your and your spouse's combined estates.

Here is how a millionaire can plan to take full advantage of the exemption equivalent. A married person can transfer free of federal tax any amount to a spouse plus up to $600,000 to anyone else. If, for example, the husband dies and his wife becomes the wealthy widow, her estate will then be taxed at her death, but the estate again will have an exemption equivalent to $600,000 (or a different amount if new legislation changes that amount). Consequently, two transfers of up to $600,000 each can be made to heirs of the couple without paying any federal estate tax on the transfer.

That is why advisers are recommending to wealthy clients that the wife (usually less wealthy) build up her assets so that she at least owns the exemption equivalent amount. Assume a husband owns an estate worth $1.2 million. He dies first, leaving a will with a $600,000 "bypass" trust (also called a "credit shelter" trust), giving the principal (in trust) to the couple's children and the income to the wife for her life. There is no federal estate tax obligation, because the $600,000 is the tax-exempt amount and the $600,000 that went to the wife was eligible for the 100 percent marital deduction. On her death later, the wife leaves $600,000 to her children. Again, there is no tax on the transfer of those assets, because that is the exempt amount. If the husband and wife have estates in the millions, there will be a tax, to be sure, but by this "credit shelter" trust planning, at least the tax on $1.2 million will have been saved.

Separate Property as a Planning Prerequisite

It should now be clear that for this arrangement to work, each spouse must own separate property at least in an amount up to the current exemption equivalent. If a wife never has owned separate property after many years of marriage, establishing her separate property ownership may seem a drastic thing to do while she is still married.

Nevertheless, in addition to the tax reasons already discussed for some separate property ownership by husband and wife, there are cogent non-tax reasons. Consider, for example, the wife who has never dealt on her own with a stockbroker, who has never decided when to buy or sell a security or whether to "roll over" a certificate of deposit or a Treasury bill, or who has never written a check on her own account. That same wife, no doubt, has never read the financial pages, never balanced a checkbook, never established a credit rating. The list could continue. The wife who wishes to develop some financial acumen, who, in the time-honored tradition, is used to relying on her husband as being more knowledgeable in financial matters, may welcome the opportunity to discuss her own investment decisions with him (while he is alive), may gain her own expertise, may even remove herself from the category of the "spouse" whose pitiable lack of expertise has been the subject of countless warnings to the other "spouse," such as: "What should be done if you believe your spouse cannot manage property? You will not want to give complete and personal control. The law permits you to put the property in certain trust arrangements that are considered equivalent to complete ownership. Your attorney can explain how you can protect your spouse's interest and qualify the trust property for the marital deduction." [*J.K. Lasser's Your Income Tax* © *1991*, J.K. Lasser Institute (New York: Simon & Schuster, 1990, p. 390).]

Regardless of these admonitions to the property-planning "spouse," we are dealing at this point with the need for the wife to have separate assets in order to establish by her will the same arrangement as that available to the husband for saving a tax on the exemption equivalent amount allowed by the federal tax. Whether the husband can tolerate this situation is for the couple to decide. As a matter of fact, if the wife does not have a job, profession, business, or other source of income, the only way in which assets can accumulate on her side of the ledger is by transfer to her sole ownership.

Ownership transfer now may be achieved with no gift tax consequences at all. This privilege for tax-free transfers between spouses was one of the major accomplishments of the 1981 tax law. Once transferred, income from the separate property owned by the wife should be maintained separately in a savings account, money fund, or the like and reserved for future investment. Income from a wife's earned outside sources likewise should be saved separately for her separate investment acquisitions. These tactics apply, of course, only in a situation where all of the income earned by the couple is not needed for living expenses. Whatever lifetime property-planning arrangements are made by a married couple, women, especially, have to be alert to advice proposed by professional consultants because of the need to overcome traditional attitudes toward the ownership of property by married women.

One major purpose of separateness, in fact, would be to establish patterns of behavior. Another purpose of transfer from the propertied spouse to the non-propertied spouse (or the less-propertied spouse) would be to take advantage of the lower prospective rate of estate taxation on the amounts so transferred.

How to Calculate the Estate Tax

Let's go back to Doris and Dan in the lawyer's office. Dan says, "All right, I understand that I have to transfer at least $600,000 worth of assets to Doris. If I do that, our net worth will look like this:" (Assume all real estate is debt-free.)

The home (Dan insists on this remaining joint) $300,000

Doris will own:		*Dan will own:*	
Beach House	$200,000	Pension	$100,000
Stocks	100,000	Condos	200,000
T-Notes	250,000	T-Notes	250,000
CD	50,000	CD	50,000

Dan wants to draw up a will giving everything to Doris. She wants to do the same. The lawyer explains that if they do that, the result could be:

Total estate = $1,500,000. Presume some final debts and administration expenses, so that the **taxable estate** could equal approximately $1,350,000.

If each spouse leaves that amount to the other, **the estate tax could be $298,500** on the death of the second spouse. There is no tax on the first transfer because it is between spouses. (Remember the 100 percent marital deduction.) If, instead, each spouse leaves the maximum exemption equivalent, or $600,000 *to the children* and the *balance* to the surviving spouse, it could equal:

Taxable estate	$1,350,000
Less	600,000 to children = no tax
	$ 750,000 to spouse = no tax

On the death of surviving spouse (with $700,000 approximately):

Taxable estate	$ 700,000 (approx.)

After computing the tax (known as the "tentative tax")
on this amount from the tax tables and then reducing
the tentative tax by the allowed Unified Credit of $192,800,
the tax equals $ 37,000

The Unifed Credit applied against the tentative tax allowed a transfer of a second amount of $600,000 tax-free in the second estate. Instead of having a tax cost of $335,500 ($298,500 plus $37,000) by using the Unified Credit, the cost of transferring all the assets in the two estates is reduced to $37,000.

"Wait a minute," says Dan, seeing the light of day. "I don't want to give my kids $600,000. I want Doris to live on all of the assets if I die first and she does not get the whole estate." "Ah," the lawyer replies. "That can be done. I was just about to explain how."

Here is the explanation: by using the full unified credit (which does not show in the example above but is part of the arithmetic that gives the final result), estate taxes are reduced considerably. The way to use this figure ($192,800) which results in an exemption equivalent to $600,000, is to designate by will that you give that amount (or assets having that value) to your children (or whomever else you name) **in trust** with lifetime income to Doris. In that fashion each estate takes advantage of the exemption equivalent.

Doris accepts the lawyer's advice readily. Dan finally is convinced reluctantly that it makes sense. He had always felt that because he had earned the money by working it all belonged to him, even though he magnanimously put it in joint ownership with his wife. She always knew that she didn't really own anything and wouldn't unless she became a widow, and she wasn't anxious to gain assets that way. True, she realized his work was "at work" while her work was "at home," but surely after forty years should be worth something. She was pretty happy about the prospect of owning some property in her own name.

Dan promised to speak to their broker about changing the ownership of the securities in their joint account to separate names and set about establishing two brokerage accounts, one for her and one for him. The ownership of the real estate had to be transferred from joint to separate and re-recorded. On this they would need help from the lawyer. Aside from legal fees it would cost very little. States do not usually exact a real estate transfer tax for transfers between spouses or, usually, even between any family members if it is a gift transfer. The re-recording fee should be minimal. Bank accounts are easily transferrable. Doris will have her own interest-bearing checking account for the first time in her married life. They can keep a joint account for convenience so that either can write checks. When Dan worries that one of them might have to act on behalf of the other if he or she becomes incapacitated, the lawyer responds that he will prepare for each a durable power of attorney (see Chapter 10). Until that is done, the simple form supplied by the bank can be used to cover incapacity hazards with regard to that bank account. The certificate of deposit at the bank which made up part of their assets might not be able to be transferred until its maturity. The bank will have to be consulted on that.

Finally, the transfers are completed, and the wills are drawn up and executed in the lawyer's office. The wills are similar. The maximum exemption equivalent amount in trust to children with income to Dan for his life (in Doris' will) and life income to Doris (in Dan's will). In each will the rest of the estate goes to the surviving spouse. Trustees and successor trustees are named. The wills can be kept in the lawyer's office, or Dan's can be kept in Doris' safety deposit box and Doris' can be kept in Dan's safety deposit box.

Many years pass. Eventually, Doris dies. Dan sadly sees how the asset transfer works. There is no estate tax to pay because of the law providing free transferability of estates and gifts between spouses, and he sees that the $600,000 that goes to the children is estate-tax free too.

However, a thought hits Dan who is now 89. "I don't need the income from the assets making up that exemption equivalent amount. Why can't I give it all to the children, principal and income too?" The answer is, "Dan, you can." Another trip to the lawyer and Dan discovers there is something known as a "disclaimer." If done in accordance with the law (requiring execution of a disclaimer within a certain period of time), the whole kit and caboodle can be handed over to the kids (who are now in their fifties). Dan never did like the idea of the children waiting to receive their inheritance from their mother until after Dan had received the "income for life." After all, Dan's needs are less, and he has the rest of Doris' estate on which to live.

Of course, the scenario might be different if Dan were a candidate for extensive medical or nursing care at this stage of life. In that case, he could have continued to receive the income from the trust because he needed it. Luckily, Dan is in the best of health and executes the disclaimer which now transfers the income without creating what would otherwise be a taxable gift. The trust is ended, and the children will receive the assets free of trust. Dan never liked, never understood, and, in fact, always mistrusted trusts anyway.

Trusts

Understanding Trusts

Lawyers love trusts. Women mostly hate trusts. Here is a definition. A trust is a form of property holding in which ownership is divided between a trustee or trustees holding *legal title* and one or more beneficiaries who hold *equitable title*. The trustees have a fiduciary duty to manage and distribute the property or its earnings to or for the benefit of the beneficiaries.

That sounds pretty formidable. By conferring legal title on a trustee, the maker of the trust (called the "grantor" or, in a will, "testator") gives the trustee the legal power to act with the outside world in the same manner that the grantor can or could. According to the powers listed in the trust document, the trustee can do a variety of acts such as: buy and sell property; lease; vote as a stockholder; borrow money; invest and reinvest; pay income or corpus (principal of the trust) to beneficiaries; exercise discretion (if granted in the trust document); and do almost anything a natural person can do.

A young parent may examine the will a lawyer drafted and find all of these legal phrases. The young parent doesn't have many of those assets anyway and wonders why there is legalese. The reason is probably to be found in the fact that the parent has minor children. The lawyer explains that it is necessary to name someone to act with regard to whatever the assets are that would fall to the children in the event the young will-maker died prematurely. Business people will not enter into business transactions with minor children because children can disavow these transactions upon reaching majority. Therefore, in the case of a trustee acting on behalf of minor children, it is absolutely essential that someone be appointed who has legal title to any assets requiring action.

Trusts are used for a multitude of purposes, not just to act for minor children. One trust that we encountered in the case of Doris and Dan was the unified credit trust, also sometimes called credit shelter trust. This, as we saw, is a trust created in a will giving a trustee legal title to the exemption equivalent amount of assets so that those assets ($600,000 worth, according to present tax law) can be **sheltered from estate taxation**. We can agree that's a pretty good reason for a trust. Of course, when planning disposition of an estate by will, if there is a great deal of wealth to be disposed of, the will-maker could give that credit shelter amount away without imposing a trust between the magnanimous giver and the eventual taker.

A trustee could be viewed as a kind of middleman. Sometimes the "middleman" serves for free, as a family member might. Sometimes there is a fee and, very often, there is a corporate fiduciary. Translated, that means something like "The Rock-of-Gibraltar Bank and Trust Company." Did you ever wonder why so many banks had as part of their name "and Trust Company"? One theory is that it stems from our early history when many people (women, spendthrift heirs, untrustworthy adult children, etc.) were not considered (by men) to be capable of handling large sums of money. Many wealthy industrialists dispensed largesse to their lesser family members only through the offices of a mahogany-paneled bank trust department. Many more people today (including women, *especially* women) do not require the services of a go-between but are perfectly capable of handling their own finances. An argument for using a corporate trustee is that they don't die, and successor trustees do not have to be named. This may simplify the language in the trust document, but it does not assure that the same trust officer working for the bank will go on for years and years paying fatherly attention to the trusts and beneficiaries in his care. He may die or move to another bank. A relationship that was built with a particular bank employee will have to be started all over again with the person's successor.

When Is a Trust Necessary?

The answer is, when no other technique is available for handling certain acts. For example, as seen, a trustee must act on behalf of minor children. There are clauses often found in wills whereby a testator gives a sizeable estate to children at certain stages of life, such as age 25, 30, 35, etc. Sometimes a wealthy person wants to protect assets from the undependable or undesirable acts of a child and puts certain instructions in the will tying up distribution of a trust corpus.

Why is it that most women do not want to have their money tied up in trusts? Because of that very result; it is tied up if it is in a trust. One woman whose late husband left all of his estate to her in trust found that she had to go to her husband's nephew who was just out of law school to plead for additional money in order to have her car repaired. That may sound extreme, but here is how it happened.

The trustee was the law firm of late husband's brother. Eventually late husband's nephew became a member of the firm, and he was given this trust to handle. No wonder the widow was furious. A person thirty years her junior was controlling her money. Don't let this happen to you. Husbands are notoriously susceptible to arguments from lawyers explaining ways in which they can restrict access to their wealth — a sort of handling-things-from-the-grave mentality. "Don't forget," they frequently were told. "You don't want a second husband to get his claws on your money!" Another reason for placing the wife's inheritance "in trust" was because husbands really did not believe the "little woman" could handle money.

One of the techniques that seems to suit the purposes of some of these husbands is something known as a qualified terminable interest property trust (QTIP). It is a mouthful, to be sure. When the Tax Act of 1981 became law providing for estate-and-gift-tax-free transfers between spouses, another provision was inserted in the law. This was a complicated device whereby spouses (read "husbands") could transfer to their heirs (children, etc.) their estates (or a portion of an estate) that would be placed in trust for the surviving spouse (read "wife") with income only to the spouse for life. Under former law, this would not have qualified for a tax-free transfer because it was for income only for life. The 1981 law said, "That's okay. Such a type of transfer to your heirs will still not incur any estate tax when it goes to your surviving spouse."

This is pretty complicated stuff. It might simplify it to remember that what the legislators probably had in mind was the fact that they had a lot of divorced, divorcing, and second-marrying constituents who were worried about being able to pass along the corpus (principal) of their estates to their kids while giving the new wife something (income) at the same time. It is important to mention the QTIP trust because it is often used by, or at least proposed to, wealthy clients who are about to enter into a second marriage. If you are the second wife, you should know about this device. It is more complicated than you think. If this happens to you and you decide you can't live with it and don't want the income while his children are waiting for you to die and you decide to give them the income too, you will find that a gift tax could be due at that time. If you say to the kids, "Here, it's yours. You pay the gift tax," they might refuse to do so, and the stage is set for a court fight. One more thing: once a QTIP is established in a will and is acted on by the testator's personal representative (executor), it is irrevocable.

In certain situations, QTIP trusts might simplify estate administration. For example, an elderly husband and wife might be suitable candidates for QTIP trust planning if their ultimate beneficiaries are the same, and the surviving spouse does not wish to manage the property. Provision for a QTIP trust in a will might eliminate or simplify administration of the second estate while preserving the estate tax advantage of the 100 percent marital deduction. As in the case of an outright bequest to the surviving spouse (but not in trust), there would be no federal estate tax until the second death.

The QTIP trust technique also is being proposed to clients as a way to prevent a wealthy and aging surviving spouse from becoming a target for undue influence by a care-giver who urges the patient to make that person (nurse, attendant, etc.) the object of his largesse in a newly drawn will. Monies left to the heirs of the first spouse to die will be protected from such a possibility while income still will be available for the surviving spouse's needs. This is a lot to consider. It will not protect the remaining assets (those owned by "declining spouse"). This is often referred to as a Groucho Marx situation because that famous comedian was known in the public press to have been the victim of just such a grasping caretaker.

What is the wife to make of all this? On the presumption that *informed decisions* are best, she should be sure to ask questions of her professional adviser. If sizeable sums are involved, it might be best to have "her" attorney and "his."

Generation-Skipping

As we have seen repeatedly, some owners of wealth are concerned that their fortunes will fall into the hands of the tax collectors rather than the hands of their own children and grandchildren. Although charities might be worthier recipients (and, of course, might be heirs of some of the estates of these wealthy people), there is a desire to keep wealth in the family. A few comments will be made here because this is an area of planning that cannot possibly qualify for do-it-yourself implementation but will require consultation and services of a highly qualified tax attorney (whose service fees the wealthy client can surely pay). Therefore, the author's comments will be minimal and, perhaps, more philosophical than the tenor of this book warrants.

An explanation of the generation-skipping tax goes like this: Property transferred by will or by lifetime gift is exposed to federal estate or gift taxes at the time of transfer. When the recipient of the property later transfers the amounts (or property) received, there is opportunity for a second tax. Assuming the first recipient (or recipients) did not use up the assets, the government gets another tax on the transfer. To avoid this second round of taxation, the donor sometimes has placed the property in a trust, reserving a life estate and giving the remainder (after the life estate is ended) to the next generation.

For example, Mrs. Dynamo puts her wealth into a trust in which her child, Horatio, and then his child, Myrtle, receive and use income from the trust, with the principal eventually going to Mrs. Dynamo's great grandchild (Myrtle's baby boy, Cuddly). In this way Mrs. Dynamo's assets will escape two generations of estate tax. In some cases estate taxes could be avoided for 100 years or more. The Staff of Congress' Joint Committee on Taxation explained, "Since such trust arrangements have been used largely by wealthier people, this failure to tax generation-skipping trusts has undermined the progressivity of the estate and gift taxes." (Blue Book of 1976 Act.) First enacted in 1976 and repealed by the Tax Reform Act of 1986, it would seem Congress had decided to forgo taxing these transfers. However, new life was breathed into the concept by the Act of 1986. In the effort to prevent wealthy families from circumventing transfer taxes through the use of complicated trusts and trust equivalents, the new generation-skipping transfer tax enacted in 1986 applied the tax to direct "skips as well as to taxable terminations and distributions" in order to simplify compliance and administration.

This is tax-speak. A direct skip means something like a transfer from a grandparent to a grandchild. In the example, Myrtle would be a "skip person." Two types of transfers are considered to be a direct skip: a transfer outright for a person at least two generations below the transferor (Mrs. Dynamo is the transferor and Myrtle the person two generations below); or, a transfer of the assets in trust for these skip beneficiaries. Had enough? There's more. A tax occurs in the event of the above scenarios or when a generation-skipping trust interest terminates, and the interest is distributed to the previously skipped person.

These transfers are taxed at a flat rate equal to the maximum estate and gift tax rate, which currently is 55 percent. That is a tax on the assets left in the nest-egg being transferred after the applicable estate and gift tax is paid on the transfer of those assets. As you can see (or maybe you can't see, but take my word for it), there is a hefty tax applied. For the donors dying to give their wealth away, however, there is a reprieve for a certain amount before being hit with the generation-skipping transfer tax. There is an exemption for $1 million of assets being thus transferred. Furthermore, the exemption is per transferor. Therefore, if there is a Mr. and Mrs. Dynamo, each can give $1 million, and none of that will be subject to the generation-skipping tax. Any future appreciation of those assets can be untaxed as to estate or gift taxes until transferred by some future generation.

There are many complex provisions in this law. This explanation is an over-simplified introduction to this means of retaining wealth within the family if that is your goal (and you are that wealthy). A great deal has been written lately about the changing patterns of family life. We have come to recognize that the third and fourth generations mentioned above are being born to parents in their thirties and forties.

Very few grandparents who are fortunate enough to know their grandchildren and who see the direction of their lives also see their great grandchildren, especially if the parent generation persists in putting off parenthood. Is it so important to provide for these unknown heirs that as infants they must be cushioned against their own possible financial indiscretions mostly for the purpose of thwarting the tax collector? The concept of the potential spendthrift heir is not new and has been the basis of many trust plans in the past in which the lawyer has assuaged the fears of a wealthy parent or grandparent that the donee child or grandchild will be protected from his bad spending habits by the terms of the trust. On the other hand, some trust drafters warn that no amount of adminis-tration by a trustee or distribution from trust assets conditioned on certain attained ages or demonstration of responsibility by the beneficiaries can create the desired productive behavior. Perhaps the wealthy donor must think again.

Marital/Nonmarital Trust

You might think we have covered trusts for wives, for children, etc. There is, however, room for a final reminder. The "nonmarital trust" is usually in the form of the "credit-shelter" trust that most agree is a necessary evil if assets of a married couple are in the million-dollar range. The "marital" trust can encompass any amount. It simply represents the amount transferred to the surviving spouse outside of the amount being sheltered from estate taxes in the estate of the first spouse to die.

The one to watch out for is the marital trust. What is that? That is the trust arrangement that embodies the fears of the spouse (husband) who thinks you (the other spouse) are not capable of handling assets or money. Therefore, all of the assets are in trusts: the nonmarital trust ("credit shelter" trust to save estate taxes — this one is okay) and a marital trust (do you want to have a trustee dole out money to you?). Beware the marital trust. Beware advice to your husband such as the following: "What should be done if you believe your spouse cannot manage property? The law permits you to put the property in certain trust arrangements that are considered equivalent to complete ownership. Your attorney can explain. . . ." [*J.K. Lasser's Your Income Tax* © *1991,* J.K. Lasser Institute (New York: Simon & Schuster, 1990, p. 390)].

The subject of trusts has not been exhausted. In fact, what is written here is intended merely as an eye-opener. Many trust arrangements are acceptable, desirable, or necessary. Make sure you acquiesce in any trust arrangement set up for you.

Wills and Probate

Is a Will Necessary?

People over and over again cannot understand why a will is necessary if they hold all of their assets as joint tenants. If you have reviewed all the possible methods of ownership and still believe joint tenancy is best for you, whether it is between spouses or between mother and adult child — or whatever — you could still need a will.

Let's take the simplest example. Joy and John, husband and wife, have $30,000 of assets between them. They have no estate tax problem. John has been married before and has one child. Joy has not been married before. There are no children of the current marriage. Joy and John have put all of their assets into joint ownership.

The couple is in a train wreck. John is killed. Joy survives six weeks, unconscious. During that time she became the survivor and sole owner of their joint assets. She might have made a will and left a portion to John's child, but she did not have the capacity. She dies, and her estate is administered in accordance with the state law of descent and inheritance for people who die without a will. All of the assets go to Joy's sister and brother, her only heirs. People who take an estate when there was no will are called "heirs-at-law," and that is what Joy's relatives are. Alas, John's child is left out in the cold. Responsible people must make wills to avoid the possibility of such a happening.

Avoiding Probate

"That is a sad story," you are saying, "but what about a situation where that is not the case but where a couple owns everything jointly and have the same children, and the surviving joint tenant takes all? Doesn't that mean that avoids probate?" The answer is yes, joint ownership avoids probate as to assets so held. Services of a lawyer might be necessary to disentangle joint tenancy ownership anyway, for example, if there is real estate and documents have to be filed. However, most states have a simplified procedure for small estate administration so that services of a lawyer are not needed in many cases. If a couple has a modest amount of assets, they may prefer to retain all in joint ownership or to separate just enough into separate ownership of each spouse so that each *separate* estate would fit within the small estate administration procedure (depends on the dollar amount of the estate) and retain joint ownership of all other assets. Some of the problems with joint tenancy property are: loss of control; possibility of creating a gift (depends on IRS rules); unintended disinheritance (of someone who did not sign the signature card at the bank, for example); possibility of a claim by someone left out of the joint ownership; inflexibility of action; impossibility of leaving joint tenancy property by will; possible exposure to creditor's claims against one joint tenant. Many couples, however, might look at these items and decide that such considerations do not pose a problem for them and feel the "togetherness" aspect of joint ownership outweighs any potential disadvantages. The aspects of freedom from "planning" ownership and avoidance of probate appeal to many people.

Estate Taxes and Joint Tenancy

A common fallacy people believe is that property passing directly to a survivor by reason of joint tenancy ownership avoids estate taxes (see Chapter 11). Many people also believe that only property going by will is taxable. Wrong again. Estate taxes apply regardless of the way in which a person's estate finds itself in the hands of the inheritors.

A **probate estate** when the person had a will is one in which property is transferred in accordance with the wishes of the will-maker. An **intestate estate** is one in which property is transferred in accordance with the state laws of intestacy (as poor Joy's was, above). An **estate created by joint tenancy ownership** is one in which the survivor takes ownership by operation of law. *In all of these situations, if the assets total over $600,000 and, therefore, equal a taxable estate, they will be subject to federal estate taxation.* If you are married, there will be no estate tax on the transfer to your surviving spouse. For other than marrieds, the rule is that all the assets are presumed to belong in the estate of the first joint tenant to die. The survivor has to prove "contribution" in order to refute this presumption. If he did not contribute, he is out of luck.

A "Simple Will"

This is almost impossible. Although clients usually want a simple will — "None of those 64-page jobs," they say — it is difficult to comply with this request. One thing that will simplify the job (if not the will) is to bring to the lawyer's office a list of names, including your children, proposed people to serve as trustee or co-trustees of any trusts, information about grandchildren, information about any beneficiaries with special problems, marital situations, an estimate of your net worth, and how your assets are held.

The last two items are essential if the attorney is to pay attention to the need for estate-planning techniques (such as those discussed earlier). The very last one is what might stump you. Don't presume that because an asset has your name and your spouse's it is a joint asset. Remember, names alone usually signify tenant-in-common ownership. Mr. and Mrs. Jones held a note when they sold their previous home. It is now a sizeable part of their assets because there is an amount of $100,000 "balloon" due on the mortgage. Only their names appear on the note. The result is that each owns half (as tenants in common). This suits their plans because the lawyer might suggest to them that they each own separate assets. The important thing about the will is that you, the client, understand it. If not, after a draft is prepared for your review, demand an explanation of every clause. You are entitled to an *understandable* document — not just legalese.

The will should be reviewed from time to time and changes made, either by executing a new will or a codicil. Changes might be necessitated by changes in your family situation or changes in the law. Always be on the lookout for tax law changes. Perhaps, at the outset of the conference, the lawyer will say to you, "Have you ever thought of a revocable living trust?"

Revocable Living Trust

More mumbo-jumbo! What is that? Actually, most people have heard of a revocable living trust, or inter vivos trust (the same thing), because banks constantly disseminate information on this device, exhorting you to pay attention to your golf game and let the bank mind your finances (and transfer your assets if you die). Such an arrangement usually is proposed as a probate avoidance device and recommended to clients instead of a will.

Some of the reasons for placing property in a living trust are: you, as grantor of your trust, can place property in the trust, observe its administration, and observe the handling of the property by a trustee or trustees, if you desire; you can control distribution of benefits (including to you); you can relieve yourself of investment decision responsibilities (if you wish); you can place the trust in operation by transferring a limited amount of assets; you can revoke the trust altogether if you decide you do not like the arrangement and you have retained that power specifically. The trust can be of great help in the event of physical or mental disability. You can put your testamentary wishes into the trust, by-passing probate as to assets in the trust. If all of your assets are transferred to trust administration, you eliminate appointing a future personal representative because your trust will take the place of your will. It will not save estate taxes.

As we have seen, a nonprobatable estate may be a taxable estate. However, if your estate is not distributed by a probate court, it is not exposed to public availability and information. If that is a concern, you will be interested in the private manner of distribution that can be achieved by means of a trust. There is, however, one side to the picture that often is overlooked by the potential grantor and minimized in publicity by the potential trustee, and that regards *fees*. Drafting a trust instrument, administering it, and providing other services can entail fees — so much so that it has been said that the practicality of a trust is limited to the value of the assets administered. Is it just for the wealthy, or is it worthwhile even for the person with moderate wealth? Remember, there is no income tax saving achieved by having your property in a trust. It is a pass-through-of-income situation so that the recipient of the income pays the income taxes. If you think being the trustee of your own trust is "neat," start with transferring title or other ownership indicia of *your* property to the trustee's name (Mary Smith to "Mary Smith, Trustee"). Caveat: some business people who deal with real estate will not conduct transactions with Mary Smith, Trustee, if there is a real Mary Smith. If, after a while, you decide you don't really like a living trust arrangement, you can revoke it. That means you transfer back all those evidences of ownership of assets and undo the trust. It's one more thing to consider.

Singles

There is one very special situation when having a living trust might appear useful and when it might be a desirable will substitute. Many people (most, in fact) one day will be a single (if they are not already by choice). Singles, especially widows and widowers, fear incapacity. For example, if you become mentally incapacitated, it is likely that someone will petition a local court for appointment of a conservator (also called "guardian"). You then become a ward of the court, usually a branch of the probate court of your state.

The need to ensure that those who conduct business with you (in your incompetent state) do not do so at their peril is as great as the need to ensure that unscrupulous people do not take advantage of you with regard to your property. Courts sometimes have a tendency to be very suspicious of caretaking relatives. A businessman who had acted for years as the agent of his 92-year-old mother was deemed unsatisfactory to act in that capacity when the mother became incompetent. He had to become the court-appointed conservator, and then his every act on her behalf had to be scrutinized by the conservator division of the probate court. He was completely trustworthy and meticulously careful in handling his mother's assets, but now as conservator he found himself swamped with paperwork to satisfy the court requirements.

How can you avoid becoming a ward of the court and have a conservator handle your property? One answer is by having established (previous to your incapacity) a revocable living trust. A trustee already would have been appointed by you, and if you were that trustee, there would have been a successor trustee named in the instrument.

Durable Power of Attorney

This is one more thing you should have on hand. Using general power of attorney authorization, you can appoint someone as your agent to handle a wide variety of matters or to handle all of your affairs.

Every state and the District of Columbia now has enacted provisions for recognition of a *durable* power of attorney. This kind of agency transcends the principal's incapacity. It is important because a general power terminates on the death or incapacity of the principal. "Durable" goes beyond that. After all, what good is it to have an agent who loses power just as you might need the agent most? A durable power of attorney in the hands of someone you trust could act together with your revocable living trust to provide for your care during a period of incapacity, avoiding any need for a court. All of these matters would have to be handled in advance of any incapacity.

Gift-Giving

A lot of singles (marrieds, too) want to give away their wealth to their children. Everyone has heard that today $10,000 may be given to anyone of your choosing free of gift tax. Such an amount may be given to a donee (the recipient of your gift) every year and to any number of donees. A husband and wife together may give such a gift in the amount of $20,000 each year. In the case of the husband-and-wife gift, a gift tax return must be filed. That is because the gift-giver must show the "consent" of the other spouse, and then the gift can be doubled. Up to $10,000 per donee ($20,000 for gifts from spouses) can be given tax-free.

You may wonder why this is such a big deal. Why tax the gift at all? The reason has to do with the federal estate tax. Although everyone can give that amount tax-free, gifts above that amount must be documented on a gift-tax return. Year by year, any gifts above $10,000 per donee are added to the amount of previously given assets or money. Eventually, the tax on such gifts might encroach on the $192,800 uniform credit.

The uniform credit was enacted to tax at the same rate gifts during life and at death (testamentary gifts). In years past, wealthy people could give away money during life at a lower tax rate than estate gifts incurred. This seemed unfair to Congress, and uniform credit was added to our estate and gift tax laws. Little by little, if the amount of gifts gets closer to that $600,000 exemption figure, the uniform credit is reduced. By continued lifetime gifts, the credit could be wiped out altogether. Not something Donald Trump will have to worry about. Few people will get near those dollars in giving away money. However, it is nice to know that if you want to give up to $10,000 a year to a child you can do so without strings. The interesting thing is that your appointed durable power of attorney could do that, in acting for you.

Convenience of Separate Assets

Before leaving the subject of the *inconvenience* of probate and even the *hardship* that the delays inherent in probate can cause, let us consider how owning some *separate assets* by a couple can help get a widow or widower over the probate hurdle. Let us go back and look into the affairs of Doris and Dan Doolittle whom we left in Chapter 6 when Dan was the surviving spouse. Presume, instead, that Doris was the surviving spouse. Remember, their home was held jointly. There will be no problem recording Dan's death and Doris' assumption of ownership as the surviving joint owner. This will not affect her immediate finances. The assets that Dan owned *separately* will have to be transferred in accordance with Dan's will and these assets will be administered by a probate court. What about Doris' separate assets? Certainly, no probate is involved there. **Doris has her own checking account.** Her other assets provide an income while waiting for re-registering of the probatable assets from Dan's estate. Many a sad widow has had to borrow from a friend or family member to pay immediate expenses because access to cash would take some time. Even a joint checking account has to be closed and money transferred to a new one in the name of the surviving joint owner. If Dan also had a separate checking account with Doris having a power of attorney for that account, it would do her no good for immediate needs. The power of attorney terminates on the death of the principal (Dan). Doris realizes that their advance planning to own some separate assets (including checking accounts) preserved her financial dignity at a stressful time. That planning eliminated for her the monetary inconvenience that other new widows she knew had faced or the need for a personal representative to petition the probate court for temporary living expenses for the widow.

9

Divorce

Divorce in Today's World

Most people are affected in some way by divorce. Either your own marriage is your concern, or that of your children, your siblings, friends, or parents. A husband and wife of many years may find their own celebration of the anniversary of a long-term happy and stable marriage is marred by the break-up of their son's fifteen-year marriage. A young couple may be distressed to learn that parents of one of them are separating. "The marriage is over. We waited until you were grown." We cannot close our eyes to the facts of divorce.

Today more marriages probably end in divorce than in the time-honored " 'til death do us part." The quoted phrase is no doubt as archaic as the old promise to "love, honor, and obey." (Obey!) Whether we deplore or applaud this change in our customs, it is sobering to remember that just a few years ago we deplored (or, at least, parents deplored) young people leaving home and setting up apartments of their own, people of different sexes living together unmarried, coed dorms, unmarried mothers, working mothers, divorced working mothers, divorced fathers having custody, and children stuck in nurseries for ten-hour days. Our mores have changed, and they will probably change again in the next generation.

If that is the case, perhaps those who want to turn back the clock will not like the idea of a baggage of separate assets for each of the two loving people who have entered into marriage; but there may be just as many who think the time has come to adopt this new attitude toward marital property as a way of life, and not because of the specter of a possible split. If cool-headed financial planning results in a decision to maintain his and her assets in separate ownership, that should not diminish the happiness and stability of the marriage — in fact, it might strengthen it. Disagreements over financial planning, how each partner views economic and budget constraints (he wants to budget rigidly, she wants to budget more flexibly), investment decisions and the like can wreck a marriage as much as accusations of extra-marital affairs. As a matter of fact, the minimization of claims of adultery today may have been a prelude to the widespread acceptance of "no-fault" divorces.

In a "no-fault" divorce, the parties merely have to convince a court that the marriage has failed and that statutory requirements have been met. The "fault" of a party is not considered in determining whether or not a divorce (and sometimes even alimony) will be granted. In granting a "no-fault" divorce, each state has certain requirements (time period, residence, criteria for living apart, etc.). Once having ascertained that those requirements have been satisfied, the court then can look to property division or, in increasingly rare instances, the granting of alimony (usually called "maintenance").

In an ideal situation, the divorcing parties establish their own agreement for dividing marital property. If that has been done, the court may accept the agreement and incorporate it into the divorce decree. If they can't agree, the court will step in and do the dividing for them. (Because this book is about property, the important matters of child support and custody are not discussed here but certainly would be a part of any divorce settlement.)

Alimony

This is where "fault" and "no-fault" may part company. Marital fault has been excluded from alimony decisions in many states. However, a finding of fault can bar alimony or may be considered a factor in some states and the District of Columbia. Alleging fault leads to acrimonious, hurtful proceedings. Invariably, there are accusations and counter-accusations. No wonder most states have barred fault in deciding whether or not to grant alimony. (It is probably still a factor in custody cases.) Some lawyers will not handle divorce actions alleging fault of a party (or will discourage a client from going down that road).

There are some historical insights into the evolution of current law. Timothy M. Tippins, author of a two-volume book called *New York Matrimonial Law and Practice* (Callaghan & Company Publishing, Wilmette, Ill., 1986 and 1988), stated, "The jurisprudential underpinnings of the concept of alimony have been traced to the common-law status of the married woman. . . . [according to Blackstone] the very being or legal existence of women was suspended during the marriage." A reviewer of the book takes this a step further: "This premise led to the view that in marriage a man and a woman become one, and that one was *the man*. Women's theoretical 'non-status' during marriage also gave rise to the early view that a wife must be supported after the marriage was ended, as well as during the marriage, since alimony . . . was the legal replacement of the husband's marital support obligation." (Sassower, Doris L., "Book Reviews," *Family Law Quarterly*, Spring '89, p. 145, Am. Bar Assn. Section of Family Law, Chicago, Ill.).

In fact, the English ecclesiastical courts and the courts in this country a century ago considered marriage a sacrament and indissoluble. However, a legal separation could be granted, in which the husband had a continuing obligation to support his wife. Remember, at that time in history, at the moment of marriage the husband automatically gained control of his wife's property and the income from that property. He retained this control after separation, and with it the corresponding responsibility for his wife's economic support. Employment opportunities for the separated wife were practically nonexistent in those days. Alimony provided her only resource for financial survival.

The first rationale for traditional alimony was that it enforced the husband's obligation to continue to support his wife. Guilt and innocence considerations also entered the picture. (If the wife was found guilty of marital misdeeds, she could not receive support, and if the husband was the guilty party, his punishment was the requirement to pay alimony.) Over the years, authorities have differed as to whether alimony also was paid to compensate the wife for her housework during the marriage, and numerous studies have been undertaken in an effort to ascribe a dollar amount to the annual services of a housewife. No published results have provided a satisfactory guideline.

"All right," you are saying, "we are no longer that fictitious 'one' that Blackstone had in mind ages ago. We're a split. When do I get my alimony?" Here are some answers: courts might award alimony (or maintenance) if the wife is too old or is disabled; the wife is the mother of young children; the wife needs transitional support so that she can go back to school to be retrained for a job; the wife gave up the opportunity to pursue her own career in deference to furthering her husband's career. Suppose she can work and the children were in day-care even during the marriage with both parents working. In fact, courts often expect that most divorced women, even those with young children, will find a way to work, especially if the wife had a pre-divorce profession, career, or job. Awarding alimony is within the discretion of the court at a divorce trial. Usually, the statutes of the various states direct or authorize the divorce courts to consider factors that relate both to support and to property division (Figure 9.1).

Figure 9.1   Factors in Property Distribution and/or Maintenance

	A States that recognize nonmonetary contributions	B States with specific statutory guidelines	C Economic misconduct considered	D: Marital fault a factor		
				1 Fault excluded	2 Fault or respective merits may be considered	3 State statutes silent re: fault
Alabama					X	
Alaska	X	X		X		
Arizona	X	X	X	X		
Arkansas	X	X				X
California	X	X	X	X		
Colorado	X	X	X	X		
Connecticut	X	X	X		X	
Delaware	X	X	X	X		
Florida	X	X	X		X	
Georgia	X	X	X		X	
Hawaii		X			X	
Idaho		X			X	
Illinois	X	X	X	X		
Indiana	X	X	X	X	X	
Iowa	X	X		X		
Kansas	X	X	X		X	
Kentucky	X	X		X		
Louisiana		X			X	
Maine	X	X	X	X		
Maryland	X	X				
Massachusetts	X	X		X[1]		
Michigan					X	
Minnesota	X	X	X	X		
Mississippi	X				X	
Missouri	X	X			X	
Montana	X	X	X	X		
Nebraska	X	X				X
Nevada					X[5]	X
New Hampshire					X	X
New Jersey[3]						
New Mexico						X

Figure 9.1   (continued)

	A States that recognize nonmonetary contributions	B States with specific statutory guidelines	C Economic misconduct considered	D: Marital fault a factor		
				1 Fault excluded	2 Fault or respective merits may be considered	3 State statutes silent re: fault
New York	X	X	X		X	
North Carolina	X	X	X			
North Dakota	X	X	X		X	X
Ohio	X	X				X
Oklahoma						X
Oregon	X	X		X		
Pennsylvania	X	X	X		X^2	
Rhode Island	X	X			X	
South Carolina					X	
South Dakota	X		X	X		
Tennessee	X	X			X^2	
Texas					X	
Utah						X
Vermont	X	X	X		X	
Virginia	X	X			X	
Washington		X		X		
West Virginia	X	X	X		X^2	
Wisconsin	X	X		X		
Wyoming					X	
Dist. of Columbia	X	X	X		X	
Puerto Rico						X
Virgin Islands				X^4		

1. Fault excluded if divorce is granted on grounds of irretrievable breakdown.
2. Fault excluded for property settlement but not for alimony.
3. These categorites are not applicable to the New Jersey statute.
4. Marital fault may be considered in awarding the possession of the marital home.
5. Recent decisions have indicated that fault may be considered a factor in distribution.

Reprinted with permission of *Family Law Quarterly,* Vol. XXIV, Number 4, Winter 1991, pp. 343-44, Amer. Bar Association-Section of Family Law, Chicago, Ill.

Many factors enter into the decision and (presumably) serve as a guide to the courts. In states providing for equitable division, it is not necessary to have alimony paid periodically to be called "alimony." Even if only "property" is divided, the property division statutes contemplate that a major consideration in its division is the "support" of one spouse by the other.

The present way of looking at alimony is that it is necessary to provide for periodic cash payments only when the property available for distribution (including cash) is insufficient for support. Some state laws specify this explicitly. Others imply it. Caveat: one divorce settlement was overturned because the court had failed to throw on the scale the *income* the divorced spouse would get from the property to be owned after the divorce. This would appeal to the divorcing husband who is only too ready to disavow the old common law rule that he is the "one." "She worked before we had kids and afterwards," he says. "Don't tell me she can't work now. If we split the property, that should be enough!"

Equitable Distribution

Most states have adopted some form of "equitable distribution" and have a variety of guidelines in their statutes to assist courts in this difficult task. Remember, courts step in only when the parties cannot come to an agreement as to property division on their own. Criteria to guide courts include: the length of the marriage; the age, health, and position in life of the parties; the occupations of the parties; the amount and sources of income; vocational skills; employability; education; the liabilities and needs of each party; the contribution of each party, including services as a homemaker in acquiring and preserving marital property and assisting in its appreciation or dissipation; and need for support in addition to property distribution or property distribution in lieu of support. The list is not all-inclusive. Each party's own lawyer will make maximum use of that state's statutes and precedents in making a case out for the client.

In an effort to be fair, or what a court perceives to be "fair," a variety of methods have been employed to arrive at a proper weighing of factors involved in determining which assets should be included in toting up his and hers. This is particularly difficult where the assets over the years have been intermingled. During the marriage, after all, especially in a first marriage, the partners are concerned with "getting ahead," with working, with acquiring the first pieces of furniture, the first home, planning for the first child and, later, perhaps for college for that child (or children). At the point in time when the marriage is beginning to fall apart — and even until the crash — assets that were originally his or hers have been put into the same pot, along with earnings from those assets. Earnings from work have been combined to buy household necessities or luxuries.

If a point has been reached in the marriage where the couple begins to acquire investment assets, it is probable that the investments will be made jointly and title held jointly. That is the traditional picture in most marriages. It is not necessary to have a marriage reach a break-up stage to start thinking about owning separate assets. You may never acquire a net worth large enough to lead to estate planning and all of the tax planning that goes into that, as set forth in Chapter 6. You may never have to face the ugly realities of dividing up property in a divorce. Therefore, why worry? Perhaps the best answer is that separate ownership as a way of life is a rational kind of planning. The conservative planner admits that, "You never know." After reading the complicated formulae and distorted reasoning of some courts, in the material that follows, it may cause you to rethink your own habitual methods of property ownership.

The laws of practically every state provide that on divorce the "marital estate" should be divided (Figure 9.2). Property included in this category often is not spelled out specifically. Frequently, lawyers have to look to court decisions to help them make out a case for a client, claiming certain assets or the dollar value of those assets are (or are not) part of "marital property." This means that once a lawyer is successful in delineating certain assets as "separate" and not part of the "marital estate," the lawyer can save those assets from being divided by the court. The solution is not necessarily found in title to assets, although title goes a long way toward establishing proof of separate ownership. In some states, in fact, title to property governs alone as evidence of separate ownership ("separate ownership" = "non-marital" and, therefore, not divisible). In other states, title to assets is evidence of the intent of the couple to keep those assets in the ownership of one or the other, or both, but equitable distribution can also impose division regardless of title. It might seem sensible to some marrieds in an ongoing marriage (with no thought of divorce) to keep some of their investment wealth in separate ownership for a variety of reasons as spelled out elsewhere in this book. Learning about the complications of divorce in the lives of others might reinforce a decision to maintain separate estates as a way of married life.

"Separate" should mean separate all the way. Earnings from separate assets should be kept separate. The simplest example would be of a certificate of deposit in the name of Mary Jones, while Bill Jones has his own certificate of deposit. Each has an account number, and interest accrues to that number. The couple still files a joint income tax return reporting the interest from both accounts. The return itself lists the accounts separately and shows the ownership, providing further evidence of separate ownership. If Mary and Bill are worried about access to the account if one should become incapacitated or ill, each can have filled out a bank form giving the other a power of attorney with regard to that particular account.

Suppose Mary is not an earner in the workplace, or suppose their earnings are unequal. That does not matter. They may decide to have equal assets by transfer-

Figure 9.2   Property Division

	A Community property states		B Equitable distribution common-law states		
	1 Equal or Presumption of equal	2 Equitable	1 All property considered	2 Only marital property considered	3 Gifts, inheritances are excluded
Alabama				X[1]	yes[1]
Alaska			X		
Arizona		X			
Arkansas				X[2]	yes
California	X[3]				
Colorado				X[4]	yes[4]
Connecticut			X		no
Delaware				X	no
Florida			X		
Georgia				X	no
Hawaii			X		no
Idaho	X				
Illinois				X	yes
Indiana			X[5]		no
Iowa			X		yes
Kansas			X		no
Kentucky				X	yes
Louisiana	X				
Maine				X	yes
Maryland				X	yes
Massachusetts			X		
Michigan			X		no
Minnesota				X	yes
Mississippi		X			
Missouri				X	yes
Montana			X		no
Nebraska				X	no
Nevada		X			
New Hampshire			X		no
New Jersey				X	yes
New Mexico	X				
New York				X	yes

Figure 9.2   (continued)

	A		B		
	Community property states		Equitable distribution common-law states		
	1	2	1	2	3
	Equal or Presumption of equal	Equitable	All property considered	Only marital property considered	Gifts, inheritances are excluded
North Carolina				X	yes
North Dakota			X		no
Ohio			X		no
Oklahoma				X	yes
Oregon			X		no
Pennsylvania				X	yes
Rhode Island				X	yes
South Carolina				X^4	yes
South Dakota			X		unclear
Tennessee				X^4	yes
Texas	X^6				
Utah			X		
Vermont			X		
Virginia				X	yes
Washington	X				
West Virginia				X	yes
Wisconsin	X				yes
Wyoming			X		
Dist. of Columbia				X	yes
Puerto Rico		X		X	yes
Virgin Islands				X^7	yes

1. Unless property is used for the common benefit of both parties.
2. Equal unless such division is inequitable.
3. Unless one party has misappropriated community property deliberately.
4. Except as to increase in value.
5. Presumption of equal division.
6. Unless the court finds equal divisions would be inequitable.
7. Personal property only.

Reprinted with permission of *Family Law Quarterly*, Vol. XXIV, Number 4, Winter 1991, pp. 335-37, Amer. Bar Association-Section of Family Law, Chicago, Ill.

ring money from one to the other so that each has an approximately equal separate estate. There are no transfer (gift) taxes between spouses.

It all seems so simple if one decides on this plan of marital ownership. However, there might be cries of pain from the wealthier spouse because that spouse thinks it is unfair. The comfortable pattern of "joint" often is followed to preserve marital peace, or even just from inertia. A workable solution would be to have some separate assets and some joint. After all, a joint checking account is a convenient way to handle joint expenses and either spouse can write checks and handle the monthly bills. The family home is held in joint ownership almost as an affirmation of love and togetherness. No one could quarrel with that. The worst mistake young marrieds can make is to have her say, "Honey, you earn more than I do. Why don't you make the investments? I'll buy the groceries from my salary."

Consider, also, the couple who does establish separate investment accounts for "him" and "her" but then fails to keep earnings separate. Here is what might happen on divorce: clients, their lawyers, and the courts might go to ludicrous extremes to define "separate." Terms like "transmutation" and "tracing" crop up. When there has been "commingling," tracing is necessary to determine what earnings or increase in value have accrued to what was considered separate property when it was acquired originally. "Transmutation" has occurred as a result of the commingling, causing what was nonmarital property to become "marital." If this sounds like mumbo-jumbo, it is.

"Marital estate" or "marital property" generally means property acquired by efforts of the spouses during the marriage. If the statutes of a particular state require division of the marital estate upon dissolution of the marriage by divorce, it would appear to be simple to divide that property, while leaving intact the property owned by either spouse prior to the marriage. But it is not that simple.

A law professor has said in a *Family Law* journal article, "Classification of property for division readily could be made if each piece of property could be characterized as marital or nonmarital on the basis of time and method of acquisition." [McKnight, Joseph W., *Family Law Quarterly*, Summer 1989, p. 206, Amer. Bar Assn.-Section of Family Law, Chicago, Ill.] For example, if a gift of stock was made by parents to a daughter on her engagement as a pre-wedding gift (after all, prospective brides used to collect trousseaux of clothing, linens, even furniture; remember the hope chest?) that clearly would be separate property of the newlywed wife. It also would be separate property of the wife if the gift is made to her years after the wedding as, perhaps, a birthday gift — or, if the property to her is an inheritance.

What often happens, however, is that the original gifted property which was separate property of the donee wife at the time of acquisition has been mingled with separate property of the husband, or put together with the joint property of the couple. The interest or dividends (or capital gains) of the original separate property, as well as its possible change in value, has been hopelessly merged so that it is impossible to separate, even after meticulous tracing of the circuitous path of that original gift over the years. The same situation might happen to separate property acquired by either of the spouses as a result of their work in their individual capacities. Unless the husband and wife think it is important, for reasons of their own and not because a divorce is contemplated, to keep separate assets separate, at a point in time when they wish to list certain assets and say, "Those are mine," they may find it is not easy to document or prove that ownership.

In Chapter 3, we discussed the usefulness of owning separate assets as a way of life for married high income individuals who might be the target of lawsuits as a way of building a wall around those assets should the other spouse ever be sued. It might appear useful, also, to a couple drawing up new wills and learning, to their dismay in the lawyer's office, that they should separate jointly owned assets. Sometimes, when the "wealthier" spouse in terms of current income is told the assets should be split down the middle in order to effectuate a tax-saving plan, he protests loudly, "I earned the money! Why should I give half to her?" That scene could be avoided if the couple understands that a plan of "his" and "hers" throughout a marriage might have some advantages.

One of the most useful guidelines for married people to be gained from a look into legislative and court attention being paid to the problem of dividing assets in divorce is the recognition of contribution as an important fact of life in an ongoing marriage. The laws have abandoned the old idea that a wife made no contribution to the couple's worldly goods unless she worked outside the home. Consider this statement by Professor Joan M. Krauskopf:

"The divorce reform legislation authorized orders dividing property so that courts could enforce sharing of . . . gains. The process meets the reformers' desire to authorize a right to property on a basis other than title. Although much litigation has questioned what benefits should be included as property, few debated the right to share in whatever gains the courts finally classed as property. The legislation clearly recognizes a right or entitlement to share in property because of contributions to the marriage.

"The contribution justification for sharing asset gains provides a valuable clue toward solving our property/support mystery. Any order for a share of an asset divided in kind or by a payment of money is a division of property *if the goal of the order is to grant a fair share of marriage assets because of contributions to the marriage.*

"Contributions to the marriage would include direct contributions to the acquisition of income and particular assets. Under statutes that list only contribution to the property, contributions to the marriage, such as homemaking, would be considered indirect contributions to the acquisition of property. Since our statutes do not indicate any weighting for different types of contribution, decision makers may weigh income production more heavily than homemaking if they wish . . .

"The issue of fault continues to rear its head no matter how hard it is stomped on. We can better understand the fault issue when we analyze it within the goal of sharing net economic gains of marriage. In addition, extreme misconduct or failure to carry one's side of the bargain in marriage not only lessens that party's contribution to the marriage, but may very well increase the other's relative contribution to the children, upkeep of the home, or attempts to preserve the marriage relation itself . . ." [Krauskopf, Joan M., "Theories of Property Division," *Family Law Quarterly*, Summer 1989, p. 259, American Bar Assn., Chicago, Ill. (italics in the original)].

Legislators appear to have imbued the deciding courts with the Wisdom of Solomon which, of course, as we all know, is not so in the real world. Just knowing of the kind of thinking that must go through a judge's mind in such situations provides a possible lesson for participants in a loving, on-going marriage. Living daily life with an awareness of the contribution that each partner makes to the marriage (which is a legal concept only tested in the waters of divorce) could promote and strengthen the marriage. One possible way of affirmation could be by dividing ownership during the marriage. Not everyone will agree, but it might be worth some thought.

This chapter has focused on some of the factors entering into property division in a divorce as those factors are weighed by courts. Many other aspects of pre-divorce life and pre-divorce economic planning of assets by the spouses are taken into consideration when the decision is made by a court. The effort to arrive at "equitable" distribution of property is often clumsy, time consuming, costly to the warring participants, and rarely satisfying to both contestants. If the parties make their own agreement as to divvying up assets on the split, of course, that makes things much simpler. If they lived their married lives according to a philosophy that sharing can mean separate (as well as joint or unequal) ownership of assets acquired during the marriage, they will have made division simpler whether the marriage ends in death or divorce.

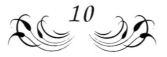

Crises

Advance Planning to Avoid Crisis Decisions

Obviously, you can't plan to avoid a crisis, but there are some types of planning possible to help in reacting to some kinds of crucial events. Everyone wants to handle his or her affairs in a responsible manner, particularly where a modest amount of assets are concerned (see Chapter 8 on wills and probate). Consider for a moment that the person needing a financial caretaker is your parent whom you never considered a candidate for financial caretaking before. A shorthand name for the problems you will be facing if you have to take on that burden is "eldercare."

Eldercare

Today's population of elderly people have presented the caring generation with a multitude of problems. The children of those elderly are perhaps themselves not young and, in fact, would like to relax and begin to enjoy the years when the pressures and financial burden of raising children, putting them through college, and the like, have eased somewhat. Now, these very "children" in their fifties and sixties must become the parents of their parents. The psychological trauma and emotional impact of seeing your once vigorous parent (or parents) become frail and insecure is something each person must handle in her or his own way. There are many sources of help in dealing with the emotional stress of aiding elderly and dependent parents. Our discussion will relate to the financial aspects of the problem, specifically asset preservation.

Durable Power of Attorney

We return to this document to emphasize the importance of advance planning in having your parents prepare this instrument while they do not yet need it (and may never need it). The durable power of attorney is a written document designating a specific person to act on behalf of the principal. It is an agency appointment. The agent is also sometimes called the "attorney in fact" (not necessarily an attorney). A power of attorney need not be "durable." It may be limited to specific acts and a specific period of time. By making it "durable," the principal indicates that the authority of the agent is to continue beyond the incapacity of the principal. The document can give you, if you are the designated agent, power to handle a long list of transactions for your parent, such as providing you with access to a safety deposit box, and allowing you to give buy and sell orders to a broker in your parent's account, to make gifts, and in some states (but not all) to handle real estate transactions.

A sample document is in Appendix 2. Should you use this or any form you can buy instead of having it drawn up by an attorney? That is a particular caution prefacing the "sample" documents. They are not intended to take the place of proper legal advice. You might look it over and then discuss it with your attorney (or your parent's attorney) to see if it meets your needs — or use it as a draft and add your own specific clauses. Many states also have special witnessing requirements.

Perhaps your parents already have engaged in the task of having properly drafted durable powers of attorney among their papers, naming each other as the agent. If possible, it might be desirable to have you, another sibling, or some other person, named as a successor agent.

Mr. and Mrs. Strong, both 75, had seen to it quite properly that their wills were in order and had followed their attorney's advice to have durable powers of attorney drawn up, naming each other as the power of attorney. Then Mr. Strong had a totally disabling stroke, and Mrs. Strong suffered an emotional trauma, making her incompetent to act in a responsible capacity. Their daughter had to take over their affairs but, unfortunately, the document had failed to name her as a successor power of attorney. Caution: cover all possibilities in such a document.

Guardian and/or Conservator

The two terms often are used interchangeably to indicate a court-appointed person to handle the affairs of an incompetent person. Consider: an agent under a power of attorney is appointed by a competent principal. A guardian or conservator is appointed by a court. Furthermore, the person appointed by the court is under the court's supervision. In the Strongs' case, the daughter had to apply to a court to be appointed conservator, because she was not named in the durable power of attorney. This designation had to have been made while her parents were competent. As a court-appointed conservator, the daughter had to file accountings with the court and get court approval for certain acts. This resulted in the expenditure of an incredible amount of effort, expense, and time. This annoyance could have been avoided by a proper designation naming her as successor power of attorney.

Is there ever a situation where it might be better to have court supervision? Yes, a single person having no one to trust and to rely on might then prefer court supervision. Of course, it is better to have that trusted person around, especially because such a person named as your agent would be more likely to know and understand your affairs, your investment philosophy, and the like. A distinction should be made with regard to a different type of power of attorney: power of attorney for healthcare. That appointee is only to handle medical decisions for the principal, including life-and-death decisions if indicated. It is not related to property and is not part of this discussion.

Other Methods of Preparing for Possible Incapacity

Many elderly people feel they have taken proper steps to have a child or other trusted person handle their affairs in event of incapacity by having that person share a joint bank account, be a joint owner of property, be a co-owner of a brokerage account. In other words, they let "joint ownership" do it. As we have seen, this is a popular misconception, a well-intentioned but misguided belief that this is the simple way. We now know that joint ownership can create hazards of exposure to your joint owner's debts (that you did not incur), can cause you to lose control, can cause tax problems, can cause disinheritance of other non-named joint owners (whom you did not wish to disinherit), and may complicate rather than simplify your financial planning.

A named durable power of attorney seems to be the preferable way to handle the possibility of a period of temporary or permanent incapacity. For simple bank account situations, it is possible to use the card supplied by your bank. You should keep your checking account or other bank account documents in your possession.

If you break your arm and can't write, you can communicate with the person you have named. If you are ill but still able to talk to your appointed agent, you can let that person know where to find your important papers. It is not a really good solution for long-term incapacity.

Conservatorship is acceptable, but you are not the one to appoint the person or to make the decision. Nevertheless, in the classic example where Dad goes to the store and buys a loaf of bread, hands the clerk a $50 bill and tells the clerk to "keep the change," adult children get alarmed and decide it is time to petition a court for a guardianship or conservatorship appointment to prevent Dad from impoverishing himself and throwing the family's assets to the winds.

The other precautionary advance step one can take is to establish an inter-vivos ("living") trust. As we saw in Chapter 7, a trust is a device to turn your assets over to a trustee who will have legal title to your property and manage the same on your behalf, as beneficiary. You can, in fact, be both trustee and beneficiary. If the purpose of the trust is to provide a legally appointed trustee to handle the assets put in the trust if you are incapacitated, it is essential to name a co-trustee or successor trustee, so that there always will be a competent person around to be the trustee. You also can name a competent corporate fiduciary such as a bank. Banks, through their trust departments (where real people act) usually insist on a certain minimum amount of assets and charge fees for their services, sometimes based on the amount of assets. Naturally, the larger the trust property, the larger the fee.

You may be saying, "I am confused. Does one need a durable power of attorney and a trust? If not, which is better? What is the difference?"

The durable power of attorney is a kind of "stand-by" document. In many states, it must be notarized, especially if the agent named in the instrument is to handle real estate transactions. In some states the document may have to be filed with the court where the property is located. It may have to be updated from time to time. If you executed such a document ten years ago, it is highly unlikely that the people who deal with your named agent will deal on the basis of such a stale appointment. If you handle your own affairs, you can see to it that the document is re-signed and dated periodically. If you are a child caring for a parent, you should see to it that you (as the agent) renew the document from time to time and update it. The principal (your parent) has to be able to sign before a notary and be competent at the time of signing. That is where advance planning becomes important. It seems a burdensome task when your parents are well and active. However, if you are the person who might be called upon to be the asset manager, you will be thankful you arranged to be appointed by a competent principal rather than a court.

Combined with a durable power of attorney, a revocable living trust could work this way: let's say your father established a revocable living trust during his busy working life to meet various investment objectives or merely to test its viability, and let's say that the trust was partially funded. The mechanism would then be in place for his agent (the durable power of attorney previously selected by him personally) to transfer additional assets (if so empowered) to the trust in order to provide funds for his care, with management by a trustee during his incapacity, avoiding any possible need for a court-appointed conservator. One adviser recommends that the exercising of the power of attorney may be contingent on a well-defined triggering event, such as incapacity certified by two licensed physicians.

There is something everyone can do to make life less complicated for a potential agent: stick to investments that do not require much management. This would be a good policy to follow, at least in the retirement years of life. Treasuries, annuities, government bonds, conservative mutual funds, and the like require less supervision than a portfolio full of volatile stocks and rental real estate. The investment philosophy should be, preserve the principal because you might need it. Stick to what the investment advisers call "cash or cash equivalents" and prefer safety of principal to yield from the invested money.

So much for thoughts about conserving principal, investing conservatively, saving, building up an estate; now we will look at the other side of the coin — when savings are depleted *by plan* in the face of a devastating health crisis.

Long-Term Illness

We may as well say the "A" word: Alzheimer's. This is the one name almost everyone associates with long-term illness and possible long-term confinement in a nursing home. In fact, it is knowledge about Alzheimer's disease that has galvanized the public into doing more and more advance planning. The difficulty is that one usually does not know the hazard of being afflicted or having a spouse or parent being afflicted long enough in advance to protect family assets. A spouse's assets may well be gobbled up before public payments, through Medicaid, will cover the expense of nursing home care for what may be many years. *Medicare,* the hospital and health insurance program based on what individuals *paid into* (like Social Security) pays very little of long-term care costs. It does not pay at all for custodial care. Medicare should not be confused with Medicaid.

Suppose your mother and father, although not wealthy, have put aside a modest amount of assets and have a comfortable income from Social Security and some conservative investments. In addition, they have a home unencumbered by a mortgage. Your father begins to display strange symptoms, and the doctor finally concludes that the illness is Alzheimer's disease. Your dad is 65 years old, strong physically, could go on for years in the mentally incapacitated state that becomes inevitable as the disease progresses. Soon the income begins to be insufficient to care for him at home, shared as it must be with a parade of helping aides because your mother is physically unable to cope with the care required. The unthinkable begins to become thinkable. You and your siblings urge your mom to apply for state assistance in a nursing home. You begin to learn a lot about applications for medical assistance from Medicaid.

The Medicaid program is funded by both federal and state governments. Usually, the federal government provides 50 percent of the funding. Medicaid is administered primarily by a state Medicaid agency in conformance with federal requirements issued and enforced by the Health Care Financing Administration (HCFA) of the United States Department of Health and Human Services. How is eligibility for Medicaid determined? In most states, the eligibility requirements of the federal cash payment program, Supplemental Security Income (SSI), are used to determine eligibility for Medicaid.

SSI is a payment to indigent persons who do not qualify for Social Security or for very little, are aged, and are disabled or blind, and at the poverty level. To qualify for SSI, a person must "spenddown." Your mom and dad, who worked hard all their lives and saved, hoping to pass something on to their children and grandchildren, must now do something they might have considered the ultimate sin — spend capital, use it up for daily living and reach the level of income allowable for Medicaid coverage of nursing home costs.

The rules for eligibility are changed continuously. There is no point in stating the exact figures at this moment. Interested people can obtain current information from a state agency.

The economic philosophy of the rules is simply this: **If one has resources to rely on, those resources must be used before the public purse will be opened.**

The word "resources" is a key buzzword in the eligibility equation. Certain resources are not counted: the home, a certain amount of household goods, an automobile needed for employment (of the well spouse), a small amount of the cash surrender value of life insurance. There is a limited period of time in which an individual must spenddown his or her income.

Assume the desired state of impoverishment finally is reached. What then? The spouse entering the nursing home must pay all of his or her income over to the nursing home. The state then pays the remaining balance of the established payment rate. The total cost, aside from the nursing home resident's contribution, is covered by the joint participation of the state and the federal government. There are certain allowances that the nursing home resident need not pay over to the home. There is a "personal needs allowance" for non-medical purposes (such as clothing, sundries, reading material, etc.). A typical amount might be $25 to $50 (monthly). There is also a monthly allowance to maintain the resident's own home if he or she may be returning there within a short period of time, and the spouse is not living there. The deduction for this purpose from the amount paid over to the nursing home can only last six months. One should, therefore, always indicate that there is an expectation of returning home. There is also an allowance for the resident's spouse if the spouse's income is below a specified amount.

Here is an example of how this Draconian budget would work out: Bill Jones has been a Medicaid resident in Tranquil Acres for a few months, but he insists that he will return home. Bill receives $800 Social Security income a month. After subtracting $30 for personal needs (the allowance in that state), $407 for his home maintenance, $29.90 for Medicare Part B deducted from his Social Security Check), and $40 for a Medicare supplemental policy, $293.10 is all that is left of his Social Security check, and this sum is his monthly share of the nursing home bill. Mr. Jones is in fair shape. He has only himself to worry about. Suppose there is a Mrs. Jones? Rather than preserving $407 for a home, Mr. Jones could provide a minimum of approximately $900 to Mrs. Jones, but this amount may be reduced by any income she has. To provide financial support to the spouse at home or to leave some assets to other family members, the prospective Medicaid recipient will need to transfer certain assets.

Transfer of Assets

There are strict rules about this. If a person expecting to become a nursing home resident and to qualify for Medicaid assistance in paying the cost of the nursing home gratuitously transfers any resource within a certain number of months (thirty as of 1990, but it might change), *it is automatically presumed that the transfer was made for the purpose of establishing eligibility for Medicaid* and that will nullify the eligibility. You may try to rebut this presumption by presenting convincing evidence that the transfer was made for some other purpose, but you may not succeed.

What can you make of all this? The only answer is, transfer assets before anyone gets Alzheimer's disease. A ridiculous solution, you might say, because people just don't *plan* to have this particular problem. Here is what one adviser says:

"The new Medicaid law encourages clients to divest themselves of their assets well in advance of any need for long-term nursing home care. For this reason, preservation planning for the middle class is now in vogue." [Barreira, Brian E., "Using Special Powers in Medicaid Trusts," *Probate & Property*, January/February 1990, p. 45, Am. Bar Assn., Chicago, Ill.]

That author views the Medicaid law as an "inheritance tax of up to 100 percent." There may be times when you should transfer assets within thirty months of going into a nursing home. You should always seek professional advice from an experienced attorney (not from the Medicaid agency) before making these decisions. It is possible that your local bar association may be able to refer you to such an attorney. One method suggested to accomplish the goal of avoiding the distasteful exercise of spending capital (perhaps accumulated over the course of a lifetime) is to first take a trip to a lawyer well-versed in setting up something known to other lawyers as a "Medicaid Trust" (but never called that in writing). Second, put your scruples behind you and convince yourself that, surely, the government never meant to take the last dollar that you and your spouse (or just you alone) saved up for your "old age." Furthermore, you must act now. Don't wait until calamity strikes.

The trust-arranging lawyer prepares a complicated document purporting to place your assets in an irrevocable trust. There are various strings attached designed to preserve your assets for your heirs while placing these assets out of reach for Medicaid purposes. The law is very complex on this subject, and it is not settled. Not many of these trusts (if any at this writing) have been tested in the courts. There is a hazard that the trust might be considered a fraudulent conveyance or that it will be deemed void because it is against public policy.

How do people feel about this? Here is one author's answer:

"The elderly have mixed emotions about the propriety and desirability of divestment planning. As to propriety, it seems a great deal depends on how it is categorized. If it is welfare, most do not want it. If it is seen, however, as an extension of Medicare — as an entitlement or as insurance — then the curse is off it. An earned benefit, transferred at life's end from a grateful state, is a lot easier to accept — or demand — than a handout. Many older, middle-class Americans feel that they have paid a great deal into the system and that they are entitled, at life's end, to take something out, if they need it. They feel that all kinds of manipulators use lawyers and fancy planning to reap undeserved rewards and that decent, middle-class people are entitled to use the same tools when such an important, and basic, entitlement is at stake." [Dobris, Joel C., "Medicaid Asset Planning by the Elderly: A Policy View of Expectations, Entitlement and Inheritance," *Real Property Probate and Trust Journal,* Spring, 1989, p. 20, American Bar Assn., Chicago, Ill.]

There is a difference of opinion as to whether or not the primary concern of the elderly who fear the possibility of encountering the need for nursing home costs is "to insure that their assets will ultimately be inherited by members of their families" (as stated in Mr. Barreira's article mentioned earlier). A letter-writer responded to that article in a later issue of *Probate & Property* (May/June 1990), stating: "Certainly senior citizens would like to provide an inheritance to their children, but this is a secondary concern." The real fear of senior citizens is their own impoverishment and that of the spouse living at home, says this letter-writer. [Strauss, Peter J., *Probate & Property* (May/June 1990), p. 5].

In addition to these moral considerations, there is a possibility that the states may remove a decision-making quandary from the families of nursing-home candidates or residents by enacting "family responsibility laws." The philosophy of such legislation would be that public funds should not be dipped into for care of an elderly parent while the children are off somewhere traveling. Of course, you should remember that the care and amenities in an institution relying on Medicaid funding may not be the same as when paid for directly.

Private Trusts

There is one technique that is spoken of in hushed tones and with lots of warnings about whom you can really trust. If it appeals to you, you can give away assets either within the $10,000-a-year ($20,000 for marrieds) gift tax exclusion or in greater amounts, using up the federal estate-tax-free exemption of up to $600,000. The gift is hedged informally with understandings that the money will be invested in "cash equivalents" and preserved for any possible future care needs of the donor.

For example, Mr. and Mrs. Planner, on retirement, decide how much they will need to live on in the manner they wish to live (trips, country club, two weeks at the beach each year, etc.). They retain assets supplying this income and keep a sufficient nest egg, together with their pension payments and social security. The rest they give away to daughter Joan and son John. Joan and John are to preserve the gifted assets and use them for the care of one or both parents if the need ever arises.

In the interim, the income belongs to Joan and John and the income tax obligation as well. This is understood by all parties. If the parents die later without ever having had to qualify for Medicaid assistance, the inheritance is where it belongs and where the parents wanted it. If there is a need for one or both of the parents to apply for Medicaid eligibility, the inheritance is still where all parties wanted it — untouched. Foresight allowed the gift to be placed beyond the reach of accountability as an available "resource." This discussion presumes such a gift takes place before the number of months within which such a transfer would be counted as a resource (according to the law in effect at that time).

Separate Assets

Suppose you really do not want to deplete your assets as the Planners did. You are married and want to take your chances that you or your spouse will never have to qualify for Medicaid assistance. The idea is so abhorrent that you refuse to plan ahead for such a possibility. (If so, you are probably in the majority of the American public.)

You should know, though, that if it does happen, the Medicaid law will treat the married couple as one financial unit, even if legally separated. Assets of the couple must be spent for the care of the institutionalized spouse down to the minimum allowed. Legal divorce would separate the couple's assets. Divorcing for this reason does not appeal to most people. There is one other possibility; the spouse who is not institutionalized may not be required to pay for the institutionalized spouse's care, although in determining the resources of an applicant for benefits, resources of either spouse, or both, are considered to be available to the applying spouse. However, during the continuous period in which the "nursing home" spouse is in an institution and after the month in which that spouse is determined to be eligible for benefits, "no resources of the community spouse shall be deemed available to the institutionalized spouse." Possibly gifts to others by an at-home spouse, while "spending down" that spouse's income would insulate those assets from accessibility to the nursing home.

A word should be said here about liens. Although the patient's home is an exempt resource under certain circumstances and may be transferred to the sole ownership of the spouse living at home, there is still the possibility of a lien hanging over the home, depending on your state Medicaid law. What does that mean? If the institutionalized spouse does not return to the home and if the spouse living there dies, the nursing home could recover Medicaid costs by collecting on the lien imposed on the home. Alternatively, the state may be able to file a claim against your estate. This lien was held in abeyance during the period of the spouse's residence (or under certain other conditions spelled out in the law), but the lien has an unlimited time span. Litigation has occurred when a nursing home was sued for wrongful death on a negligence claim. If the members of a family or a personal representative of the deceased nursing home patient sues and wins a negligence award, such an award might be considered income and a resource; the nursing home or the state might be able to obtain part of the award back as a claim against the estate to recover the Medicaid costs for the nursing home care. Bizarre as it seems, such a result has occurred.

If there is any conclusion a thoughtful individual can take away, it might be that preparation for unexpected and unwanted events requires some choices of action that also might be unwanted. Some could feel the solution offered is more distasteful than the potential problem. If it does have some appeal, it is one more thought to put in your "separate" file.

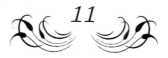

Taxes

Life and Taxes

Yes, of course, the saying goes, "Only two things are certain: death and taxes." However, it is almost more axiomatic to aver that *life* and taxes are certain, because we rarely get through life without having paid some attention from time to time (or *all* the time) to taxes.

Although advisers invariably tell their clients never, never to plan just for tax reasons, their clients almost invariably do plan for tax reasons. On the other hand, there might be just as many who ignore tax consequences of their financial planning acts and wish they had not. Looking back at many of the topics covered in previous pages, it is obvious that thoughtful people must take into consideration the tax aspects of certain transactions.

A brief run-down of some tax concepts is offered here with a very stringent caveat: tax laws are one of the most unstable foundations for business or personal financial planning. Alas, this has been the most repeated cry of the taxpayer — along with pleas for a moratorium on tax changes. Taxes are too fertile a political field for Congress to just let them alone (and look to reducing spending as a path toward fiscal responsibility). Therefore, at our peril, we ignore taxes.

Basis

When you give someone a security, whether by using your funds to purchase the security and labeling it joint or by making the security an outright gift, you should tell the donee your basis (the price you paid for the security). If someone gives you a security as a gift, you should ask the donor for his/her basis. "Unthinkable!" you are saying. "How could I ask dear Aunt Agatha what she paid for the shares of XY Zipper Company she gave me for my graduation from high school? And why should I?"

Aunt purchased the stock twenty years ago. You have a conversation with a classmate at your twentieth high school reunion and discover that very stock is now selling for $50 a share. You want to sell. You call your broker the next morning and he says, "What did you pay for the stock?" Answer: "I don't know! It was a gift from Aunt Agatha — 500 shares. I can't ask her; she died ten years ago."

Your broker will have to do some research to try and find out what the cost basis was for the stock. You do have to pay a tax on the gain. The gain is the difference between the cost and the selling price. As a gift recipient, you take the donor's basis. If Aunt Agatha was observing the rules when she gave you the stock, she might have had to file a gift tax return but only if the value of the gift on the date of the transfer to you was greater than the amount of the gift tax exclusion at that time. If she had filed such a return, it might not help you in reporting your gain because the value of the stock at the date of the gift is not significant — only the donor's cost price.

Adjusted Basis

Suppose instead of stock, Aunt Agatha, that beloved aunt, gives you her cottage in the mountains. She knows how much you love the mountains, and at 86 she has hung up her skis. You go up to the mountain cottage one day and learn that the Realresorts Developers, Inc., has its eye on the mountaintop and is gobbling up cottages for its development plans. You can sell for a huge price. You have to know what Aunt Agatha paid for the cottage so that you can calculate your gain.

Now change the facts a little. Aunt Agatha, instead of giving you her cottage in the mountains, is giving you her investment one-bedroom condominium that she bought when her apartment building went condo. She lived in one apartment and bought another as an investment. She has had it for five years and has depreciated it according to the calculations of her accountant. She paid $50,000 for the condo and has taken depreciation under the depreciation rules in effect for the five years she held the apartment. It now has a cost basis of $40,000. You don't want to manage an apartment and can use the money for another purpose. You put it on the market and sell it for $55,000. Your gain is the difference between $40,000 and $55,000. What you have had to use as the cost basis was an **adjusted basis.**

Stepped-Up Basis

Suppose now that dear Aunt Agatha died and left you the condominium in her will. You have no problem with estate taxes, because her will directed her executors to pay any estate taxes due out of her residual estate. At her death, the condominium is valued at $60,000 (assuming a still increasing real estate market). It is transferred to you, and you place it on the market for sale. If you sell for $60,000, you will have no income tax to pay on the sale. Along with the condominium you received a stepped-up basis. If you sell for $65,000, you will have realized a capital gain of $5,000. This is because your basis for the sale is the date-of-death value, or $60,000. That is your stepped-up basis. Inherited property is transferred to the inheritor with a stepped-up basis, assuming it has increased in value, which is the date-of-death value. If it is adjusted because of depreciation allowed on investment real estate, the depreciation is not taken into account. The person who receives the property just takes the date-of-death value in computing the capital gain. This rule may change. Congress has been trying desperately to change this part of the Internal Revenue Code, and some day it may succeed. An effort several years ago failed because it proved unworkable — but this is still one of the targets in tax legislation.

Tax Traps

Suppose Aunt Agatha, that wily and sophisticated widow, was not so generous with her property but decided to keep the rental condominium for herself as an investment. Over the years she took the depreciation deduction as an expense of rental property. Let's assume she paid $50,000 and depreciated it down to a tax basis value of $40,000. That would be her adjusted basis. The market changed for real estate, and she needs some cash and sells for $45,000. Does she have a $5,000 loss? No. She has a $5,000 capital gain.

Taxes and "Joint"

We have seen that labeling an asset can have an income tax consequence as well as an estate tax consequence. If Aunt Agatha buys a property and puts all of the money into it herself and lists as owners "Aunt A and Niece N, Joint Tenants," Niece N owns one-half from that time on and owns one-half of the income that the property earns. If Aunt A dies and has a taxable estate (over $600,000), all of the value of the property will be included in her estate for federal estate tax purposes. The reason for this is the Internal Revenue Code rule that presumes a jointly owned asset belongs in the estate of the first joint owner to die unless the co-owner can come forward and prove contribution to the acquisition of the asset.

The way to circumvent this surprise result (which Aunt Agatha won't be around to lament over) is to have Aunt Agatha wearing her financially sophisticated hat and very much alive go to her attorney or tax adviser and have a gift tax return prepared to document the gift of one-half of the property to N. This might involve encroachment on the unified credit allowable against estate taxes on A's estate, but it will complete the documentation necessary to prove that A gave N a gift. Furthermore, the appreciation between the date of the gift and A's death will never be a part of A's estate (although the appreciation of A's one-half will be).

Estate Planning and Basis

This type of planning is often a part of estate planning considerations between parents and children. The decision is whether to give a lifetime gift of appreciating property to (adult) children or leave the property within the estate until death. The "joint" situation discussed above is one of the most frequent routes taken by family members. Either widowed mother or father gives one-half of the family home to a child or children (to avoid probate) and continues to live there, or gives the entire ownership to a child or children and continues lifetime occupancy of the home.

In the first case, estate tax inclusion results from the rule that places a jointly owned asset in the estate of the first to die. In the second situation, occupying the home for life assures estate inclusion for federal estate tax purposes because such occupation fits within the "gift with a retained interest" clause of the Internal Revenue Code [Sec. 2036]. In either case, completion of the documentation (gift tax return, showing application of the potential gift tax against the unified credit), and having the parent living in the home pay rent to the child or children who now own the home, will avoid estate tax inclusion. Don't forget; if you decide this is a poor decision and you forego this gift to a child or children, the house will receive a "stepped-up basis" at your death. If the next generation later sells the house, there will be an income tax advantage because the house will have a date-of-death value as its basis.

Spouses and Taxes

If you are wondering how much of this applies to husbands and wives, the answer is, "None of the above." The rules are very different as to estate taxation of jointly owned property if the joint owners were married. In that case, there is no estate tax incurred on the death of one spouse, because of the change in the tax law enacted by Congress in 1981 when the 100 percent marital deduction came into existence.

There is an income tax consequence of joint ownership that should be weighed by couples when deciding on "joint" or "separate." This has to do with the basis the surviving spouse is handed along with the property that passes to the spouse who owned the assets JTRS with the decedent spouse. According to the law in effect at this time, only one half of the value of any property held in a joint tenancy between a husband and wife will be included in the estate of the first to die. Because of the unlimited marital deduction, this property would pass to the survivor free of any federal estate tax.

Why is it important that only one-half is included in the estate? It is important because this affects the income tax basis of the property that the surviving spouse inherits. As to that portion (one-half) of the jointly owned property, the surviving spouse's basis will be the date-of-death value. The effect is that as to that half, when the property is sold by the survivor, there may be a smaller (or no) income tax capital gain tax to pay, presumably because date-of-death values are often greater than original purchase values (at least, this probably would apply to real estate). Although, of course, values can decline. Date-of-death values give the heirs a "stepped-up basis," if the facts warrant it.

For example, in 1950 a couple purchased a property for $25,000. There is no mortgage due when the husband dies in 1991. The property was held in joint tenancy by the husband and wife. When the husband dies, it is worth $200,000. The wife is the JTRS survivor, and the property passes to her.

As to the one-half that she owned as part of the original purchase, her basis is $ 12,500 (1/2 of the price).

As to the one-half that she inherits, her basis is $100,000 (her basis if she sells)
Total $112,500.

If she sells for $112,500, there will be no tax to pay. If she sells for above that amount, the capital gain will be the difference between $112,500 and the sale price less any expenses of the sale, such as commissions.

The big question: would the widow be better off if her late husband had owned the property separately? In that case, the stepped-up date-of-death value would be $200,000. If she sold at that amount, there would be no capital gains tax to pay. If she had owned one-half as described above, and sold at $200,000, the taxable gain would be $87,500, which would be taxed as income (the difference between $112,500 as the basis and $200,000, the sale price). Should husband and wife each own investment property separately? It will take crystal-ball gazing to know who will inherit from whom. At the time of investment in a certain property, one does not usually think of that as a factor. It is, however, a side effect of a possibly changing mode of holding property for spouses, doing it "separately" instead of "jointly." Food for thought.

The oversimplified example shows basis as merely cost price. This basis usually applies in a purchase of personal property, such as securities. If the asset in question is investment real estate, a factor for depreciation must be taken into consideration. Depending on the dollar amount of the depreciation deductions taken over the years the property was an investment, the basis would have been reduced. This would apply to the one-half of the original purchase (as JTRS owners) by the husband and wife that, according to the current tax law, the wife owns (and does not inherit when her husband dies). This would change the basis figure for her half, but it would not change the basis figure for the half that she receives on her husband's death, which is the stepped-up date-of-death value. The latter value also would apply to the entire property if it had been owned as separate property by the husband. The depreciation deductions do not apply, and the widow who inherits the husband's separate property receives the fair market value for estate tax purposes (the date-of-death value or the alternate six-months-later value) as the basis, not reduced by depreciation deductions.

This basis, as we have seen, affects her income tax obligation on a later sale of the property. These are complicated concepts, but for one who is interested, depreciation on investment real property, basis, and stepped-up value all provide additional factors to be considered in deciding how to own property. Whether or not the property is depreciable may be of importance in reaching a decision.

Freedom to plan marital property ownership was enhanced by the 1981 tax law, which created an unlimited marital deduction. An explanation prepared by the staff of the Joint Committee on Taxation states:

"Because the maximum estate tax marital deduction generally was limited (under prior law) to one-half of the decedent's adjusted gross estate, the estate of a decedent who bequeathed his or her entire estate to the surviving spouse was often subject to estate taxes even though the property remained within the marital unit. When the surviving spouse later transferred the property (often to the children), the entire amount was subject to transfer taxes. The cumulative effect was to subject their property to tax one and one-half times, i.e., one half upon the death of the first spouse and again fully upon the death of the second spouse. This effect typically occurred in the case of jointly held property. Because this additional tax fell most heavily on widows, it was often referred to as the 'widow's tax.'

"Although the Congress recognized that this additional tax could be minimized through proper estate planning, it believed that an individual generally should be free to pass his or her entire estate to a surviving spouse without the imposition of any estate tax. For similar reasons, the Congress believed it appropriate generally to permit unlimited lifetime transfers between spouses without the imposition of any gift taxes.

"In addition, the Congress determined that substantial simplification of the estate and gift taxes would be achieved by allowing an unlimited deduction for transfers between spouses. Under prior law, it was often extremely difficult to determine the ownership of property held within the marital unit and to determine whose funds were used to acquire that property. These problems generally will not arise with an unlimited marital deduction." [General Explanation of the Economic Recovery Act of 1981, Staff of the Joint Committee on Taxation, Dec. 31, 1981, pp. 233-34.]

Divorce and Taxes

Transfers between spouses during marriage is a nontaxable event. This was one of the great gifts to married people by Congress in its enactment of the 1981 tax law. Remember, the name of this enlightened provision was the 100 percent marital deduction, which applied to lifetime transfers (gifts) or deathtime transfers (via joint tenancy survivorship, will, or intestacy). In 1984, Congress decided to make the *end* of marriage by divorce a nontaxable event as well.

No gain or loss is recognized on the transfer of property from one person to another who is a former spouse, if the transfer is part of a divorce settlement or separation agreement. The nonspouses are treated somewhat the same as spouses at the time of transfer. However, the similarity ends there. The parties become nonmarrieds, and the transfer is for income tax purposes treated as a gift. In other words, the transferee former spouse takes the basis of the transferor spouse. There are many other tax considerations in divorce, and transfer of property is only one of them. For example, both parties should know the rules for sharing or taking separately the lifetime exclusion of $125,000 of capital gain on the sale of a residence. Tax advice is important in divorce planning.

As we learned in the chapter on divorce, some courts include *all* property, regardless of how titled, in distribution of property on divorce. This may not be as calamitous as it sounds, when you know that along with a court-ordered transfer of assets to satisfy a property distribution scheme, the basis in the hands of the titled owner also is being transferred. Timing is important because certain time frames apply to the divorce-ordered transfer or transfer agreed-upon between the parties. For example, transfers pursuant to a written agreement concerning marital and property rights are exempt from gift taxes but only if the divorce occurs within three years (I.R.C.S. 2516).

Life Insurance

One form of property that, if handled properly, can provide a tax-free windfall for beneficiaries is life insurance. Naming the *owner* of a life insurance policy is extremely important in assuring that the proceeds are not included in the estate of the named insured and thus available for possible estate tax inclusion. Life insurance is one of those assets that transfers outside of probate but if owned by the decedent is a part of that person's estate. The way to avoid this is to have the policy owned by a spouse or a trust on behalf of children.

An insured must not hold an "incident of ownership" in the policy at death or within three years of death. The best way to be certain that an insured will not be considered to have held these "incidents of ownership" is to make certain that the insured never holds an incident of ownership. What is an "incident of ownership"? The insured must not pay the premiums, have the ability to change beneficiaries, borrow against the cash value, etc. In other words, there must not be "ownership" types of control over the policy. How are the premiums paid? If a spouse has separate assets and earnings from those assets, that person can pay the premiums. If a trust is established on behalf of minor children, income-generating assets must be transferred irrevocably to the trust so that the trust can pay the premiums. This is complicated planning, and your lawyer can help you. A type of life insurance being offered today provides for insuring the life of the last-to-die of a husband and wife. In that way, money is available after the marital deduction has been used on the first death (remember, no federal estate tax on a transfer at death between husband and wife) in order to pay estate taxes due when the second spouse dies, leaving a taxable estate.

Life insurance has not been dealt with in great detail because it is usually a part of early-in-married-life planning, especially in a family where there are minor children. The income-earner (or earners) may want to assure that funds will be available for college for those children in the event of the early demise of the income-earners. At a later stage in life, separate assets of each spouse can provide that spouse with a separate income in the event of the demise of the other owner of assets. Buying insurance on the life of the "second-to-die" is a way of providing funds for estate taxes if due.

Taxes and the Future

Everyone would like to have a crystal ball. Failing that, it is important to keep on top of the news of the activities of the tax-writing committees and sub-committees, and pronouncements of the congressional leaders, etc. Comments in this chapter on taxes have been minimal. More information would be gained by conferring with your own tax adviser, especially if important moves are being contemplated either with regard to your finances or property or changes in your life.

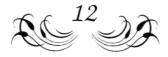

The Psychology of "Separate"

The previous chapters have taken you on a trip through various life situations you might encounter in which it may (or may not) be desirable to own separate property. There has been no attempt to make this a complete, all-inclusive treatise. Discussions of title, creditors' rights, estate-planning, trusts, divorce, wills, probate, and the like have been intended merely to serve as an introduction to these subjects. Forms of ownership have been focused on to introduce the reader to an acknowledgement that the form of ownership of assets is significant.

Ownership for Husbands and Wives

We are looking at the 21st century, but many married people are locked into the customs and habits of the 19th century. More than 100 years ago, legislatures in the various states of this country began removing the shackles that tied husbands and wives into knots of "oneness" that people had accepted as the normal way of owning property. "Oneness" meant that when a man and woman married they became *one*, literally, for certain legal purposes, including property ownership. "One" meant that although it might take two to convey property on a sale to a buyer, only one was in control, and only one was in possession in the eyes of the law. That one was the husband.

In 1977, a case came before the Supreme Court of Alabama, bringing into issue a provision in the state constitution that denied a wife the power of conveying her own land to a buyer when her husband had refused to assent and concur in the sale. Without his concurrence, the conveyance to the buyer would be void. The court found that such provision violated Alabama's constitution which guarantees citizens equal protection of the laws. It also violated the United States Constitution which preserves the right of equal protection for all citizens. In deciding, the Alabama court said:

> "There is no provision of the Constitution which would permit the legislature to deny to married women rights possessed by all other adults. Its authority to do so . . . cannot rest upon an ancient myth that married women are presumed to be more needful of protection of their own interests than other adults, male or female." [*Peddy* v. *Montgomery,* Ala. 345 So. 2d 631.]

Most states have removed impediments thwarting the free action of married women with regard to property. The difficulty is that many marrieds still act as though the common law presumption that the husband is the dominant party to the marriage still exists.

Unmarrieds

As we have seen, unmarried women have been the deferring, disinherited, and also dominated members of the family since Biblical days, dominated by their fathers before marriage and by their husbands after. Independent ownership of assets has been a fairly modern phenomenon. The psychological goal of independent thinking may yet have to be achieved.

Freedom from Guilt

The biggest difficulty for men and women in adopting a plan of separate ownership of assets is, perhaps, the onus of guilt that clings to the partner who suggests such a financial plan. He thinks, "Why does she want her separate stocks? Is she thinking of divorce?" She might think, "Why doesn't he want me to have a separate brokerage account? Doesn't he trust me?"

Conclusion. If the guilt, doubt, suspicion, timidity, and fear are removed from joint planning, perhaps decisions can be arrived at that will be mutually agreeable and that are based on cool-headed unemotional design. If this book leads to a consideration of *how* assets should be owned or rearranged to implement a particular plan, it will have served a useful purpose.

Appendix 1

Summary of State Laws Affecting Property

Introduction

The summaries in this appendix are not all-inclusive. A great deal more of state legislation affects property than will be summarized here. Rather, the summaries cover some of the subject of property as that subject has been dealt with in the preceding text. For example, the topic "Marriage" only specifies whether or not the given state recognizes common-law marriages. Other statutory material under "Marriage" would have to do with the legality of certain marriages, the legal age of participants, requirements as to health tests, etc., none of which is deemed pertinent to readers of this book. Therefore, bear in mind that this appendix is a capsule reference to certain state laws. For more complete coverage, refer to *Martindale-Hubbell Law Digests, United States Law Digest,* © 1990 by Reed Publishing (USA), Inc., the source of the information listed here. This reference can be found in some public libraries.

Topics Covered in This Appendix

The following topics are covered. Not every state uses the same nomenclature, and for some states there are subjects not on this list. Some version of the following types of subjects, however, will be found for each state:

❖ curtesy

❖ dower

❖ divorce (or dissolution of marriage)

❖ husband and wife

❖ marriage

❖ personal property

❖ real property

❖ taxation

❖ wills (having to do with election or statutory share)

How to Use This Appendix

Coverage under each topic is intended to give only a quick look. Under "Wills," for example, you will not find the precise amount of a surviving spouse's statutory share (or elective share against the will), because the information in the statute itself includes references to children of the deceased, children of the deceased from other marriages, surviving parents of the deceased, and so on. The percentage would change depending on the existence of other potential heirs. You will learn, however, which states allow a surviving spouse to take an elective share or to waive this right.

It is also important to remember that laws undergo frequent changes and that court decisions establish legal precedents further embellishing and interpreting statutory law. The material presented is current up to 1990; but anyone whose planning depends on the up-to-the-minute law should consult an attorney for the latest update on legislation in a particular state or on case law affecting the matter at hand.

You may find that a quick look at this appendix will be very useful in some situations. Here is an example. You have inherited a house in township X of state Y. You alone have inherited this property from your late grandmother. You do not want it or need it. It is an old building in need of repairs. It is not rentable unless expenditures are made for these repairs. You find, however, that it is salable. The owner of the house next door wants to buy it quickly, because he also has an opportunity, and may choose instead to buy the house on the other side. You have to make an immediate decision and decide to sell. Your husband, however, is out of the country, and he may be unreachable at the time of settlement. A quick look at the law in state Y indicates that dower has been abolished. You may sell the house and convey good title without having your husband's signature on the deed.

Here is another scenario. Your niece, Betty Smith, is getting married. She is your late brother's child, and you want to give a sizable present. However, the prospective bridegroom, George Gambler, is not to your liking and you have serious doubts that the marriage will last. What if you give the young couple the gift you have in mind and they later get divorced? You quietly go to the summary for your state and find that property owned by either party prior to the marriage is not subject to distribution on divorce. Of course, the law of your state (presumably where the marriage will take place) may not be the law followed in the state in which the couple might be living if there is a divorce, but a little further search reveals that most states follow that rule. You quickly call your broker and tell him to buy 1,000 shares of Good Corporation Stock in the name of Betty Smith, now. She is getting married next week. If Betty has looked into this matter, she might be inclined to retain the stock in her separate ownership.

The material in this appendix is informational only and in capsule form. Do not overlook the importance of and necessity for proper legal or other professional advice.

ALABAMA

Curtesy and Dower

Abolished in Alabama.

Divorce

Property acquired before marriage or by gift or inheritance may not be considered in making allowance for the support of either spouse out of the estate of the other spouse unless such property or income from it has been used during the marriage for the spouses' common benefit. This is also the rule if divorce is granted for misconduct of the other spouse. Misconduct may be considered in determining the amount of allowance to either spouse from the estate of the other spouse, but the excepted property (property acquired before marriage or by gift or inheritance) may not be considered in determining the amount of allowance. This rule also is followed in property distribution. Again, property used regularly for the common benefit of the spouses during marriage may be awarded in a property settlement. Factors considered in determining amount of alimony (and in making equitable division of property) include earning ability of parties, future prospects, age, health, duration of marriage, accustomed standard of living, source, value and type of property, and conduct of parties as related to marriage (473 S0.2d 1091).

Husband and Wife

Alabama is a separate property state. All property acquired by the wife before or after marriage and all earnings received by her from third persons are the wife's separate property, and are not subject to husband's debts. Antenuptial agreements are valid but scrutinized for informed consent and equity to the spouse (386 S0.2d 749). Spouse must waive statutory right to share of spouse's estate to allow assets of first marriage to go to first marriage's children.

Marriage

Common-law marriages are recognized, but mere cohabitation is not enough to establish a common law marriage. They also must have a mutual intent to be married.

Personal Property

Tenancy by the entirety does not exist in Alabama, but joint tenancy with right of survivorship does exist in personal property.

Real Property

Tenancy by the entirety does not exist in Alabama.

Survivorship as an incident of joint tenancy has been abolished except when the document (a deed, for example) uses "with right of survivorship" or other words after "joint tenants." (This means that an instrument creating a joint tenancy between two or more parties is construed to mean a tenancy in common unless the survivorship right is included and spelled out, and the instrument shows the intention to create a survivorship right.)

Taxation

There is no inheritance tax in Alabama, but there is an estate tax. That tax is imposed on net estates passing by will or under the intestacy laws, equivalent to the amount of the full credit or deduction allowable in computing federal estate taxes under the federal act in effect at the time. Alabama also imposes a tax on generation-skipping transfers.

There is no gift tax.

Wills

A surviving spouse has the right to take an elective share, but that right may be waived.

ALASKA

Divorce

In Alaska, courts may divide property obtained during the marriage. Furthermore, courts may, for equitable distribution reasons, divide property obtained by either spouse prior to the marriage. Upon dissolution of the marriage as declared by the court, the court may decree for division between the parties the joint property of the parties, or separate property of each in such manner "as may be just."

Dower

Dower has been abolished.

Husband and Wife

Each married person may own and manage his or her own property. Rights in property acquired by gift or inheritance are not subject to debts of the other spouse. In other words, Alaska is a separate property state. Either spouse may convey his or her real property by separate deed as though unmarried, but there are special rules for joining in a conveyance of the family home ("homestead") owned by either spouse.

Note, however, that if real property is conveyed *to* a husband and wife, the ownership is as tenants by the entirety unless expressly declared otherwise.

While Alaska is not a community property state, there is a statutory provision that if a married person dies holding property that was deemed community property under the laws of another jurisdiction, one half of this property is deemed to belong to the surviving spouse. The other half is the decedent's property, subject to testamentary disposition.

Marriage

Common-law marriages are not recognized in Alaska.

Personal Property

Joint tenancy may be maintained as to interests in personal property.

Real Property

Joint tenancy has been abolished. All persons having undivided interests in realty are tenants in common. However, joint interests in personalty have not been abolished. Also, tenancy by the entirety is recognized for a husband and wife, and may be created by a husband and wife between themselves. Alaska has made estates held by the entirety (other than homestead) liable for the debts of either or both tenants.

Taxation

The inheritance tax has been repealed. An estate tax is imposed to absorb the federal allowance for state death taxes.

ARIZONA

Curtesy

Abolished.

Deeds

Arizona is a community property state, and a conveyance of community real property is not valid unless that conveyance is executed and acknowledged by both husband and wife. However, a married person may convey his or her separate property without being joined by his or her spouse in such conveyance. A husband and wife must join in a conveyance of the family homestead.

Descent and Distribution

The surviving spouse has no right to take an elective share.

Dissolution of Marriage

A court may assign each spouse his or her sole and separate property, and divide community, joint tenancy, and other property held in common equitably without regard to marital misconduct. Property acquired outside Arizona is considered community property if it would have been community property in Arizona at the time of acquisition.

Dower

Abolished.

Husband and Wife

All property, real or personal, owned by either spouse before marriage and any property acquired by gift or inheritance after marriage and the appreciation and profits from such property are the separate property of that spouse. The separate property of a spouse is not liable for the separate debts of the other spouse, and the separate property of a spouse may be conveyed without having the other spouse join in the conveyance. Each spouse has sole management, control, and disposition rights of his or her separate property.

All property acquired by either the husband or wife during marriage is community property. This applies if the spouses are living in Arizona at the time they acquire the property or if they are residing in a state that has a similar community property law. This does not include property described above as separate property.

A spouse owns his or her separate property and his or her share of community property, and this property passes by testamentary disposition at death or by intestacy if no will was left.

Spouses may create a joint tenancy between themselves by an agreement that the property should be treated as jointly owned. Any conveyance of community realty requires the joining of both spouses.

Marital rights in property acquired in Arizona during the marriage by persons who were married outside Arizona and then moved into the state are controlled by Arizona law.

Marriage

Common-law marriages are not legal in Arizona but are recognized if valid where they were contracted.

Antenuptial agreements are valid if they are not contrary to law or "good morals"; they may affect rights in and to community property.

Personal Property

Tenancy by the entireties is not recognized.

Real Property

A conveyance to two or more persons creates a tenancy in common, but joint tenancy with right of survivorship may be created by express words. A grant to a husband and wife is presumed to establish a community tenancy, but it may create a joint tenancy between the husband and wife if the deed of conveyance contains language expressly creating such an estate and the wording is such as to indicate that the husband and wife show knowledge of that provision.

Taxation

There is no inheritance tax. The estate tax is gauged to the allowance for state death taxes in filing a federal return or paying federal estate taxes.

ARKANSAS

Curtesy

Common law curtesy has been abolished, but in its place there is a statutory allowance that is still called curtesy. The allowance is the same as the widow's dower. No conveyance by a spouse without the concurrence of the other spouse can pass title free of curtesy or dower.

Descent and Distribution

The surviving spouse takes a percentage dependent on the existence of other survivors, such as children, and on the length of time that the spouses were married. There is also a provision with regard to community property of another jurisdiction. If personal property was acquired as community property in a community property state and/or real estate located in Arkansas was acquired with proceeds from or is traceable to community property acquired in another jurisdiction, then one half of such property belongs to the surviving spouse. The other half is the property of the decedent spouse and is not subject to the surviving spouse's right to elect against the will, and no estate of dower or curtesy exists in that half.

Divorce

On a final decree of divorce, each party receives the "undisposed" property that he or she brought into the marriage. One half of marital property is distributed to each party unless the court finds such division inequitable. Marital property is defined as all property acquired by either spouse after marriage. However, it does not include property acquired by either spouse by gift, bequest, devise, or descent; property derived from or exchanged for such property; property acquired after a decree of divorce; property excluded by valid agreement of the parties; and increase in the value of property acquired before the marriage.

Dower

Dower is still a legal estate in Arkansas, and, as was stated under "Curtesy," it applies to both spouses. If a married person dies "intestate" (without a will) leaving a surviving spouse and a child or children, the surviving spouse receives (is "vested of") a life interest in one-third of all the real property that the decedent spouse owned and fee title in one-third of the personal property that the decedent owned. The percentage changes if there are no surviving children. The Arkansas statute mentions creditors; the proportion that the surviving spouse receives "as against creditors" is roughly one-third (depending on the nature of the property). There is also a specific provision relating to timber, oil, gas, and mineral property. A married person may release dower or curtesy in real estate by joining in a spouse's deed.

Husband and Wife

A married woman may acquire and hold property of any kind and do business as a "feme sole." Separate property is not liable for a husband's debts. If a married person permits his or her spouse to have control and management of separate property, this raises the presumption that the spouse is acting as agent. But if a wife allows her husband to use her separate property as his own (and thus he contracts debts based on his apparent ownership), she is *estopped* to claim it. The word "estopped" involves the legal doctrine of "estoppel." The statutory provision is mentioned here to alert anyone interested to seek further legal information.

A married person may convey or release rights in homestead, dower, or curtesy through a duly appointed power of attorney. If a husband conveys to himself and his wife, that creates the estate of entirety. Spouses may enter into antenuptial contracts, and the rights mentioned above may be released legally in such an agreement. Neither spouse is liable for debts of the other contracted prior to the marriage, nor is a spouse's separate property liable for debts of the other spouse in trade or business.

Marriage

Common-law marriages in Arkansas are not recognized, but Arkansas does recognize as valid a common-law marriage that was contracted and is valid in another state.

Antenuptial agreements establishing rights and obligations concerning property of either or both parties are valid and enforceable if executed voluntarily and with proper disclosure of financial data.

Separate property owned prior to marriage and property received after marriage by gift or inheritance, or by his or her own business or labor, and income from such separate property remains the separate property of that spouse. Such property may be sold or transferred without interference of the other spouse. Separate property of a married person is not liable for debts of his or her spouse.

Personal Property

Tenancy by the entirety exists in personal property, in shares of corporate stock, in bank accounts, and in savings accounts.

Real Property

Joint ownership by husband and wife creates an estate by entirety. Conveyance to a husband and wife creates an estate of entirety with right of survivorship. A conveyance to two or more people (not spouses) creates a tenancy in common unless a joint tenancy (with right of survivorship) is specified.

Taxation

There is no inheritance tax. The estate tax in Arkansas is equal to the credit allowable on the federal estate tax return.

Wills

The surviving spouse may elect between will and any part of property that would have been taken on intestacy (meaning statutory allowances), including dower or curtesy and homestead rights.

CALIFORNIA

Community Property

California is a community property state.

Curtesy and Dower

There is no dower or curtesy right. A surviving spouse of a nonresident decedent has the same right to take a share of noncommunity real property against the decedent's will as though such property were situated in the decedent's domicile.

Descent and Distribution

The surviving spouse takes an outright share of the separate property of the deceased spouse if not disposed by will. The percentage depends on who the other takers are — surviving children, parents, and so on.

Dissolution of Marriage

California is a community property jurisdiction. The parties may by written agreement divide their property or may stipulate in open court as to property division. Otherwise, the court must, in decreeing legal separation, equally divide community, quasi-community, and homestead property. The court may also award a particular asset to one party to effectuate substantially equal division or may make an additional award where one spouse has been determined to have deliberately misappropriated the community property of the other spouse. A single-family residence acquired during the marriage in joint tenancy is, upon legal separation or dissolution of the marriage, presumed to be community property. All real property situated in California and personal property wherever situated, acquired during the marriage which is not separate property, is community property. Upon dissolution or legal separation, property acquired in joint form, including tenancy in common, joint tenancy, and tenancy by entirety is presumed to be community property. Presumption may be rebutted by written evidence that it is separate property.

Husband and Wife

A husband and wife may hold property as joint tenants or tenants in common or as community property. Either a husband or wife (or both) may have separate property. An inventory of the separate personal property of either spouse may be recorded in the office of the county recorder in the county where the parties reside, and such a record is evidence of the title of such property. The separate property of either spouse is not liable for debts secured by community property unless there is a special assent in writing making separate property liable. A conveyance or encumbrance (mortgage) may be made by a married woman in the same manner and has the same effect as if she were unmarried. Joinder of the husband in a wife's conveyance or encumbrance of her separate property is not necessary. A married woman must join with her husband in a deed to release homestead rights or convey or encumber community property.

The community property system applies in California. All property owned by either spouse before marriage and acquired by either spouse after marriage by gift or inheritance, together with earnings on that property or enhancement of its value, is the separate property of that spouse and may be conveyed without the consent of the other spouse. All real property situated in California and all personal property wherever situated acquired during marriage by a married person while domiciled in California is community property.

Quasi-community property is all real and personal property wherever situated acquired by either spouse while domiciled elsewhere that would have been community property if the acquiring spouse had been domiciled in California or property that has been received in exchange for such property. (This puts the parties on notice that records should be kept if there is a desire to designate some property as separate.)

Property taken in the names of a husband and wife as joint tenants may be considered joint and not community property if the parties intend it to be joint and this is documented. However, there is a presumption in the law that property acquired by a husband and wife is community property. Unless the husband and wife carefully designate otherwise, a purchaser is protected in his reliance on the community ownership of the husband-and-wife seller.

Management and control of community personal property as to his or her share may be exercised by either spouse. A spouse operating or managing a business or interest in a business that is community property has sole management and control. As to community realty, either spouse has management and control, but both spouses must join in a lease for more than one year or in a conveyance on a sale. On the death of either spouse, one-half of the community property belongs to the surviving spouse. If there is no testamentary disposition by the decedent, the decedent's share also goes to the surviving spouse. For those who are domiciled in California, this also applies to personal property, wherever situated, and to real property situated in California even though it may have been acquired while the decedent was domiciled elsewhere, if it would have been community property acquired while the decedent was domiciled in California.

Community property going to a surviving spouse may do so without probate or administration, but in that case the surviving spouse is personally liable for debts of the deceased spouse chargeable against the community property. A surviving spouse may elect that the interest of the decedent spouse in community property be probated, and for that purpose procedures exist for determining what is community property and for apportioning debts.

Marriage

Common-law marriage cannot be contracted in California but is recognized if it was valid in the state in which it was contracted.

Personal Property

Tenancy by the entirety in personal property is not recognized. Joint tenancies in safe-deposit boxes are prohibited (c.c. 683.1).

Real Property

Tenancy by the entirety is not recognized. Joint tenancy and tenancy in common are recognized and defined, but a joint tenancy is created only when it is declared as such.

Taxation

The inheritance tax and gift tax were repealed effective June 9, 1982. An estate tax is imposed in California to accord with the maximum allowable state death tax credit under federal estate tax law.

Wills

A surviving spouse has no right of election between a testamentary provision, if any, and a share of the separate property of the decedent (as in the case of intestacy). However, if a spouse attempts in his or her will to make a disposition of more than half of community property, then the surviving spouse must elect whether to take under the will or to take his or her half of the community property. The surviving spouse may take property given that spouse under a will as well as his or her community share.

COLORADO

Curtesy

Tenancy by curtesy does not exist in Colorado.

Dissolution of Marriage

Property is distributed upon dissolution by giving each spouse his or her separate property and then dividing marital property in the proportions that the court deems just. The court is to disregard marital misconduct. The court is to consider these guidelines: contributions (including contributions as homemaker); the value of the property set aside for each spouse; the increase, decrease, or depletion of property; and the economic circumstances of each party.

Dower

Abolished.

Husband and Wife

A married woman retains the separate real and personal property she owned at marriage and property that comes to her by gift or bequest, and income therefrom. Such property is not liable for her husband's debts. Nuptial agreements are valid and enforceable provided that fair and reasonable disclosure of assets and financial obligations is made. Neither spouse requires the consent or joinder of the other in order to convey or encumber his or her separate property.

Marriage

Common-law marriage is recognized.

Personal Property

A joint tenancy in personal property may be created by a declaration of joint tenancy in the instrument evidencing ownership.

Real Property

Joint tenancy and tenancy in common are recognized. Tenancy by the entirety is not. Tenancy in common is presumed unless the instrument or will conveying the property specified joint tenancy.

Taxation

An inheritance tax did exist, but it does not apply to the estates of decedents dying after December 31, 1979. The gift tax also does not apply to transfers by gift occurring after December 31, 1979. The Colorado estate tax is based on the credit for state death taxes allowable under the federal estate tax.

Wills

A surviving spouse may exercise an election, notwithstanding a will, to take possession of up to one-half of the decedent's estate by filing a petition for his or her elective share, but property already received by the surviving spouse is charged against the elective share.

CONNECTICUT

Curtesy

Abolished.

Dissolution of Marriage

The court may assign to either the husband or wife all or part of the property of the other. The court may pass title to real property to either party or to a third person, or it may order the sale of such property when, in the judgment of the court, sale of the property is proper to effectuate the court's decree. In fixing the nature and value of the property to be assigned, if any, the guidelines that the court is to consider are: the length of the marriage; the cause of dissolution; the age, health, station, occupation, amount and sources of income, vocational skills, employability, estate, liabilities, and needs of each party; and the opportunity of each party to effect future acquisitions of capital assets and income. The court is also to consider each party's contribution in the acquisition, preservation, or appreciation in value of the parties' respective estates. The statute gives the court broad discretion in assigning property upon the dissolution of marriage.

Dower

Abolished.

Husband and Wife

Either spouse may dispose of his or her property without having the other spouse join in the conveyance. A wife may convey and receive the conveyance of real and personal property in her own name. A wife's separate earnings are her sole property.

Marriage

Common-law marriages are not recognized.

Personal Property

There is no statutory authorization for tenancy by the entireties in personal property.

Real Property

A conveyance to more than one person is deemed to create a tenancy in common unless the words "as joint tenants" follows the names (this means joint tenants with right of survivorship). In reverse, a joint tenancy (with right of survivorship) may be converted into a tenancy in common by conveyance, mortgage, attachment and execution on a judgment, or dissolution of marriage. Tenancy by the entirety is not recognized in Connecticut.

Taxation

No inheritance tax is named as such, but a transfer tax is in the statute. An estate tax is imposed on the transfer of a decedent's estate that is equal to the amount allowed as a credit against federal estate taxes. There is no gift tax in Connecticut.

Wills

A provision in a will for a surviving spouse is deemed to be in lieu of a statutory share unless a contrary intention appears from the will. The surviving spouse must, in writing, elect to take one-third of the estate for life, if desired. When a spouse elects to take a statutory share in lieu of the provision for that spouse in a will, general legacies are first taken to satisfy that share before specific legacies are disturbed. In the absence of such election, the spouse is deemed to have accepted the will and is barred from taking the statutory share.

DELAWARE

Curtesy

The estate of curtesy has been abolished.

Divorce

Marital property is divided as follows: "Upon request of either party in divorce or annulment proceedings, court shall divide equitably all marital property without regard to marital misconduct as it deems just."

Agreements between husband and wife relating to support or adjustment of property rights will be upheld, even though such an agreement was made in contemplation of divorce, if there was no collusion and the agreement was not conducive to the procurement of divorce. The *Law Digest* states: "Law prefers private settlement of marital obligations at time of separation." (287 A. 2d 413, aff'd. 336 A. 2d 216).

Dower

The estate of dower has been abolished.

Husband and Wife

A married woman holds her property as a separate estate that she may sell, transfer, encumber, and so on. Deeds of real property executed by a married woman are valid "as if she were sole."

Marriage

Common-law marriages are not valid in Delaware. Delaware follows the law of most states that do not recognize common-law marriages but will recognize such marriages if contracted by nonresidents of Delaware elsewhere, and if valid in the state where contracted.

Personal Property

Tenancy by the entirety may exist.

Real Property

Both joint tenancies and tenancies in common are recognized. There is a statutory presumption in favor of tenancies in common (except with regard to executors and trustees); but a joint tenancy can be created by express statement that the property is to be held in joint tenancy rather than as a tenancy in common. A conveyance to a husband and wife gives them an estate by the entirety "as at common law."

Taxation

There is an estate tax and inheritance tax. If a gift has been made in contemplation of death, the gift tax is the same as the inheritance tax. The estate tax allows a credit for the inheritance tax paid to Delaware or other states, and this is deductible from the maximum credit allowable under federal estate tax law. The remainder, if any, constitutes the Delaware estate tax.

Wills

A surviving spouse has the right to take a one-third share of the elective estate, less the amount of the transfers that have been made to the surviving spouse by the decedent.

DISTRICT OF COLUMBIA

Curtesy

Abolished (see "Dower").

Divorce

Upon the final decree of divorce, each party is assigned his or her sole and separate property acquired prior to marriage, and his or her sole and separate property acquired during marriage by gift, bequest, devise, or descent. All other property acquired during marriage, regardless of how titled, is distributed in an equitable manner. Among the guidelines are the duration of the marriage, age, health, occupation, employability, assets, debts, and provisions for the custody of minor children. Fault in ending the marriage may or may not be a consideration in property distribution.

Dower

The right to dower applies to the husband or wife. Neither may convey or encumber his or her real property without joinder of the other spouse. No dower attaches to land held in joint tenancy. Dower entitles the surviving spouse to a one-third interest for life in real estate owned by the deceased spouse during the marriage. A spouse may release the dower right by joining in the other spouse's deed. The intestate share of the surviving spouse in real estate is in lieu of dower unless he or she files a written election to take dower. In a divorce, the court may retain to the spouse obtaining the divorce his or her right of dower in the other spouse's estate.

Husband and Wife

Each spouse may hold property separately of the other and dispose and convey "as if unmarried." However, this must be read together with statements regarding the married person's rights and obligations under "Dower."

Conveyance of property is not impaired by the marital state of the seller, but attention must be paid to the necessity for release of dower.

Antenuptial contracts specifying property rights at the death of a spouse or on divorce are not void, but such contracts will be scrutinized by a court, which will determine its validity after examining fairness, voluntary entrance of both parties to the agreement, and full disclosures of assets.

Marriage

Common-law marriages are recognized.

Personal Property

Tenancy by the entirety exists.

Real Property

Conveyance to a husband and wife as joint tenants (unless otherwise specified) creates a tenancy by the entirety. If not expressly designated as a joint tenancy, a conveyance to two or more persons (including a husband and wife) is a tenancy in common; however, an estate vested in executors or trustees, as such, is a joint tenancy, unless expressly stated to be a tenancy in common.

Taxation

An estate tax is imposed to obtain the credit allowed by federal estate tax laws for state death taxes.

Wills

A surviving spouse who files a written renunciation of the decedent spouse's will becomes entitled to the share of the decedent's estate to which he or she would have been entitled had the decedent died intestate (with dower if this is elected in lieu of real estate). The intestate share applies if the decedent made no devise or bequest to the surviving spouse or if any estate of the decedent is undisposed by will. Otherwise, the will of the decedent spouse applies unless the surviving spouse renounces it.

FLORIDA

Curtesy

Abolished in Florida.

Divorce

The court has the power to adjudicate property rights only where these are made an issue by the parties. The terms of any valid property settlement agreed to by the parties generally may not be modified by the court. Where the parties are unable to agree on the disposition of property, the court has power to determine disposition, based on legal and equitable principles. Florida courts recognize special equities and equitable distribution doctrines. Courts may enforce an antenuptial agreement to arbitrate a dispute.

Dower

Abolished in Florida.

Elective Share of Surviving Spouse

The surviving spouse of a person who dies domiciled in Florida has the right to an elective share of the estate of the deceased spouse. No elective share exists in the Florida property of a decedent who was not domiciled in Florida. The size of the elective share is detailed in the statute.

Husband and Wife

Real or personal property may be held in the name of either the husband or wife or both. A married woman may contract, sell, convey, mortgage, etc., her real and personal property (except homestead property) without joinder of her husband. Both spouses must join in the sale, gift, or mortgage of homestead property. (It is important to consider this provision because you may not think of the Florida condominium as the family "homestead." If you think of buying from a married seller, make sure that the spouse signs the deed, because the condominium might be their homestead.)

Marriage

Common-law marriages are invalid (if entered into after 1968).

Personal Property

Personal (and real) property may be held by a husband and wife as tenants by the entirety.

Real Property

All interests in real estate that were recognized by common law are recognized in Florida. Survivorship as to joint tenancies has been abolished unless the instrument expressly provides for it. Where property is conveyed to a husband and wife, however, they are presumed to take as tenants by the entirety (with resulting survivorship). In case of divorce, former spouses become tenants in common.

Taxation

There is no inheritance or gift tax in Florida. The tax on the estates of resident and nonresident decedents is equal to the amounts allowed as credits or deductions from similar taxes levied by the United States or any state.

Wills

If an election is filed, the remaining assets of the estate after payment of the elective share (as indicated under the topic "Elective Share of Surviving Spouse") are distributed as though the surviving spouse had predeceased the decedent. Wills made by a husband or wife whose marriage to each other has been dissolved subsequent to the date of the will are void as to the divorced former spouses.

GEORGIA

Curtesy

No tenancy by curtesy in Georgia.

Divorce

Property acquired by the parties during marriage is subject to equitable division. Interspousal gifts made during the marriage also are eligible for equitable division. After separation, no transfer of property by either party (except in payment of preexisting debt) will pass title to defeat the vesting of property according to the verdict of the jury or court in a divorce action. Agreements as to property, alimony, etc., made between the parties in contemplation of the divorce are valid.

Dower

The right of dower has been abolished by Georgia laws.

Husband and Wife

The property of the wife at the time of marriage remains her separate property, and any property acquired by her (or earnings, etc.) during marriage remains separate and is not liable for any debt of the husband. When a transaction between a husband and wife is attacked as a fraud on the creditors of either the husband or wife, the burden is on the married person to show that the transaction is fair, and not in a fraudulent act. Discrimination by a lender in extension of credit on the basis of marital status is prohibited. Either spouse may convey or encumber his or her real estate without joinder or consent of the other. A wife must join in her husband's conveyance of real property to which he holds record title in trust for her.

Marriage

Common-law marriages are recognized.

Personal Property

Joint tenancy with survivorship as under common law (including tenancy by the entirety) has been abolished. However, rights of survivorship may be created by contract. An instrument of title in favor of two or more is construed to create an interest in common without survivorship unless the instrument expressly refers to the takers as joint tenants or as taking jointly with survivorship.

Real Property

The word "heirs" is unnecessary to create a fee simple estate. Every properly executed conveyance creates a fee simple estate unless a lesser estate is mentioned. Thus, estates for the life of a tenant may be created by an express agreement or by operation of law. Any conveyance to two or more persons is construed to create a tenancy in common unless the instrument contains reference to joint tenants. Tenancy by the entirety is not recognized.

Taxation

There is no inheritance tax and no gift tax in Georgia. The estate tax is equal to the credit allowed on the federal estate tax return, and credit also is allowed for death taxes paid to another state on the transfer of property outside Georgia.

Wills

A surviving spouse and minor children are entitled to "support from the estate for one year." A legatee having a claim adverse to the will must elect whether to claim under the will or against it (unless that legatee is also a creditor).

HAWAII

Curtesy

Hawaii has adopted the Uniform Probate Code, which has provisions for election by a spouse to take the prescribed share, but the section abolishing curtesy was not adopted. However, for rights in the property of a married person that accrued prior to July 1, 1977, the husband has a life interest in one-third of the lands owned by the wife in fee simple at her death and an absolute right to ownership of one-third of her remaining property. During her life, he has no curtesy right, inchoate or otherwise. (This, therefore, indicates that there are still some remaining male marital rights in Hawaii.)

Divorce

A court has discretion to divide and distribute any property of the divorcing spouses, real, personal, mixed, joint, or separate.

Dower

Although Hawaii has adopted the Uniform Probate Code, for rights accruing prior to July 1, 1977, a wife has a dower right to one-third of the land owned by her husband at any time during the marriage. She also is entitled to ownership of one-third of his remaining property at his death. After July 1, 1977, Hawaii law allows the wife only one-third of lands owned by the husband at any time during the marriage prior to July 1, 1977, that are not included in his net estate; the remaining property is then subject to the spouses' elective share provisions as set forth in the Uniform Probate Code as adopted in Hawaii.

Election

Both spouses have the right to elect the statutory share or dower. The election to take dower precludes the surviving spouse from taking a testamentary bequest.

Husband and Wife

A married woman may contract as if sole and may control her property, both real and personal, as if sole. Agreements and deeds between spouses in contemplation of divorce or separation are valid. Agreements for support and maintenance made in contemplation of divorce or separation are valid if approved by the court, but are subject to modification if changed circumstances are shown.

A husband may not release the wife's dower right by power of attorney from the wife. Prospective spouses may enter into premarital agreements.

Marriage

Common-law marriages are not recognized in Hawaii.

Personal Property

Common law rules are followed. Tenancy by the entirety exists for shares of corporate stock, automobiles, and so forth. However, a motor vehicle registered in two or more names presumes ownership in joint tenancy.

Real Property

A conveyance or devise to two or more persons is construed to create a tenancy in common unless it appears from the instrument that it was intended to create a joint tenancy or a tenancy by the entirety.

Inheritance and Estate Tax

The inheritance tax is repealed for estates of decedents dying after June 30, 1983. After that date, the only state death tax that is imposed is the amount of the credit allowed on a federal return for estate taxes. There is a pro rata calculation taxing estates of nonresident decedents on their real property located in Hawaii.

There is a provision for reciprocal exemption from tax if the decedent is a resident of a jurisdiction that exempts a Hawaiian nonresident from tax on personalty that has an intangible situs in the decedent's state of residence.

An additional tax is imposed on the transfer at death of real property situated in Hawaii and of tangible personal property having an actual situs in Hawaii even though owned by a nonresident of Hawaii. Reciprocal enforcement of death taxes is provided in the case of nonresident decedents.

There is no gift tax (except for a tax on gifts made in contemplation of death).

IDAHO

Community Property

Idaho is a community property state. The specifics are covered under the topic "Husband and Wife."

Curtesy

Abolished. Spouses have a right of election.

Descent and Distribution

Idaho has a provision regarding quasi-community property. This is defined as "all personal property, wherever situated, and all real property situated in Idaho which has heretofore been acquired or is hereafter [after 1972] acquired by the decedent while domiciled elsewhere and which would have been the community property of the decedent and the surviving spouse had the decedent been domiciled in this state at the time of its acquisition . . ." The law also includes "all personal property, wherever situated, and all real property situated in this state" acquired in exchange for property that would have been community property had the decedent been domiciled in Idaho at that time. Specific provisions stipulate that 50 percent of quasi-community property belongs to the surviving spouse, while the other 50 percent is subject to the testamentary disposition of the decedent or goes directly to the surviving spouse if it is not disposed of by the will of the decedent.

An "augmented estate" consists of a restoration of property or its value to a decedent's estate if the decedent "gave" the property to a person other than the surviving spouse without the consent of that spouse. The statute also spells out other ways in which a decedent might have removed property that would otherwise have been part of the community property of an estate. The elective share is based on the "augmented estate." A surviving spouse may renounce or waive the elective share, and this also may be done before or after marriage by a written contract, after fair disclosure. Such a waiver also is allowed as part of the property settlement entered into after or in anticipation of separation or divorce.

Divorce

A court presiding over a divorce divides community property "as may be just." Agreements as to property transfer that may have been made during the marriage to take effect on death are revoked by divorce.

Dower

Dower does not exist.

Husband and Wife

All money or other property owned by either spouse before marriage or received afterward by gift or inheritance and earnings or proceeds from such property are that spouse's separate property. Spouses may by written agreement specifically provide that all or specified property shall be the separate property of one spouse or the other. A community obligation incurred by a husband or wife without the consent in writing of the other spouse will not obligate the separate property of the nonconsenting spouse. One spouse may convey real property to the other spouse, and thereafter it is presumed to be the separate estate of the grantee spouse. The grantor spouse executes and acknowledges the conveyance. All property acquired after marriage is community property. This includes the rents and profits of separate property of either spouse, unless the instrument by which such property is acquired by one spouse provides that the rents and profits are for that spouse's sole and separate use. A husband and wife have joint management and control of community property. If community real property is placed in a revocable trust, it retains its community property character.

Neither a husband nor a wife may sell, convey, or mortgage community real property unless the other spouse joins in by executing and acknowledging the deed or other instrument of conveyance.

In connection with property succession on the death of a spouse, real property in another state owned by a domiciliary of Idaho would be included as quasi-community property if the laws of that state permit the descent and distribution of such property to be governed by the laws of Idaho.

Marriage

Common-law marriages are recognized. A common-law marriage exists when the parties consent to be married and mutually assume marital rights, duties, or obligations. When properly executed and recorded, marriage settlements may vary the rights of spouses from those listed in statutes.

Personal Property

The presumption is that all property acquired during marriage is community property. Tenancy by the entirety does not exist.

Real Property

Conveyance to two or more persons creates a tenancy in common unless the document expressly declares that a joint tenancy is being conveyed or unless the property is acquired as partnership or community property.

Taxation

Although there is an inheritance tax, it is not levied on community property transferred to a surviving husband or wife.

There is no gift tax, but the inheritance tax applies to gifts that are made in contemplation of the donor's death or that are to take effect after the donor's death.

There is an estate tax in an amount equal to the federal credit and is imposed on the transfer of a taxable estate.

Wills

Renunciation of property left by will is permitted. Written waiver of the right to renounce also is permitted.

In settling the estate of a decedent, expenses are not to be charged against the survivor's share of community property. Where the estate consists partly of separate property and partly of community property, community debts are charged to community property and separate debts to separate property. Administration expenses are apportioned and charged against the different kinds of property in proportion to their relative value.

ILLINOIS

Curtesy and Dower

Abolished in Illinois.

Dissolution of Marriage

A marital property distribution system is used in the disposition of property. Marital property is all property acquired by either spouse subsequent to the marriage whether it is held individually or in some form of co-ownership. Certain property is excepted from this category and considered "nonmarital," regardless of whether title to that property is held individually or in some form of co-ownership. Increase in the value of nonmarital property during the marriage because of the owning spouse's personal effort does not cause the property to become marital. If nonmarital and marital property are commingled into newly acquired property, however, such property will be marital. A right to reimbursement exists, but the spouse's contribution must be traceable by clear and convincing evidence. In a proceeding for the dissolution of marriage, the court assigns each spouse's nonmarital property to that spouse and divides marital property (without regard to marital misconduct) "in just proportions." Here are the relevant factors that the court is to consider: each party's contribution to the acquisition of the property; the value of the property; the duration of the marriage; the economic circumstances of each spouse; obligations and rights arising from prior marriages; any antenuptial agreement; the parties' ages, health, occupations, needs, and so on; custodial provisions for children; whether apportionment is in lieu of or in addition to maintenance; the reasonable opportunity of each spouse to acquire future assets and income; and the tax consequences of property division.

Marriage

Common-law marriages are invalid.

A married woman is entitled to her own earnings. She may make contracts and incur liabilities as if she were unmarried. A married woman may hold real and personal property, and dispose of the same to the same extent that a husband may deal with his property.

Personal Property

Tenancy by the entirety does not exist in Illinois. To create a joint tenancy with right to survivorship in personal property, that intent must be expressed in establishing the tenancy.

Real Property

All common law estates are recognized. Tenancy by the entirety has been abolished. Joint tenancy with right of survivorship can be created only by an express declaration that the estate is a joint tenancy and not a tenancy in common. A grantor can create a joint tenancy with right of survivorship even though he is also a grantee. (This means that someone owning property as a sole owner can convey it to himself and another as JTRS, if desired.)

Taxation

The inheritance tax was repealed for decedents after December 31, 1982. An estate tax is imposed that is equal to the state death tax credit for federal estate tax purposes.

Wills

A surviving spouse may renounce the decedent's will and take a statutory share. (The size of that share depends on what other descendants remain.)

INDIANA

Curtesy and Dower

Common law curtesy and dower have been abolished. A joint deed of a husband and wife is sufficient to convey any interest of either spouse or both spouses in lands held by them. A married man may execute a deed to his separate property as if he were unmarried, without the spouse's joinder. Married women have the same rights concerning real and personal property that unmarried women have.

Descent and Distribution

Since common law dower and curtesy have been abolished, a surviving spouse has the right to take a statutory share.

Dissolution of Marriage

The system of property distribution is marital. A court must divide the divorcing parties' property in a just and reasonable manner, based on: the contribution of each spouse to its acquisition; the extent to which it was acquired prior to the marriage; the economic circumstances of the spouses; the conduct of the parties during the marriage as related to the disposition of property; and the earnings or earning ability of each party.

As to common-law marriages, a court decision held that claims brought as a common-law spouse under current Indiana law would not be actionable, but that recovery could be based on contractual or equitable grounds (410 N.E.2d 1325). Common-law marriages are not recognized in Indiana.

Husband and Wife

All the legal disabilities of married women with regard to the making of contracts were abolished in 1881. A married woman may acquire, convey, and encumber real and personal property in her own name and may retain her separate property as income and profits from her separate property, business, or service.

A married person may sell, mortgage, lease, or execute any instrument of any kind affecting his or her property as if he or she were unmarried.

When a husband and wife take title to real estate jointly, an estate by the entireties is created. Each will own an equal and unseverable interest. Upon the death of either, the survivor holds the entire estate. Real estate purchased by husband and wife under a written contract is deemed to be held by them as tenants by the entireties.

Personal Property

Estates by the entirety do not exist for personal property, except when such property is derived directly from real estate held by the entirety (such as crops).

Personal property owned by two or more persons is owned by them as tenants in common unless the instrument expressly states that a joint tenancy is being conveyed. However, a survivorship interest is presumed in the case of personalty that is conveyed to a husband and wife jointly (unless a contrary intent is expressed clearly in writing).

Real Property

A conveyance or devise of land or an interest in land is taken to create a tenancy in common and not a joint tenancy, unless a contrary intention is expressed. A conveyance to a husband and wife (or to executors or trustees) is, however, held by them in joint tenancy.

Taxation

An inheritance tax is imposed on transfers by will, by intestacy, or by lifetime transfers made within two years of death (and presumed to have been made in contemplation of death.)

The Indiana estate tax equals the federal death tax credit minus the state death taxes paid.

Wills

A surviving spouse may not be deprived by will, without consent, of an absolute interest in half of both the real and personal property of the decedent. However, if the surviving spouse is not the decedent's first spouse and had no children by the decedent (who had surviving children by a previous spouse), then the amount to elect is one-third of personal property and a life estate in one-third of the real estate.

In electing against the will, the surviving spouse is deemed to renounce all other interests in the property of the decedent spouse. The surviving spouse may consent to be deprived by the will.

IOWA

Curtesy and Dower

Abolished in Iowa.

Dissolution of Marriage

With regard to division of property of spouses, the ultimate question before the court is whether distribution of property and assets is "equitable" under the specific facts of the case. Where the accumulated property is not the product of the joint efforts of both parties, or where one party brings property into the marriage, that property does not have to be divided. Otherwise, the court may make such order in relation to children, property, parties, and maintenance of parties "as may be just."

Husband and Wife

All disabilities of married women have been removed.

A married woman may own in her own right real and personal property and manage and dispose of it in the same manner as the husband can dispose of property belonging to him. But the right of either spouse to a distributive share in the realty of the other cannot be affected by a conveyance or mortgage in which he or she does not join.

Antenuptial contracts are recognized under Iowa law and should be construed liberally to carry out the intentions of the parties (174 N.W.2d 368).

Common-law marriages are recognized whether contracted in or out of the state.

Personal Property

Tenancy by the entireties is not permitted.

Real Property

Common law estates are recognized, but tenancy by the entirety is not recognized. A conveyance to two or more is construed as creating a tenancy in common unless the intent to create a joint tenancy is expressed.

Taxation

There is an inheritance tax.

There is no gift tax, but an inheritance tax applies to gifts made in contemplation of death or to take effect after death. (Gifts made within three years of death are presumed made in contemplation.)

There is an estate tax not exceeding the maximum credit allowed by the federal estate tax law.

Wills

A surviving spouse may elect to take or refuse to take under a will (electing a statutory share instead). The share depends upon the nature of the property (real or personal) and whether any surviving children also were issue of the surviving spouse.

KANSAS

Curtesy and Dower

Abolished. The husband has the same interest in his deceased wife's property as a wife has in her deceased husband's property. A surviving spouse is given the right to receive an undivided one-half interest in all of the real estate in which the deceased spouse *at any time during the marriage* had a legal or equitable interest.

A conveyance by one spouse who has title does not defeat the inchoate interest of the nonowning spouse. This inchoate interest is defeated or extinguished only by one of the following: when the nonowning spouse has consented in writing (usually by joining in the conveyance); by an election to take under the grantor's will; when the real estate is taken by a legal proceeding (as a judicial sale on execution of a judgment); and if the nonjoining spouse was not a resident of Kansas at the time of the conveyance and was never a resident during the marriage.

Any purchaser from the spouse who has title receives the entire fee simple subject to the inchoate right of the nonjoining spouse. The inchoate right becomes an absolute right on the death of the grantor (titled) spouse. (It appears that although dower and curtesy are abolished in Kansas, they actually are preserved in this statutory form.)

Divorce

The court is to divide real and personal property of the parties, regardless of whether acquired separately prior to or during marriage or acquired by joint efforts of the married couple. In making division of the property, the court is to consider the age of parties; the duration of marriage; the property owned by the parties; their present and future earning capacities; the time, source and manner of acquisition of the property; family ties and obligations; allowance of maintenance or lack thereof; dissipation of assets; and other necessary factors.

Husband and Wife

The following are separate property: all property owned by the spouse before marriage, and the rents and profits from that property; property acquired by descent, devise, or bequest and the rents and profits from such property; and property acquired by gift, except from the other spouse. A spouse's earnings are also separate property. However, if a divorce action is filed, all property becomes marital property for purposes of the divorce action. Spouses' interests vest at commencement of the action; the extent of the vested interest is determined by the court.

A married person may buy, sell, and contract with respect to that person's separate property.

It is not necessary for husband and wife to join in conveyances by one of them, except to bar the inchoate statutory interest or where the property being conveyed is a homestead.

Marriage

Common-law marriage is recognized.

The Uniform Premarital Agreement Act was adopted in 1988. It applies to agreements executed on or after its effective date. Before that enactment, common-law principles were in effect. The law in Kansas is that contracts made either before or after marriage that set forth property rights between husband and wife are not against public policy unless the terms encourage separation of parties. Such a contract is interpreted liberally to carry out the parties' intentions if the contract was fairly made and its terms are equitable.

Personal Property

Tenancy by the entirety does not exist.

Real Property

Common law estates exist. Joint tenancies and estates by entirety were abolished in 1891. Therefore, conveyance to two or more creates a tenancy in common unless the language used makes it clear that a joint tenancy is intended. Joint tenancy may be created by a grant from an owner to him or herself and another.

Taxation

There is an inheritance tax. Taxable transfers include all passing of property or property interests. Transfers within one year of death are deemed to have been made in contemplation of death. Transfers to or for the benefit of a surviving spouse are exempt from transfer tax.

An estate tax is imposed on the estate of every decedent in an amount that will enable the state to absorb the maximum credit allowed under the Internal Revenue Code.

There is no gift tax.

Wills

A surviving spouse who has not consented to the testator's will in the testator's lifetime may elect whether to take under the will or by law of intestate succession, but is not entitled to both.

KENTUCKY

Antenuptial Agreements

Written antenuptial contracts are enforceable and favored in Kentucky if full disclosure has been made of the extent of property owned by each party and principles of contract law have been followed.

Curtesy and Dower

A surviving spouse has an estate of one-half of surplus real estate owned by a decedent spouse at death if the decedent died without a will. Also, a surviving spouse takes an estate for life in one-third of the real estate owned by the decedent during life but not so owned by the decedent at death, unless the interest has been relinquished. The survivor also has an estate in one-half of personalty. This right is barred if the surviving spouse had joined in deeds of conveyance, as to land.

Dissolution of Marriage

Factors are set forth in the law for court-ordered declaration of separate property of the parties and division of marital property. Marital misconduct is to be disregarded (but case law holds otherwise and fault may still be a factor in division) [460 S.W.2d 821].

Husband and Wife

A married woman may acquire and hold property, real and personal, in her own name and may sell, encumber, and dispose of her personal property.

Either spouse may sell, convey, or encumber his or her real property, but the other spouse retains the right to curtesy or dower unless he or she joins in the instrument or releases the right by separate instrument. Gifts or assignment of personal property must be recorded to bind third parties.

Marriage

Common-law marriages contracted in Kentucky are not recognized as valid.

Personal Property

Tenancy by the entirety in personal property is recognized.

Real Property

Joint tenancy is recognized, but the common law right of survivorship between joint tenants is abolished (meaning if survivorship is intended, it must be spelled out in the document "JTRS and not as Tenants in Common").

The same thing applies to a conveyance to husband and wife. There is no mutual right to the entirety by survivorship between them, but they take as tenants in common unless tenancy by the entireties with survivorship is provided for expressly in the conveyance or document.

Taxation

There is an inheritance tax on the transfer of property passing by will or by the intestacy laws of the state.

There is no gift tax, but the inheritance tax applies to gifts deemed in contemplation of death, or to take effect at or after death.

In addition to the inheritance tax, an estate tax is imposed for the purpose of taking "full advantage of the credit allowed for state succession duties by federal estate tax law."

Wills

A surviving spouse may, within six months after probate, renounce the will of the deceased spouse and take the dower or curtesy share of the estate as if no will had been made. If the decedent held real estate in fee simple at death, the elective share is only one-third of such real estate.

LOUISIANA

Curtesy and Dower

Neither exists in Louisiana.

Descent and Distribution

When a person dies after December 31, 1981, and leaves no will, property descends to various persons by law, depending on the classification of the property as community or separate property of the deceased. A surviving spouse inherits the community property share undisposed of by the deceased spouse if there are no descendants. If there are descendants, the undisposed share of the community property is inherited by such descendants.

Divorce

After filing a petition for separation or divorce, either spouse may be awarded occupancy of the family home pending partition of their community property. The court considers the relative economic status of the parties and the best interest of the family. The concept of fault exists. The party against whom a separation has been pronounced loses all advantages to which he or she might have been entitled in considering contributions to the marriage. The party who obtains the judgment preserves the consideration given his or her contributions, even if such contributions were made reciprocally.

Husband and Wife

Separate property of a spouse consists of property acquired prior to the establishment of the community property regime, acquired individually by inheritance or gift, or acquired as a result of a voluntary partition of community property during the existence of the community property regime. A separate property regime may be established by agreement or by a judgment of separation. Each spouse may use and dispose of separate property without the concurrence of the other spouse.

Louisiana law specifically states (in the *Martindale-Hubbell Digest,* p. 26 of Louisiana section): "A married woman, whether a resident of this state or not, is competent to contract debts, purchase, sell and mortgage and to bind and obligate herself personally, and with reference to her separate property; to sell, alienate . . . mortgage and pledge . . . her separate property. . . . She may also open bank accounts, deposit funds therein and withdraw the same by check *as though unmarried."*

A community property system applies to spouses domiciled in Louisiana. Unless modified or terminated by agreement, this system provides that each spouse owns a present undivided one-half interest in the community property. Spouses may, without court approval, voluntarily partition community property in whole or in part during the existence of the community regime. Property acquired by such partition then becomes separate property. Each spouse may manage, control, or dispose of community property unless otherwise provided by law.

The Louisiana law does allow spouses to enter into matrimonial agreements (antenuptial contracts) modifying the legal community property regime, but such agreements may not renounce or alter the marital portion or the established order of succession.

Marriage

Common-law marriages are not recognized in Louisiana.

Personal Property

Tenancy by the entirety in personalty is not permitted in Louisiana.

Real Property

Louisiana law is based on French civil law and not English common law. Therefore, Louisiana does not recognize any of the common law estates, such as tenancy in common, joint tenancy, tenancy by the entirety, etc. There is, however, a form of ownership (called a "usufruct"), similar to the common law life estate, in which the title is vested in another.

Taxation

An inheritance tax is levied on all inheritances, legacies, and gifts (called "donations") in contemplation of death.

An estate tax equalizes the state inheritance tax and federal estate tax allowance for state death taxes. The difference between the credit and amount of state inheritance tax (if less) must be paid to the state.

There is a gift tax, with certain lifetime and annual exclusions. Above those exclusions a tax is due on all transfers by gift, with varying rates depending on the amount of the gift.

Wills

In Louisiana there are limitations on disposition by will. The law reserves to descendants of a property owner ("forced heirs") a certain portion of the estate (termed "legitime"). These heirs create a limitation on the disposable (by will) portion of the estate according to a particular percentage detailed in the law.

MAINE

Curtesy and Dower

Abolished.

Descent and Distribution

A surviving spouse takes a distributive share in the estate of a deceased spouse who dies without a will. The share depends on the relationship of other surviving heirs. The surviving spouse of a person who died while domiciled in Maine has a right of election to take against the will.

Divorce

All property acquired subsequent to marriage and prior to legal separation or divorce is presumed to be marital property unless shown to be otherwise. The court has broad powers over disposition of marital property. A divorce decree filed in the registry of deeds office for the district where real estate is located will extinguish the claim of a nonowner spouse and establish any rights in real estate acquired by the divorce decree.

If a divorce decree fails to dispose of marital property, such property is deemed to be held by both parties as tenants in common.

Husband and Wife

A married woman has the same rights and liabilities as a man. All disabilities of marriage have been removed. A married woman may hold any property, real or personal, as her separate property, and her control over her property is as absolute as the control of her husband over his property. A married person may convey separate property, real or personal, without a spouse's joinder or consent. Real estate conveyed from one spouse to the other does require joinder. A married woman may contract with her husband or any other person as though unmarried, but a husband and wife cannot be business partners.

Antenuptial contracts are allowable.

Marriage

The law is unclear on common-law marriages, but they probably would not be not recognized. Out-of-state common-law marriages probably would be recognized (45 Me. 367).

Personal Property

There is no statutory provision for tenancy by the entirety in personalty.

Real Property

Tenancy by the entirety is not recognized. The presumption is that a conveyance to two or more persons creates an estate in common, unless an estate in joint tenancy and the intention to create such an estate is shown clearly by the language of the document. Thus, deeds naming two or more grantees as joint tenants are construed as vesting a fee simple estate in them *with survivorship*.

Taxation

An inheritance tax was imposed. However, it does not apply to estates of persons whose death occurred after June 30, 1986. A "new" estate tax applies for the estate of one whose death occurred after June 30, 1986. Generally, the tax is equal to the amount of federal estate tax credit for state death taxes.

There is no gift tax.

Wills

The Uniform Probate Code has been adopted with modifications.

MARYLAND

Antenuptial Agreements

These agreements settling or barring rights in real or personal property are valid if full disclosure is made of the value of property rights being waived.

Curtesy and Dower

Abolished in 1970.

Divorce

The Maryland divorce court is empowered to make certain disposition of property in cases filed after January 1, 1979. The court may exercise this power after a foreign divorce was granted in another state if one spouse was domiciled in Maryland when the foreign proceeding commenced and the foreign court exercised no jurisdiction over that spouse or property at issue.

The Maryland court, when granting either divorce or separation, may order partition or sale of jointly owned personal property but may not transfer ownership. When granting an absolute divorce, the court has the same powers to determine the value of marital property (acquired during the marriage other than by inheritance or gift) and may grant a monetary award as an adjustment of the equities of the parties concerning marital property.

Some of the factors to be considered in balancing the equities are: monetary and nonmonetary contributions of each spouse; military pensions or retirement benefits; determination of which property is the family home and family use personal property. The court may issue orders as to the use or possession of such property regardless of how it is titled or owned.

Husband and Wife

All disabilities of married women are removed.

Property belonging to a woman at the time of marriage and all property she may acquire or receive after marriage is protected from the debts of her husband. Property of the husband is his own and free from claims of his wife or her creditors.

Husband or wife may convey, transfer, or encumber separate personal or real property without the consent or joinder of the other. There are no restrictions on contract made by a married woman or man, and they may contract with each other. A husband is no longer liable for a debt or contract incurred or entered into by his wife on his credit.

Marriage

Common-law marriage is not permitted but will be recognized in Maryland if valid in the state where it is contracted.

Personal Property

Tenancy by the entirety is recognized. Husband and wife may acquire personal property as tenants by entireties, and conveyance to a husband and wife is presumed to be held as tenants by the entirety unless a contrary ownership is designated. Also, property purchased with entirety money is entirety property.

An instrument in writing must expressly provide joint tenancy if such ownership is intended (instead of entirety ownership).

Real Property

All common law estates in real property are recognized. If a document purports to create other than tenancy in common, there must be language indicating that joint tenancy is intended. Any deed or devise to a husband and wife creates a tenancy by the entirety unless otherwise provided. An owner or owners, including husband and/or wife, may convey to themselves or others without using a straw man. In this way ownership and title can be changed.

Taxation

There is an inheritance tax imposed on the value of all tangible or intangible property, real or personal, having a taxable situs in Maryland, passing on the death of a resident or nonresident decedent, or by gift made within two years of death (if in contemplation of death). This includes property in which the decedent had an interest as a joint tenant or tenant in common and property over which the decedent had retained dominion during his lifetime. Property held by a husband and wife as tenants by entireties or as joint tenants that passes to the surviving spouse is exempt from inheritance tax. Other exemptions: real property passing from decedent to a surviving spouse; interest in property that passes by right of survivorship; insurance payable to a named beneficiary.

There is no gift tax, but the inheritance tax applies to gifts in contemplation of death or intended to take effect at or after death or made within two years before death.

A tax is imposed on the transfer of a "Maryland estate." That tax equals the amount, if any, by which the credit under federal estate tax law exceeds the aggregate of state death taxes payable out of the Maryland estate of the decedent.

Wills

Dower and curtesy are abolished. Either surviving spouse may elect to take a statutory share in election against the will.

MASSACHUSETTS

Curtesy

Curtesy has been abolished in Massachusetts. Curtesy and dower rights are merged together and called dower. A surviving husband is given the same dower rights as a surviving wife. Dower is limited to real estate owned by the deceased spouse at the time of death. Mortgage encumbrances take precedence over dower rights.

Descent and Distribution

A surviving spouse must file an election of dower in the offices of the probate registry. This situation applies only to real estate and personal property not disposed by the decedent's will. If dower is not elected, other statutory shares apply.

Divorce

Alimony may be awarded to either party. In determining the amount, the following factors must be considered (not precluding other factors): length of marriage; conduct of parties during marriage; age, health, station, occupation, amount, and sources of income; vocational skills, employability, estate, liabilities, and needs of each party; and opportunity of each party for future acquisition of capital and income. Discretionary factors are: contribution of each of the parties in the acquisition, preservation, or appreciation in value of their respective estates; and contribution of each of the parties as homemaker to the family unit.

Division of property of the spouses may be ordered in addition to or in lieu of alimony, following application of the same factors. Property is subject to division irrespective of how title is held or how it was acquired.

Dower

The merged-together limited dower and curtesy rights that remain in Massachusetts are obtained by filing a claim in the registry of probate within six months after approval of an administrator's bond. Dower applies only to real estate owned by the decedent spouse at the time of death. Any encumbrances made during life take precedence over dower rights. The probate court may assign dower. A tenant by dower is entitled to possession and profits of an undivided one-third of the decedent spouse's real estate until the assignment is made.

Husband and Wife

All disabilities of married women are removed.

Real and personal property owned by any person upon marriage remains that person's separate property. A married person may receive, receipt for, hold, manage, and dispose property, real or personal, as if such person were sole.

Either spouse may convey property individually.

Antenuptial contracts designating certain property to remain or to become that of a husband or wife must be recorded before or within ninety days after marriage. Otherwise, such contracts are void. They are valid (even without recording) between the parties or their heirs and personal representatives.

A conveyance or transfer by will to a husband and wife jointly creates a joint tenancy unless the document expressly states the husband and wife are to take as tenants by the entirety.

Marriage

Common-law marriages are not recognized.

Personal Property

There is no statutory provision, but case law indicates that tenancy by the entirety exists with reference to personal property (293 Mass. 67, 199 N.E. 383).

Real Property

Common law estates exist in real property. A conveyance or devise to two or more persons (except a mortgage or conveyance or devise in trust) creates a tenancy in common unless the instrument states explicitly (or by inference) that a joint tenancy is intended to be created in the takers. After August 30, 1979, a conveyance or devise to two persons as tenants by the entirety creates a joint tenancy (and not a tenancy in common) if they are not married to each other.

Taxation

An estate tax is imposed to absorb credit for state death taxes allowed by federal revenue laws.

Wills

A surviving spouse may file in the registry of probate a written waiver of the will's provisions and take a statutory share of the decedent spouse's estate. (For example, if a testator leaves children, the surviving spouse is entitled to one-third of personal and real property.)

A surviving spouse is not entitled to dower in addition to taking under the provisions of the will (unless the will-maker showed a different intention).

MICHIGAN

Curtesy

Abolished.

Descent and Distribution

The right of a surviving spouse to an intestate share may be waived by written agreement made before or after marriage.

Divorce

The divorce court may award to either party all or part (as it deems just and reasonable) of the real and personal property (or its monetary value) that came to either party by reason of the marriage. If the property awarded to either party is insufficient for suitable support and maintenance of either party and the children, the court may make a further award to either party of the property of either party. The factors to consider are ability, character, and situation of the parties and all other circumstances. A husband and wife who own realty as joint tenants or as tenants by the entirety become tenants in common. If a party contributed to the acquisition or improvement of the other spouse's property, the court may award that party all or an equitable portion of such property.

Dower

Dower is recognized. It is the widow's right to use one-third of all the estate of inheritance owned by her husband during the marriage. If a husband attempted to transfer that property during the marriage, the property would still be subject to the widow's dower at the husband's death. The value would be the value at the date of transfer. However, the dower right will not prevail against a purchase money mortgage given by the husband. A nonresident wife is not entitled to dower in lands conveyed by her husband during his life but only in those he owned at his death. A wife may contract with her husband for release of dower. By joining in her husband's deed, a wife relinquishes and bars her dower right in that property. She may also bar dower by conveyance to her husband or by antenuptial agreement for certain property rights in lieu of dower.

A court granting divorce must include in its decree a provision in lieu of the wife's dower right to the husband's property. This extinguishes claims the wife might have in present or future property of husband.

Husband and Wife

Property owned by a husband or wife before or after marriage (unless joint) is his or her separate property, with the right to manage and dispose of it alone. Separate property of either spouse is not liable for the debts of the other. Exception: a husband's real estate is subject to his widow's dower. A married woman may enter into a written contract, jointly or severally, with another person.

Property may be held by the entireties. Unless otherwise expressly provided, real property conveyed to husband and wife is deemed to be held by entireties. Personal property in the form of stocks, bonds, debentures, notes, mortgages, and other evidences of indebtedness payable to a husband and wife is deemed to be held jointly with right of survivorship in the same manner as real estate held by the entireties; but this presumption does not extend to bank deposits, insurance, or other simple contracts.

To convey or encumber property held by the entireties, a husband and wife must join in the same instrument. A husband need not join in a deed of his wife's separate property. A wife's dower is barred by the wife's joining in the husband's conveyance or may be barred by a separate instrument expressing this intention.

A married woman may enter into a contract with respect to her separate property and carry on business for her own account. She may contract directly with her husband, including partnership with him. A married woman may enter into a written contract assigning her separate property as security for the debt of another (including her husband). A contract relating to property made by persons in contemplation of marriage remains in force after marriage.

The community property system no longer prevails in Michigan. The repealing act became effective May 10, 1948.

Marriage

Common-law marriages are not valid if contracted after January 1, 1957. A common-law marriage valid where contracted is valid in Michigan.

Personal Property

Common law estates are recognized. As to tenancy by the entirety, it is unclear whether such tenancy possesses all the elements of tenancy by the entirety in real property (such as immunity from partition). Joint tenancy with rights of survivorship can exist in bank accounts, securities, and contents of safety deposit boxes. However, the intent to create such a tenancy must be shown clearly by agreement of the tenants.

146 🏶 Appendix One

Real Property

All conveyances of lands made to two or more persons (except executors or to husband and wife) are construed to create estates in common and not in joint tenancy. A joint tenancy between husband and wife is a tenancy by the entirety, and a conveyance to husband and wife creates such a tenancy. One spouse cannot sever a tenancy by the entirety except by conveyance to the other spouse. The right of survivorship cannot be destroyed if expressly declared in the conveyance creating a joint tenancy. A joint tenancy between others is severed by a conveyance by one tenant.

Taxation

There is an inheritance tax. In cases where the inheritance tax does not equal or exceed the maximum credit for death taxes allowable under federal estate tax law, an additional tax is imposed to absorb the full credit.

Wills

A surviving spouse (widow) may elect to take dower right or to take intestate share or under the will. The election right and the right to inherit may be waived by either spouse by written agreement before or after marriage.

MINNESOTA

Curtesy and Dower

Abolished. Surviving spouses are entitled to the same share as in case of the intestacy of a deceased spouse.

Dissolution of Marriage

The marital property system of distribution generally applies. The court may make such disposition of marital property as is just and equitable without regard to marital misconduct. With certain exceptions applying to dissolution proceedings started on or after August 1, 1988, the divorce court is to value marital assets as of the day the dissolution proceedings began. If the court finds that either spouse's resources or property, including that spouse's share of marital property, are so inadequate that they cause an unfair hardship, the court also may distribute up to one-half of nonmarital property not excluded by a valid antenuptial contract. All property acquired during the marriage is presumed to be marital property, including vested pension benefits. Nonmarital property is any property acquired as gift, bequest, devise, or inheritance made by a third party to one but not both spouses. Nonmarital property also includes: property acquired before the marriage; property acquired in exchange for, or increase in, nonmarital property; property acquired after a decree of legal separation; or property excluded by a valid antenuptial contract.

Husband and Wife

A married woman retains the same legal existence after marriage as before.

A married woman may hold any property, real or personal, as her separate property.

A married woman may make (and is bound by) any contract she could make if unmarried.

A husband and wife may convey real estate of either by joint deed. Either spouse may, by separate deed, convey any real estate owned by that spouse (except the homestead), subject to the statutory right of the other spouse. (Conveyance of assets does not defeat a spouse's rights at the death of the grantor spouse.) However, either spouse may, by separate instrument, relinquish rights in real estate conveyed by the other spouse.

An antenuptial contract may be entered into prior to the day of marriage, provided there is full and fair disclosure of earnings and property of each party and the parties have the opportunity to consult legal counsel of their own choice. The contract must be in writing and may determine the rights of each party in nonmarital property upon dissolution of the marriage, legal separation, or death. A contract affecting rights to real property may be recorded with the county recorder to protect those rights against a subsequent purchaser.

Marriage

Common-law marriages entered into after 1941 are void.

Personal Property

Tenancy by the entirety does not exist.

Real Property

Tenancy by the entirety is not recognized. A grant or devise to two or more persons creates a tenancy in common unless the instrument expressly creates a joint tenancy.

Taxation

An inheritance tax was repealed for estates of decedents after 1979. A gift tax also was repealed for gifts after 1979.

For estates of decedents who died after December 31, 1985, Minnesota applies a "pick-up" tax which is based on the federal credit allowed for state death taxes.

Wills

A surviving spouse who elects to take against the will takes the same share he or she would take in case of intestacy. If the decedent left no children, the surviving spouse takes only one-half, and not all, of the estate (prior to 1987). This was changed in 1986. For estates of decedents dying after December 31, 1986, the surviving wife's share is one-third.

Minnesota adopted the elective share provisions of the Uniform Probate Code. Those provisions apply to the estates of decedents who died after January 1, 1987. These provisions are intended to preserve a spouse's elective share against transfers by the decedent during the marriage which would have reduced the survivor's share (if the survivor had not joined in the transfer).

MISSISSIPPI

Curtesy and Dower

Abolished.

Divorce

Mississippi is not a community property state. Property is distributed on the basis of title and special equity.

Husband and Wife

All property of a married woman (except the homestead) is her separate property with which she may deal as though "feme sole." Disabilities of married women have been abolished totally.

In a conveyance or encumbrance by one spouse of separate property, the other spouse need not join in (except if the property is the homestead).

Antenuptial contracts made "upon consideration of marriage" must be in writing.

Marriage

Common-law marriages were valid before 1956 but now are presumed to be invalid if contracted after that date. There is no provision for recognition of out-of-state common-law marriages. Certain marriages are deemed void. Persons whose marriage is void can be imprisoned for cohabitation.

Personal Property

Tenancy by the entirety is recognized.

Real Property

Conveyances or devises of land made to two or more persons, or to husband and wife, are construed to create estates in common and not in joint tenancy or entirety, unless it appears from the instrument that it was intended to create an estate in joint tenancy or entirety with right of survivorship. An estate in joint tenancy or entirety (to husband and wife) with right of survivorship may be created by a conveyance from the owners to others or to themselves.

Taxation

There is no gift or inheritance tax. An estate tax is imposed, and such tax is not to be less than the credit allowed on a federal estate tax return.

Wills

A surviving spouse cannot be disinherited. If a will does not make "satisfactory" provision, a spouse can renounce and take the intestate share. However, if the surviving spouse has separate property equal in value to what would be his or her lawful share, then that surviving spouse cannot renounce the will and take a statutory share of the estate.

MISSOURI

Curtesy

The estate of curtesy is abolished, but a widower is given the same rights of inheritance, allowances, and exemptions as a widow.

Dissolution of Marriage

The court shall distribute to each spouse his/her property and shall divide marital property as the court deems "just." The relevant factors to consider include: the contribution of each spouse to the acquisition of marital property including contribution as a homemaker; the value of property set apart to each spouse; the economic circumstances of each spouse at the time the property division is to become effective; and the conduct of the parties during the marriage. The court is to consider the desirability of awarding the family home or the right to live there for reasonable periods to the spouse having custody of any children.

Dower

The estate of dower is abolished. A surviving husband has the same rights in a wife's real estate as a widow has in the husband's real estate, including the right of election. According to case law, however, a wife may defeat such rights as to her separate property by her conveyance without his joinder. She may release her marital rights in real estate by joining in a deed with her husband or by prenuptial contract.

Husband and Wife

A married woman may hold as her separate property any property, real or personal, owned by her at the time of marriage; thereafter acquired by gift, bequest, devise, or descent, or purchased with her separate money or means; anything due her as wages; any rights of action; and all income, increase, and profits of her separate property. Such property is not liable for the debts of her husband.

A spouse should either join in or give consent in writing (acknowledged) to a conveyance of the other spouse's separate real property. This would not be necessary if marital rights have been released by prenuptial contract. However, failure to join will not prevent loss of marital rights (unless fraud was present). Because of difficulty in establishing the separate character of property, a joinder is deemed advisable for an effective conveyance.

Antenuptial contracts must be in writing.

Marriage

Common-law marriages are null and void, but they are recognized if legal where originally contracted.

Personal Property

Tenancies by the entireties are recognized.

Real Property

Tenancies recognized are tenancy in severalty, tenancy in common, joint tenancy, tenancy by the entirety, homestead, and life estates. A grant or devise to two or more persons (except executors, trustees, or spouses) is deemed to create a tenancy in common unless the instrument expressly declares the conveyance to be in joint tenancy. Real estate may be conveyed by an owner or owners to himself or themselves or others or a combination. The conveyance has the same effect as to whether it creates a joint tenancy, tenancy by the entireties, in common, etc., as if it were granted by a stranger to the persons named as grantees.

Taxation

There is no inheritance tax.

An estate tax is equal to the maximum credit for state death taxes on the federal estate tax return. The state also imposes a generation-skipping tax on a generation-skipping transfer equal to the credit allowed by the Internal Revenue Code.

There is no gift tax.

Wills

A surviving spouse can elect to take against the will. In determining the spouse's share when there is an election, all property is considered even if it is not subject to probate, such as trust property, insurance, profit-sharing plans, and joint property.

MONTANA

Curtesy

No right of curtesy.

Dissolution of Marriage

Montana has a special equity type of system. The court shall equitably apportion property without regard to marital misconduct or recorded ownership, and may protect children by setting aside separate funds for their welfare.

Dower

Abolished.

Husband and Wife

Husband and wife shall support each other out of their property and labor, including nonmonetary support provided by a spouse as homemaker. Otherwise, neither has any interest in the property of the other.

Property of a married person owned before or acquired after marriage is his/her separate property. Earnings after marriage are his/her own. Neither husband nor wife is liable for debts of the other, but property of both is liable for necessary family expenses and children's educational expenses.

A wife may convey or encumber her separate property without the consent of the husband. He may do the same with his property. However, both must join in any conveyance or encumbrance of the homestead.

The Uniform Premarital Agreement Act has been adopted in Montana. A premarital agreement is enforceable without consideration.

Disabilities of married women have been removed in general.

Marriage

Common-law marriages are recognized.

Personal Property

Tenancy by entirety ownership is not permitted with regard to personal property.

Real Property

Ownership of real property by more than one person may be as joint interests, partnership interests, or interests in common. Every interest in favor of several persons, including husband and wife, is an interest in common, unless expressly acquired in partnership for partnership purposes or declared in its creation to be a joint interest.

Taxation

There is an inheritance tax.

An estate tax is imposed to provide the state with the full benefit of the maximum tax credit allowable against the federal estate tax.

There is no gift tax.

Wills

There is a right of election to take against a will.

NEBRASKA

Curtesy and Dower

Abolished.

Dissolution of Marriage

Nebraska follows the marital property system of property division. The court may include inherited property and retirement plans in the marital estate. When dissolution or separation is decreed, the parties can enter into a written property settlement regarding support, maintenance, and property as to themselves and any minor children. The agreement (except with regard to support and custody of minor children) is binding on the court unless the court finds the agreement to be unconscionable. Unless the agreement provides to the contrary, it becomes part of the decree. Terms of the agreement can be enforced by all available remedies. Alimony may be ordered in addition to a property settlement. If parties do not agree, the court may award alimony and/or property using similar criteria, but the two serve different purposes and are to be considered separately. Except for terms regarding minor children, a decree may preclude or limit modification of its terms.

Husband and Wife

Property that a woman owns at the time of marriage and any increase in value of such property, as well as property she receives by inheritance or gift from another (not her husband), and property she acquires by purchase, is her sole and separate property and is not liable for her husband's debts.

A married woman may sell and convey her real and personal property and enter into any contract concerning the same as freely "as a married man." Her contract must explicitly state the intention to bind only her separate property. She may carry on any trade or business and perform any service on her own account; her earnings are her sole and separate property, to be used and invested by her in her own name. Parties may enter into an antenuptial contract barring inheritance rights upon death. However, an agreement for forfeiting rights upon divorce is invalid as against public policy, but it may be admissible evidence in divorce.

Both husband and wife, if Nebraska residents, must join in a conveyance of each other's real estate to cut off statutory rights. A married woman who joins in the conveyance of her husband's property for the sole purpose of relinquishing her statutory rights is not bound by covenants in the deed.

Marriage

Common-law marriages cannot be contracted in Nebraska (since 1923). Common-law marriages valid in other states are recognized in Nebraska.

Personal Property

Tenancy by the entirety does not exist.

Real Property

Tenancy by the entirety is not recognized. Tenancy in common and joint tenancy are recognized. There is a conclusive presumption of co-tenancy when interest in real estate is conveyed to more than one person.

If both husband and wife are residents of Nebraska, each must join in a conveyance of the real estate of the other in order to cut off his or her statutory rights in such real estate. The statutory rights are spelled out in the Uniform Probate Code provisions adopted in Nebraska. Both husband and wife must join in the conveyance of real estate which is the homestead.

Taxation

There is an inheritance tax on all property, including life insurance payable to an executor or administrator, passing by will or intestate laws or by transfer in contemplation of death when such property is part of an estate. Interests passing to a surviving spouse by will are not subject to tax. If joint property was acquired by gift from a third person, only the fractional part owned by the deceased is included in that person's estate. The value of assets is determined as of the date of death.

In addition to the inheritance tax, an estate tax is levied on the estate of every resident decedent based on the state tax credit allowed by the federal estate tax.

There is no gift tax, but the inheritance tax applies to gifts made within three years of death.

NEVADA

Community Property

Nevada has a community property system.

Curtesy and Dower

Abolished.

Divorce

The residence requirement is six weeks prior to the commencement of the action. There must be actual physical presence within the state of Nevada for the required time (corroborated by a credible local witness).

Nevada is a community property jurisdiction. Property rights are determined by the court. It may make such disposition of community property as appears equitable. The court also may set apart such portion of the husband's property for the wife's support, or the wife's property for the husband's support (if he is disabled or unable to provide for himself), or the property of either spouse for the support of their children. Agreements settling property rights are looked on favorably and usually are approved. A property settlement agreement made when divorce is pending or immediately contemplated is not invalidated by a provision therein that it shall become effective only in the event of divorce. It may be merged in the divorce decree unless the decree specifically provides that the agreement not be merged.

Husband and Wife

The unity of husband and wife and the rule that the residence of the husband is that of the wife unless, having ground for divorce, she establishes a separate residence, are recognized by Nevada courts.

Real or personal property may be held by husband and wife in joint tenancy, tenancy in common, or as community property.

All property of each spouse owned before marriage, and all acquired afterward by gift or inheritance and profits from those are the separate property of that spouse.

If a married person is a resident of Nevada, an inventory of separate property may be recorded in the county of residence. If real property in a different county is included in a recorded inventory, then the inventory also must be recorded in that county. Recordation is very important because failure to record such an inventory of separate property of one spouse might fail to prevent a sale by the other spouse.

Either spouse may, without the consent of the other spouse, convey encumber, or in any manner dispose of his or her separate property.

Community property is all property acquired after marriage by either husband or wife, except that acquired by gift or inheritance (or as an award for personal injury damages), together with profits of such property. Other exceptions from community property are property arrangements set forth in a written agreement between spouses, effective only as between them; by a decree of separate maintenance; or by written authorization from one spouse to the other for separate earnings to be appropriated to his or her own use.

Either spouse, acting alone, may control community property, with a power of disposition such as the acting spouse has over his or her separate property. Neither spouse, however, may devise or bequeath by will more than one-half of the couple's community property. Neither spouse may give away community property without the other spouse's consent. Some other requirements are: community real property can be conveyed or encumbered only by an instrument executed and acknowledged by both spouses; a contract to purchase community real property must be joined in by both spouses; both spouses must join in a contract of sale; neither spouse may acquire, sell, convey, or encumber assets of a business (including real property and goodwill) where both spouses participate in management without the consent of the other. However, a husband or wife may give a written power of attorney to the other to sell or convey any property held as community property.

On the death of either husband or wife, an undivided one-half interest in community property is the property of the surviving spouse and that person's sole separate property. The remaining interest is the decedent's property and is subject to the testamentary disposition of the decedent. In the absence of testamentary disposition, that portion goes to the surviving spouse and is the only portion that is administered by the probate court. The Uniform Premarital Agreement Act was adopted in 1989.

Marriage

Common-law marriages are prohibited. There is no statutory provision as to local recognition of out-of-state common-law marriages.

Personal Property

Tenancy by the entirety does not exist.

Real Property

Tenancy by the entirety is not mentioned in statute but appears to be abolished by implication. Real estate may be held in joint tenancy, tenancy in common, as community property of husband and wife, and/or in condominium. A grant or devise to two or more persons (other than executors and trustees) creates a tenancy in common, unless the instrument expressly declares the estate granted or devised to be a joint tenancy. Joint tenancy may be created without the intervention of a straw man.

Taxation

There is no inheritance tax or gift tax. There is a tax on the transfer of an estate to equal the maximum credit allowed by the federal estate tax law.

Wills

In Nevada the surviving spouse has no right of election to take under intestacy law and against the will (see "Community Property").

The divorce or annulment of the marriage of a testator (the one who made a will) revokes every interest given to the testator's former spouse by a will executed before the divorce decree unless a separate property agreement or former will was approved by the court in divorce proceedings.

NEW HAMPSHIRE

Curtesy and Dower

Abolished.

Divorce

Upon a decree of divorce, the court may restore to the wife all or any part of her estate, and may assign to her such part of her husband's estate as may be deemed just. Property includes both tangible and intangible, and real and personal property, regardless of how it was held. The court may order "equitable" division of property between the parties which need not necessarily be "equal," depending upon how the court analyzes certain factors.

Husband and Wife

A married woman holds for her own use, free from the interference or control of her husband, all property at any time earned, acquired, or inherited by or given to her either before or after marriage. Every married woman has the same rights and remedies, and is subject to the same liabilities in relations to her property, as if she were unmarried, and she may convey, make contracts, etc., as if she were unmarried.

Real estate may be conveyed directly by a husband to his wife, or a wife to her husband, without the intervention of a third person. A married woman may convey her real estate. A married man or woman who is "justifiably" living apart from his or her spouse because such spouse has been guilty of conduct that constitutes cause for divorce may apply by petition to the probate judge for the county in which real estate owned by that person is situated for a license to convey to bar the homestead rights of the "guilty" party.

If a woman has resided in New Hampshire for six months and is the wife of a man residing in another state, assuming she is residing in New Hampshire separate from her husband, she may convey all real and personal property held by her in New Hampshire, the same as if she were sole and unmarried.

Common-law marriages are not recognized.

Personal Property

Tenancy by entirety in personal property is not recognized.

Real Property

Tenancy by entirety in real property is not recognized. A deed that names grantees to be tenants by the entirety creates a joint tenancy. Conveyances and devises of real estate to two or more persons are construed to create an estate in common and not in joint tenancy unless joint tenancy is provided expressly in the instrument. A conveyance to a husband and wife as tenants by the entirety creates a joint tenancy.

Taxation

An inheritance tax is imposed on all property within the jurisdiction of New Hampshire, real or personal, belonging to domicilaries of the state. It also is imposed on all real estate within the state belonging to a nonresident decedent, that is transferred by will, by intestate succession, or by gift made in contemplation of death. Transfer to the survivor of jointly held property is deemed a taxable transfer as though the whole property had been owned by the joint owners as tenants in common and had been devised or bequeathed to the survivor.

In addition to the inheritance tax, an estate tax is imposed on the transfer of all estates subject to an estate tax under the provisions of the federal Internal Revenue Code to equal the credit allowed for state death taxes.

There is no gift tax except on a transfer to take effect on the death of the donor.

Wills

Any devise or bequest to a surviving spouse is held to be in lieu of all his or her rights in the estate of the deceased spouse unless it appears by the will that such was not the intention. A surviving spouse may, instead, file a waiver of testamentary provision for that spouse, and in lieu of that provision receive a distributive share of the estate.

NEW JERSEY

Curtesy

On the death of his wife, a widower takes a life estate in one-half of the real property she owned at any time during marriage prior to May 28, 1980, whether children were born or not, unless he has released his right of curtesy by joining in a deed or conveyance directly to his spouse. An absolute divorce terminates the right of curtesy.

Effective May 28, 1980, all rights of dower and curtesy are abolished with respect to real property acquired subsequent to that date. As to such property occupied jointly with a spouse, which is the home, every married person has a right of joint possession during marriage. This right of possession may not be released, extinguished, or alienated without the consent of both spouses or court judgment.

Divorce

Pending suit for divorce, brought in New Jersey or elsewhere, or after judgment for divorce, wherever obtained, the court has the power to make orders awarding alimony and to revise the same from time to time. The court may award alimony to either party; in doing so the court shall consider the need and ability to pay of the parties, the duration of the marriage, the history of financial or nonfinancial contributions to the marriage, interruption of one's career or educational opportunities, and equitable distribution of property. In addition to alimony and maintenance, the court may effectuate an equitable distribution of certain real and personal property acquired by either party during the marriage.

Dower

On the death of her husband, a widow takes a life estate in one-half of the real property he owned at any time during marriage prior to May 28, 1980, unless she had released her right of dower. There is no dower in an estate by joint tenancy except in favor of the wife of a surviving joint tenant.

A widow's right of dower may be released by a deed executed and acknowledged in the manner prescribed by law. Conveyance by a married person directly to a spouse releases inchoate or possible future curtesy or dower in lands conveyed if the conveyance so provides. Absolute divorce terminates the right of dower.

Effective May 28, 1980, all rights of dower and curtesy are abolished with respect to real property acquired subsequent to that date. As to such property occupied jointly with a spouse as their principal matrimonial residence, every married person has a right of joint possession during marriage. This right of possession may not be released without the consent of both spouses or court judgment.

Husband and Wife

A married woman's real and personal property owned at the time of marriage or acquired after marriage is her separate property as though she were unmarried. A wife is entitled to earnings of her separate employment and investments. A wife's separate property is not liable for her husband's debts.

A married woman may execute and deliver any instrument relating to her real property with the same effect as if she were unmarried, and any such instrument is valid without her husband's joinder or consent. However, no conveyance or act of such married woman can affect any estate or interest of her husband in such property. Either spouse may convey directly to the other real estate or any interest in it. The conveyance is valid, although the grantee spouse does not join in or acknowledge the same. Such conveyance extinguishes the dower or curtesy interest if specifically released. A conveyance by either spouse to himself or herself and the other spouse of real estate held in severalty shall be construed to vest an estate by the entirety in the husband and wife.

A married woman may contract with her husband to form a partnership or business and will be bound by partnership contracts to the same extent as though unmarried.

As to antenuptial contracts, all contracts made in contemplation of marriage remain in full force after marriage.

Marriage

Common-law marriages are not recognized unless contracted before December 1, 1939.

Personal Property

Tenancy by the entirety in personal property is recognized if the husband and wife acquired the interests under a written instrument designating both their names as husband and wife.

Real Property

Tenancy by the entirety in real property is recognized. A grant or devise to two or more persons creates a tenancy in common unless an intention to create a joint tenancy and not a tenancy in common is expressly stated in the instrument. (A grant or devise to trustees always creates a joint tenancy.) A grant or devise to a husband and wife creates a tenancy by the entirety unless it is otherwise expressly stated. Joint tenancy may be created by conveyance from a grantor to himself and others. An absolute divorce changes tenancy by the entirety to tenancy in common.

All rights of dower and curtesy are abolished as to real property acquired by married persons during the marriage after May 28, 1980, but rights of dower and curtesy established prior to May 28, 1980 still exist.

Taxation

An inheritance tax is imposed on the transfer of all real and tangible personal property situated in New Jersey. It also is imposed on the transfer of all intangible property (including an interest in jointly owned property) wherever situated of resident decedents (and on certain property located in New Jersey of nonresident decedents) by will or intestate laws or in contemplation of death (within three years).

An estate tax is imposed in addition to an inheritance tax to equal the credit allowed on a federal return for state death taxes paid.

There is no gift tax, but the inheritance tax applies to gifts in contemplation of death or to take effect at or after death.

Wills

All rights of dower and curtesy are abolished as to real property acquired by married persons after May 28, 1980, but rights of dower and curtesy attached to real property acquired prior to that date are not affected.

A spouse to whom realty is devised takes the same in lieu of dower and curtesy, but he or she may file a written refusal renouncing such devise, and then is entitled to dower or curtesy. There is no statutory provision as to the effect of a gift of personalty. If expressed in a will to be in lieu of dower or curtesy, the surviving spouse may instead elect to take the intestate share.

NEW MEXICO

Curtesy and Dower

Abolished.

Community Property

New Mexico follows the community property system.

Descent and Distribution

The surviving spouse owns one-half of the couple's community property. The other one-half can be disposed of by will. Community property is subject to community debts.

Dissolution of Marriage

The court has the power to make division of spouses' property. This may apply on permanent separation, even without dissolution of the marriage. Community property must be divided equally.

Husband and Wife

Separate property can include: property acquired by either spouse before marriage; property acquired by gift, devise, bequest, or descent; property designated as separate by written agreement of the parties; property held as co-tenants or in joint tenancy or tenancy in common; or property designated by a court as such, with all rents, issues, and profits from such property. Property acquired during marriage by the wife by an instrument in writing in her name alone (or in her name and name of another party not her husband) is presumed to be the wife's separate property if the instrument was executed prior to July 1, 1973.

Either spouse may convey his or her separate property without the other joining, or may dispose of it by will. As to community property, only one-half can be disposed of by will; the surviving spouse owns one-half.

All property acquired by either spouse after the marriage (except as listed above as "separate") is community property. A husband and wife may take title to realty as joint tenants. As to dealing with respect to her separate property, there is a conclusive presumption in favor of a person dealing in good faith and for valuable consideration with a married woman that she is the owner of the separate property.

As to community property, a husband and wife must join in all deeds of community real property (except from one spouse to the other). Either party may manage and control personal community property, unless one spouse is named in the document of title or in an agreement with a third party as having sole management and control. In the latter cases, only the spouse so named may manage or control that property. Where the document of title is in the names of both spouses, both must join in the transaction with regard to that property.

As for antenuptial contracts, a husband and wife can alter their property relations (but not their own legal status). Nuptial contracts that attempt to alter legal relations of parties are generally void either for lack of consideration or as against public policy.

Marriage

Common-law marriages are not recognized.

Personal Property

Tenancy by the entirety is not recognized specifically by statute.

Real Property

Tenancy in common and joint tenancy are recognized. A grant or devise to two or more persons creates a tenancy in common unless it is declared expressly in the instrument that they take as joint tenants. Husband and wife may hold realty as joint tenants.

Taxation

There is no inheritance tax; there is an estate tax equal to credit allowed on a federal return for state death taxes.

There is no gift tax, but a form of "succession" tax applies to gifts in contemplation or to take effect upon death.

Wills

Upon the death of a spouse, the entire community property goes to the surviving spouse if the decedent did not exercise power of testamentary disposition over one-half. An omitted spouse who married the testator after execution of the testator's will takes the intestate share unless omission was intentional, or the testator made provision for the spouse by transfer outside the will with intent that transfer would be in lieu of a testamentary provision.

NEW YORK

Curtesy and Dower

Abolished (since 1930).

Divorce

The court determines the respective rights of the parties in separate and marital property, and orders disposition as follows: separate property is to remain as such; marital property is to be distributed equitably between the parties, considering the facts and circumstances of the case. "Marital property" means all property acquired by either or both spouses during marriage (and before the divorce action began), regardless of the form in which title is held. "Separate property" includes property acquired before the marriage or acquired by inheritance or gift (from other than the spouse), and property derived from the separate property (as an exchange, increase in value, etc.) unless the appreciation was due in part to the other spouse's contributions. The divorce court may, in its discretion, make a distribution where equitable distribution is impracticable to carry out. The court may make an order regarding the use and occupancy of the marital home regardless of ownership form.

Husband and Wife

A married woman has all rights with respect to real or personal property, including acquisition and disposition. She also has a right to make contracts with regard to her property and is liable on such contracts (and judgments) as if she were unmarried. A husband and wife may agree in writing as to ownership or disposition of separate and matrimonial property, including testamentary provisions.

As for antenuptial contracts, written contracts in contemplation of marriage remain in full force after the marriage. Agreements made after July 1, 1980 are valid and enforceable if in writing and able to be recorded. The provisions of such an agreement may include waiver of election right to take against a will, specific testamentary provisions, and matters relating to ownership or distribution of both separate and marital property. A court, to uphold such an agreement, considers whether the terms were fair and reasonable, not unconscionable, etc.

Marriage

Common-law marriages are prohibited but are recognized if entered into in New York before April 29, 1933, or if valid where created.

Personal Property

Tenancy by the entirety is not recognized.

Real Property

Tenancy by the entirety is recognized. A conveyance or devise to two or more persons (not husband and wife) creates a tenancy in common unless expressly declared to create a joint tenancy (except that estates vested in executors or trustees is held by them in joint tenancy). Conveyance to a husband and wife creates a tenancy by the entirety unless expressly declared to be a joint tenancy or a tenancy in common.

A conveyance to two persons who are not legally married but describe themselves as "husband and wife" creates a joint tenancy unless the terms expressly state they take as tenants in common. (This would be significant information for nonmarrieds buying property together. It is important to state their ownership preference or the law will do it automatically.)

Taxation

There is no inheritance tax.

There is an estate tax. A New York gross estate consists of the federal gross estate, whether or not a federal return is required, excluding the value of real and tangible personal property situated outside New York whose amount is included in the federal gross estate. Gifts made within three years of a decedent's death are included in a New York gross estate.

A gift tax is imposed on the transfer of property by gift; it is modeled after the federal gift tax, but unification of estate and gift tax rates has not been adopted.

Wills

A surviving spouse has the right of election to take the intestate share.

NORTH CAROLINA

Curtesy and Dower

Abolished. After July 1, 1960, a surviving spouse may elect to take an interest similar to common law dower in the estate of a deceased spouse in lieu of an intestate or testamentary share.

Divorce

Separation agreements are valid (but the court may exercise independent judgment regarding spouses' agreement as to the care and custody of child). In the absence of a separation agreement, either spouse may petition for an equitable distribution of marital property. However, before, during, or after marriage, the parties may enter into a written agreement providing for distribution of marital property in a manner deemed by the parties to be equitable.

Husband and Wife

A married person may hold property free from the debts of his or her husband or wife. A married woman can contract and deal with regard to her separate real and personal property in the same manner as if she were unmarried. However, every conveyance or other instrument affecting the estate, right, or title of any married persons in lands or real estate is subject to the elective life estate of either the husband or wife. This right to elect may be waived by execution of the deed or by executing a valid separation agreement authorizing conveyance without the consent of the other spouse.

Certain conveyances are valid without joinder of the grantor's spouse. These are: conveyance by one spouse to the other; conveyance by either spouse to both spouses (which creates tenancy by entireties unless a contrary intent is expressed in the conveyance); and conveyance by one tenant in entirety to the other (which dissolves the estate by entireties in the property so conveyed).

Effective January 31, 1983, a husband and wife have equal right to the control of, use, income, and profits of real property held in tenancy by the entirety. Neither spouse may sell, lease, mortgage, or convey any property so held without a written joinder of the other spouse.

Personal Property

Tenancy by the entirety does not exist in personal property.

Real Property

Tenancy by the entirety does exist. Common law estates are recognized.

Taxation

There is an inheritance tax.

In addition to the inheritance tax, an estate tax is imposed on the transfer of the net estate of every decedent where an inheritance tax imposed is less than the maximum state death tax credit allowed by federal estate tax law so that the aggregate amount of tax due the state of North Carolina is equal to the maximum amount of credit allowed by federal law.

There is a gift tax, but charitable gifts are exempt. Also, North Carolina follows federal law in allowing a $10,000 exclusion, including consent by spouses to each use his or her annual exclusion. Gifts by nonresidents are taxable to the extent that the property given is located within the jurisdiction of North Carolina.

Wills

Any surviving spouse may, by timely election, dissent from the will of the decedent spouse and receive the same share he or she would have received had the deceased spouse died intestate, up to a maximum of one-half of the deceased spouse's estate before deduction of estate taxes. There is an exception to this: where the surviving spouse receives one-half or more in value of all the property passing upon the death of the deceased spouse (including property passing under the will and property passing outside the will), there is no right of election.

NORTH DAKOTA

Curtesy and Dower

Abolished.

Divorce

When a divorce is granted, the court is to make an "equitable distribution" of real and personal property of the parties as may seem "just and proper." Either party may be required to provide the other with an allowance for support during life or for a shorter period, and the court may modify its orders from time to time. Where a husband or wife has a separate estate sufficient to provide proper support, the court, in its discretion, may withhold any allowance to that person out of the separate property of the other spouse. The court may assign the homestead to the innocent party either absolutely or for a limited time. The Supreme Court of North Dakota has held that, in determining the question of alimony or division of property, the court is to consider ages of the parties, their earning ability, duration of the marriage and the conduct of each spouse during the marriage, their station in life, circumstances and necessities of each, the parties' health and physical condition, and their financial circumstances. As to the last-named criterion, the court is to consider the property owned, its value and income-producing capacity, and whether it was accumulated or acquired before or after the marriage.

Husband and Wife

Separate property of either spouse is not liable for the debts of the other. Each is liable for his/her own debts contracted before or after marriage. The earnings of one spouse are not liable for the debts of the other. Husband and wife are jointly and severally liable for debts contracted by either while living together for certain necessary household expenses and education of minor children.

Either husband or wife may enter into contracts with each other or with third persons that either might enter into if unmarried. Either spouse may convey or encumber their separate property without the consent or joinder of the other except that both must join in encumbrance of the homestead.

Marriage

Common-law marriages are invalid.

Personal Property

Tenancy by the entirety is not permitted in personal property.

Real Property

Tenancies in common and joint tenancies are recognized. Tenancies by the entirety are not recognized.

Taxation

There is no inheritance tax or gift tax; there is an estate tax equal to the federal tax credit (but only with respect to the properties within North Dakota).

OHIO

Curtesy

Common law curtesy is abolished. A husband has dower interest the same as a wife.

Divorce

The court may grant permanent alimony payable in gross or in installments, in either real or personal property, and to either party. The court is to consider various factors prior to grant of alimony. The court also considers marital conduct. The court may grant alimony for the following causes: adultery; any gross neglect of duty; abandonment without good cause; ill treatment; habitual drunkenness; sentence to and imprisonment in a penitentiary.

Ohio divides marital property.

Dower

A surviving spouse has a life estate in one-third of all real property the decedent spouse owned during marriage. If the decedent spouse had encumbered the property, the surviving spouse's dower interest is computed on the basis of the amount of the encumbrance. The spouse of the owner of real property may be made a party to any action involving a judicial sale of real property to satisfy creditors' claims. A spouse's dower interest may be subject to sale without the spouse's consent, with the court determining the present value and priority of the dower interest. These provisions do not apply to a tax lien or sale for delinquent taxes. The dower interest of either spouse terminates upon granting of absolute divorce. Either spouse may release his or her dower right by joining the other spouse as a grantor in a deed, mortgage, etc., or by separate instrument.

Husband and Wife

Neither husband nor wife has any interest in the property of the other, except the right of support, dower, and to remain in the homestead after the death of either. Either spouse may receive, hold, or dispose of his/her separate property. No joinder is necessary, except to bar dower rights in real property.

Antenuptial agreements must be in writing to be enforceable. Such agreements must be entered into freely without fraud or duress, after full financial disclosure, etc. Antenuptial agreements providing for certain financial arrangements must not be unconscionable at the time of divorce or separation.

Marriage

Common-law marriage is recognized.

Personal Property

Tenancy by the entirety does not exist.

Real Property

Tenancy by entireties may be created by language in a conveyance or grant.

Joint tenancy is not presumed, but express provisions in the instrument creating a joint tenancy will be given effect (otherwise, a tenancy in common is created).

Taxation

An inheritance tax only applies to estates of decedents who died before June 30, 1968.

There is no gift tax. An estate tax applies to gifts in contemplation of death or intended to take affect after death.

An estate tax applies to estates of residents dying on or after July 1, 1968. The value of a gross estate is similar to valuation for federal estate tax. A gross estate includes property transferred within three years of death (unless such transfer is shown not to be made in contemplation of death). There is a $10,000 per transferee per year gift exclusion. There is also a tax on a generation-skipping transfer in an amount equal to the credit allowed on a federal estate tax return for taxes paid to any state in respect to any property included in a generation-skipping transfer. The estate tax generally is intended to absorb the credit for state death taxes allowed by federal estate tax laws.

Wills

When a surviving spouse is the sole legatee or devisee under a will, no election is required, but one may be made. In all other cases, the surviving spouse must elect to take under the provisions of a deceased spouse's will or under the statute of descent and distribution.

OKLAHOMA

Curtesy and Dower

Abolished.

Divorce

Permanent alimony may be awarded to either spouse for support. Alimony allowed by a divorce judgment must be based on the parties' circumstances at the time of divorce and constitutes a final determination; it is not to be modified by subsequent changes in condition. "Open-end" alimony awards are not permitted in Oklahoma.

Division of property of spouses may be made by a court even though divorce is not granted. Jointly acquired property is disposed by the court as "deemed reasonable" regardless of the legal owner. A spouse's interest in joint property acquired during marriage becomes vested upon divorce.

Separation agreements are not binding on the court. They may be upheld after close scrutiny to determine whether they are "reasonable, just, and fair."

Husband and Wife

The *Oklahoma Law Digest* states: "Husband is the head of the family and selects the place of living. He is under the duty to support her, although a wife must support an infirm husband."

After this, the *Digest* states: "Married women retain the same legal existence and personality after marriage as before."

Except as to the right of support, neither husband nor wife has any interest in the separate property of the other, although neither may be excluded from the other's residence. Husband and wife may hold property as joint tenants or tenants in common or as community property. However, the Oklahoma Community Property Law, which became effective July 26, 1945, was repealed effective June 2, 1949. Prior to June 2, 1952, a husband and wife whose property interests were affected by the law could record an agreement specifying the rights acquired by either party under the prior law. The topic now (in 1991 and beyond) seems moot. There still are references to "community property" in the *Digest*.

Antenuptial contracts to alter property claims must be in writing, executed prior to marriage, be fair, and give full disclosure.

Personal Property

Tenancy by the entirety exists between husband and wife.

Real Property

Joint tenancy in real or personal property may be created by a single instrument, will, or transfer document when expressly declared that a joint tenancy is being created. Joint tenancy may be created by transfer to persons as joint tenants from an owner, or a joint owner to himself and one or more persons, or from tenants in common to themselves. Such an estate may be created by or for persons who have elected to become bound under any community property act now in existence or that may be enacted in the future. Tenancy by the entirety, in real or personal property, exists between husband and wife.

Taxation

There is no inheritance tax and, effective January 1, 1982, no gift tax.

An estate tax is levied on the transfer by will or intestate laws or any transfer taking effect at death (any transfer made within three years of death is deemed a transfer in contemplation of death unless shown to be otherwise).

Wills

Prior to July 1, 1985, if a married person attempted to devise or bequeath away from his or her spouse less in value than would be taken through succession by law, the surviving spouse might elect to take under the will or by succession.

For deaths occurring after July 1, 1985, a spouse cannot bequeath and devise away from a surviving spouse so much that the surviving spouse receives less than one-half of property acquired through joint efforts during the marriage. In such a case, the surviving spouse has the right of election to take one-half of joint industry property instead of under the will.

A valid antenuptial agreement will override this provision.

OREGON

Curtesy and Dower

Abolished for the surviving spouse of person who dies after July 1, 1970.

Divorce

The term "alimony" no longer is used. Support, during divorce litigation and permanent, may be allowed. Permanent support may be ordered paid in a lump sum or in installments. A decree as to future support may be modified with changed circumstances.

The marital property system of distribution prevails. The court may approve a voluntary property settlement agreement providing support. In distributing property by court, the court must consider the spouse's contribution as home-maker as a contribution to marital assets, and the tax consequences and costs of sale of assets occurring in divorce property division. The court must also presume equal contribution (but that is rebuttable), and full disclosure of assets is required. Division of property by decree is not a taxable sale or exchange. Fault in causing dissolution of the marriage may not be considered.

Husband and Wife

Neither spouse is responsible for liabilities of the other spouse incurred before the marriage or incurred separately during the marriage (except for family expenses or education of children).

Parties to an intended marriage may enter into prenuptial agreements in writing concerning their respective personal and real property holdings; these agreements will be binding on the parties and their heirs. Prenuptial agreements prohibiting alimony are enforced unless the spouse waiving alimony has no other reasonable means of support. Court approval of such an agreement can be modified if circumstances change.

The Community Property Law of 1947 was repealed April 11, 1949. Former community property may be converted into property held in common, by the entirety, or separately, by an agreement in writing signed by both spouses. On the death of either spouse after April 11, 1951, all property which would have been separate prior to the 1947 law can be distributed by will or by the state (if decedent died intestate) as though the community property law had never existed. (This apparently was a short-lived period of community property law in Oregon.)

Marriage

Common-law marriage cannot be entered into in Oregon but will be recognized if valid in the state where entered into.

Personal Property

Tenancy by the entirety does not exist in personal property. Oregon considers conveyance to a husband and wife with right of survivorship as creating concurrent life estates with contingent cross remainders. A joint tenancy in personal property may be created by written instrument. It does not negate the rights of creditors.

Real Property

Joint tenancy is abolished, and use of the term, without more, creates a tenancy in common. The right of survivorship, however, may be created by express agreement of the parties. Joint property rights may be created directly without the use of an intervening conveyance to a straw man. A husband and wife may own property as tenants by the entirety or as tenants in common.

A conveyance to husband and wife as husband and wife creates a tenancy by the entirety.

Taxation

Inheritance tax is subject to a gradual phase out and does not apply (except for a tax equal to the state tax credit on a federal estate tax) to estates of decedents dying after December 31, 1986.

For estates of persons dying before January 1, 1987, an inheritance tax was imposed on the right to receive beneficial interests in property by right of survivorship, will, or gift intended to take effect after the death of the decedent, and also on the right to receive proceeds of insurance policies on the decedent's life if the decedent possessed incidents of ownership. A tax also was imposed on the transfer of property within three years of death (including the amount of any gift tax paid on such transfer). No tax is imposed on one-half of jointly held property passing to a surviving spouse.

There was a gift tax but none was imposed on the creation or severance of a joint interest with right of survivorship by spouses. (On severance, each spouse receives an undivided one-half interest, thus becoming tenants in common.) No gift tax applies to gifts made after December 31, 1986.

Wills

A surviving spouse has the right to elect a percentage of the decedent's net estate but forfeits certain rights under the will of a decedent spouse, if an election is made.

PENNSYLVANIA

Curtesy

Curtesy in Pennsylvania is the share of the deceased wife's estate which is allotted to a surviving husband by the rules of intestate succession or by election against the will.

Divorce

The marital property system of distribution prevails. Upon request of either party in divorce or annulment proceedings, the court must equitably divide all marital property without regard to marital misconduct as the court deems just. Marital property is subject to division regardless of how title is held.

Dower

Dower in Pennsylvania is the share of the deceased husband's estate allotted to a surviving wife by the rules of intestate succession or by election against the will.

Husband and Wife

In 1985, the Pennsylvania legislature passed a law repealing "out of date" statutory provisions relating to married women. Married women have the same right and power as married men to acquire, own, possess, control, use, convey, mortgage, etc. any property.

Either husband or wife may convey to both as tenants by entireties; both together may convey to either spouse alone.

For purpose of determining property subject to the elective share of a surviving spouse, a married person can convey title to individually owned real property without the necessity of the other spouse joining in the deed to the extent adequate consideration is received.

For the purpose of determining marital property in a divorce or annulment proceeding, real property conveyed or disposed of in good faith for adequate consideration before divorce proceedings is excluded from "marital property."

As to her own property, a married woman is not liable for her husband's debts. Separate earnings of a wife belong to her.

Antenuptial contracts, if challenged as to validity, are presumed valid and enforceable provided reasonable provision was made for the spouse challenging and the other spouse had disclosed his or her worth fully and fairly.

Marriage

Common-law marriages are recognized.

Personal Property

Pennsylvania recognizes tenancy by the entirety in personal property.

Real Property

A joint tenancy with right of survivorship may be created if such intention is expressed or can be inferred clearly from express directions. In the absence of a clear intention to create a joint tenancy with right of survivorship in the instrument of conveyance, such instrument would create a tenancy in common.

Unless a contrary intention is stated clearly, real estate in the name of a husband and wife creates a tenancy by the entirety.

Taxation

An inheritance tax is imposed on transfer of any property by will or by intestacy by a resident or nonresident, and is imposed on certain inter vivos transfers. Property held in joint tenancy with right of survivorship is taxable. The share of inheritance tax pertaining to each surviving joint tenant's ownership is determined by dividing the value of the whole property by the number of joint tenants in existence immediately prior to the death of the decedent. An exception to this is property held by husband and wife with right of survivorship (unless the co-ownership was created within one year of the death of a co-tenant).

In addition to the inheritance tax, an estate tax is imposed on estates of resident decedents (and on estates situated in Pennsylvania of decedents who resided elsewhere) in order to absorb the full credit allowed on a federal estate tax return.

There is no gift tax, but the inheritance tax applies to gifts made within one year of death (with a $3,000 exclusion).

Wills

A surviving spouse may elect to take against the will of a deceased spouse and in such case is entitled to one-third of the probate estate. The right to elect is personal to the spouse and may be exercised in whole or in part during his or her lifetime (or by his or her agent as power of attorney).

PUERTO RICO

Antenuptial Contracts

Future spouses may enter into an antenuptial contract prior to marriage setting forth an agreement as to ownership of present and future assets. The terms may not be contrary to law or to "established customs as to authority of spouses within family." The contract must be in the form of a public instrument executed before a notary public and may not be amended after the marriage occurs.

Curtesy

Does not exist in Puerto Rico.

Divorce

The community property system prevails in Puerto Rico. Dissolution of marriage requires dissolution of the conjugal partnership and distribution of community property assets to the spouses. Upon filing a divorce action, neither spouse may contract debts or effect any settlements to be paid from community property without court approval.

Dower

Does not exist in Puerto Rico.

Husband and Wife

Separate property of spouses is property brought into the marriage by either spouse as his or her own; property acquired during the marriage by gift or inheritance; property acquired by exchange for other separate property; and property bought with money belonging exclusively to either the husband or wife. Each spouse has the right to manage and dispose of his or her separate property, but gifts between spouses (except "moderate" gifts on "festive" days) are void.

Community or conjugal property belongs in equal parts to both spouses. Such property is property obtained by the earnings or wages of each spouse; property purchased with money of the marriage partnership; and the earnings obtained during marriage from the separate property of each spouse. Marriage partnership property does not include capital gains from the sale of private property of either spouse. Marriage is considered a co-partnership, but a prenuptial agreement may provide otherwise. Unless agreed to the contrary, both spouses are administrators of conjugal partnership property. Neither spouse may alienate or encumber community property without the written consent of the other spouse. The rules apply to immovable property in Puerto Rico (regardless of the place of marriage). When a marriage partnership is dissolved by death or divorce, property covered by it is divided equally between the spouses. Each spouse may by will dispose of one-half of the couple's community property.

Marriage

Common-law marriages are not recognized in Puerto Rico.

Real Property

In Puerto Rico law, the term "real property" is unknown. The term "immovable" categorizes real property. Dominion title is roughly the same as fee simple.

Common law estates of joint tenancy and tenancy by the entirety are unknown. Co-ownership is governed by contract. There is no concept analogous to joint tenants with right of survivorship.

Taxation

There is an estate tax patterned somewhat on the U.S. Internal Revenue Code. (Puerto Rico taxation involves a unique situation requiring special interpretation of U.S. law.)

A gift tax is imposed on gifts of property wherever situated if the donor is a resident of Puerto Rico. If the donor is a nonresident, the tax is imposed on gifts of property situated in Puerto Rico.

Wills

The surviving spouse has, in addition to half of all marriage partnership property, a life interest in a portion of the estate, varying according to the number of children (who have a share).

Only part of the decedent's estate may be disposed of freely by will; a certain portion goes to the heirs by operation of law (these are "forced heirs"), depending on their relationship.

The surviving spouse has no right to take against the will except as to portions allotted by law as forced heir.

RHODE ISLAND

Curtesy and Dower

Common law estates of curtesy and dower are abolished. A surviving spouse is entitled to a life estate in realty owned by the deceased spouse at death, subject to encumbrances. The life estate takes precedence over any will provision or creditor's claim (except those secured by a lien), if the surviving spouse elects that right. This life estate, by statute, replaced dower and curtesy; the right of spouse to a distributive share of the estate apparently does not bar a life estate in realty (which replaced dower and curtesy).

Divorce

The court may assign to either spouse (in addition to or in lieu of alimony) a portion of the estate of the other. Property held prior to the marriage is not assignable (but income from it is); property inherited before, during, or after the marriage may not be assigned. After a complaint for divorce is filed, the court may permit either party to sell or dispose of his or her separate real estate free of dower or curtesy.

Husband and Wife

A married woman has the same rights and powers (as well as liabilities) as to her own property as if she were unmarried. Separate property acquired by a married woman either before or after marriage remains her sole and separate property free from the control of her husband.

A married woman may convey to or take title from any person, including her husband, except in fraud of creditors.

Antenuptial contracts are recognized. Rhode Island has adopted the Uniform Premarital Agreement Act.

Marriage

Common-law marriages are recognized.

Personal Property

Common law rule is presumed to govern the validity of tenancies by the entirety in personal property. There are no decisions.

Real Property

Common law estates in land are recognized, with statutory modifications. All transfers to two or more persons are deemed to create a tenancy in common and not a joint tenancy, unless the intent to create a joint tenancy is declared expressly. Joint heirs are deemed to be tenants in common. Tenancies by the entirety are recognized. A husband's creditors may attach a husband's interest as a tenant by the entirety, but they may not sell it. Rhode Island also recognizes the common law estate of "fee tail." A devise in fee tail is limited to the first taker (lawful issue of the donee); after that it becomes an estate in fee simple. (This is a holdover of English law.)

Taxation

The inheritance tax was eliminated in 1980.

An estate tax is imposed on the estates of decedents dying after October 1, 1980. The tax is on transfers by will, by intestate succession, and inter vivos transfers in contemplation of (or to take effect at) death. Additional taxes are imposed to equal the amount of credit allowed under the Federal Revenue Act for state estate taxes if Rhode Island estate taxes are less than the credit.

Wills

Where a will fails to indicate an intention that provision for a surviving spouse is in lieu of the statutory life estate in real estate of the deceased, then the surviving spouse takes such statutory life estate in addition to such will provision.

SOUTH CAROLINA

Curtesy

Abolished.

Divorce

The Family Court settles all legal and equitable rights of parties to real and personal property of the marriage in marital litigation. A law providing for equitable distribution of marital property (with emphasis on title) was amended to provide that "marital property" is to be distributed regardless of how title is held. The Family Court is allowed (if petitioned to do so) to freeze all marital assets within the state. Professional or other degrees or licenses are not to be classified as marital property. Inherited property itself is not marital property (unless certain circumstances cause inherited property to lose its nonmarital character).

Family court settles legal and equitable rights of parties in real and personal property of the marriage. The title theory was the basis of distribution with property ordinarily set aside to the spouse with clear title. Exceptions to the title theory were recognized on the basis of other legal doctrines. For example, recent case law allows a wife to claim a contribution as a homemaker as the basis of "special equity."

Dower

Dower and jointure abolished by statute May 31, 1985.

Husband and Wife

The real and personal property of a married woman, held by her at the time of marriage or acquired after marriage, is her separate property and not subject to her husband's debts. A married woman has all rights incident to her separate property as if she were unmarried "or a man."

A spouse acquires a vested interest in marital property which is subject to apportionment in marital litigation. Nonmarital property is not subject to apportionment.

Marriage

Common-law marriage is recognized.

Personal Property

Tenancy by the entirety does not exist in personal property. Joint tenancy with right of survivorship for stocks and other securities has been repealed as of January 1, 1989.

Real Property

The estates recognized are fee simple, tenancy in common, joint tenancy (instrument must expressly provide for survivorship), and life estate.

Taxation

Effective for decedents dying after June 30, 1991, a tax equal to the maximum amount of federal credit allowed under the federal Internal Revenue Code of 1986 is imposed on transfers of resident decedent's taxable estates.

A gift tax is based upon and similar to federal gift tax provisions (with certain exceptions).

Wills

If a married person domiciled in South Carolina dies, a surviving spouse has a right to take an elective share of one-third of the decedent's probate estate (in lieu of the share provided in a will).

SOUTH DAKOTA

Curtesy and Dower

Abolished.

Divorce

All property of spouses, including inherited property, regardless of which spouse holds title, may be considered marital property and may be divided between spouses at the court's discretion. Factors to be considered by the court are duration of the marriage, value of the property, ages of the spouses, health of the spouses, competency of the spouses to earn a living, contribution of each spouse to the accumulation of property, and the income-producing capacity of each spouse's assets. The court is not to take fault into account in awarding property unless fault is relevant to the acquisition of property during the marriage.

Husband and Wife

Neither husband nor wife has any interest in the property of the other except the homestead, and neither can be excluded from the other's dwelling (if separate). Each has respective rights for support as provided by law. Each spouse retains after marriage all civil rights and property rights of a single person (except as to the homestead). Earnings of the spouse are not liable for debts of the other spouse, and separate property of a spouse is not liable for debts of the other spouse contracted before or after the marriage. Either husband or wife may contract with each other or any other person regarding property, just as either might if unmarried. There is no requirement for joinder of a spouse with regard to encumbrance of separate property.

Antenuptial agreements are allowed with certain qualifications relating to spousal support.

Marriage

Common-law marriages are not permissible if initiated after July 1, 1959. Before that date, they were recognized and valid.

Personal Property

Joint tenancy is permitted in personal property. Tenancy by the entirety is not recognized.

Real Property

Tenancy by the entirety is not recognized. An interest in property created in favor of several persons is an interest in common unless expressly declared in the document to be an interest in joint tenancy. A joint tenancy is the only estate with survivorship rights. A creditor's rights are preserved against a surviving joint tenant. South Dakota law also specifically includes partnership interests as a type of joint ownership.

Taxation

An inheritance tax is imposed on all property of resident decedents passing by will or inheritance. It is also imposed on all property of nonresident decedents located in South Dakota and on all property transferred in contemplation of death. Property passing to the survivor of a joint tenancy is subject to inheritance tax (including property held by husband and wife as joint tenants).

An estate tax is imposed equal to the maximum allowable credit against federal estate taxes for state death taxes paid.

Wills

Unless there is a clear provision in the will requiring an election by the surviving spouse between the will provisions and homestead rights, the surviving spouse may take both.

South Dakota law has some specific (and unusual) provisions regarding the statutory rights of a surviving spouse. A "homestead" may be any structure (i.e., theater or hotel building) that is partly adaptable for living quarters. A surviving spouse may require administrators of the decedent's estate to pay off an encumbrance against such homestead (if there are sufficient funds). (Anyone interested in this aspect of South Dakota law should have an attorney look into it.)

TENNESSEE

Curtesy

Curtesy, unless vested, was abolished as of April 1, 1977.

Divorce

Tennessee is a marital property state. The court presiding over a divorce action is to divide equitably and distribute marital property without regard to fault; it may divest and reinvest title where necessary or order the sale with proceeds to be divided between the parties. Guidelines provided are to be followed. The law does not affect the validity of an antenuptial agreement or preclude incorporation into the divorce decree of a property settlement agreement made by the parties themselves. The court may award the home and household effects to either party but must give special consideration to the parent with custody of the children.

Dower

Dower, unless vested, was abolished as of April 1, 1977.

Husband and Wife

A married woman may acquire, hold, manage, control, and dispose of all property, real or personal, as though "not married."

A married woman may contract with her husband or any other person. Husband and wife may transact business with each other. Antenuptial contracts and settlements regarding property must be registered. Such contracts are enforceable if entered into freely in good faith and without duress or undue influence. Postnuptial agreements regarding property are void as to existing creditors.

Either spouse may convey his or her real estate "(except the husband's homestead)" without joinder of the other. Mortgage by one spouse without joinder of the other will not defeat dower or curtesy. (Presumably, that means dower or curtesy, *if vested.*)

Marriage

Common-law marriages are not recognized but are considered valid if contracted in a state where such marriages are valid.

Personal Property

Personal property may be owned as tenants by the entirety.

Real Property

Tenancy by the entirety is recognized, as are all usual common law estates. Survivorship in joint tenancy has been abolished. Heirs of property jointly held take as tenants in common. However, the right of survivorship may be created expressly and, if so created in the instrument, will be valid.

Taxation

There is an inheritance tax on the following: transfer from a resident decedent of Tennessee of real property situated within the state, tangible personal property (unless it is outside the state), all intangible personal property, insurance proceeds, proceeds of certain employee benefit plans, and property in which the decedent had a "qualifying income interest for life," as defined by statute. When the transfer is from a nonresident decedent, a transfer of real property located within Tennessee is taxed, as is tangible personal property located within the state. These transfers are taxed whether by will, by intestacy statutes, or by gift within three years of death. For jointly held property, the rules are similar to the rules for federal estate taxation.

An estate tax is imposed to take full advantage of the credit for state death taxes allowed on a federal estate tax return.

There is a transfer tax on gifts of real property within the state and tangible personal property located within the state (even if the donor is a nonresident) and on gifts of intangible personal property where the donor is a resident. There is also a tax on generation skipping transfers keyed to provisions in the Internal Revenue Code.

Wills

A surviving spouse may elect to take one-third of a decedent spouse's real and personal property after estate administration expenses.

TEXAS

Curtesy and Dower

Curtesy and dower do not exist in Texas.

Divorce

The court presiding in a divorce case may make division of property in such way as seems "just and right," having due regard for the rights of each party and their children. Texas is a community property jurisdiction.

Husband and Wife

Marriage creates certain responsibilities, duties, and privileges. There are no disabilities of married women. A married woman has full powers to make contracts and sue or be sued in her own name.

All property, real and personal, owned by either of the parties before marriage and that acquired afterward by gift, devise, or descent and increase in the same are the separate property of that individual. Separate property of a spouse is not subject to liabilities of the other spouse unless both spouses are legally liable. Rents and profits arising out of separate or community property are community. This includes cash dividends from stock and interest on bonds. However, bonus money and royalties payable with respect to oil and gas leases covering separate property are separate.

Persons about to marry or those already married may by written instrument, from time to time, partition between themselves all or part of their property, present or future, and set aside to each spouse separately such property, including the income from such property, provided such action is not taken to defraud pre-existing creditors. Spouses may create a joint tenancy with right of survivorship if property is partitioned into each spouse's separate property but cannot create joint tenancy with right of survivorship with community property.

If one spouse makes a gift of property to the other spouse, the gift is presumed to include all income or property that might arise from that gift.

The Texas law gives management and control of separate property to each spouse and of community property to the spouse who would have owned it had both spouses been single. Property in a spouse's name is presumed to be subject to his or her management or control.

Each spouse has sole management, control, and disposition of his or her separate property, real and personal, and may convey or encumber the same without joinder of the other spouse. Community property may be conveyed by the spouse who would have owned it had both been single.

Parties intending to marry may enter into a marital property agreement concerning their property then existing or to be acquired, listing such stipulations as they desire.

The Uniform Premarital Agreement has been adopted. All property acquired by either a husband or wife during marriage is the common or community property of the husband and wife. The exceptions are: property defined in the law as separate property, and property contracted to be "separate" between the parties.

Marriage

Common-law marriages, both those contracted in Texas and out-of-state, are recognized.

Personal Property

Tenancy by the entirety is not recognized.

Real Property

Tenancy by the entirety is not recognized. Where property is owned jointly and one joint owner dies, that person's interest does not go to the remaining joint owner(s) but to the decedent's heirs. However, a right of survivorship may be created in writing.

Taxation

The inheritance tax law was changed so that for estates of decedents who die after September 1, 1983, a tax will be imposed on the transfer at death of property of every resident of Texas (and on property within Texas of a nonresident) equal to the amount of the federal credit for state death transfer taxes.

There is no gift tax. There is a tax on property included in a generation-skipping transfer.

Wills

If the will of a husband or wife attempts, by explicit language, to dispose of the entire community property, or any part of the community property, the surviving spouse has a right to elect whether to take the provision in the will or to retain his or her right in the community property against the will. Election may be express or implied, by word or act, but must be made with a showing of knowledge that the right to elect exists. There is no right to elect between a testamentary provision (in a will) and a distributive share under the statute of descent and distribution (which applies when there is no will).

UTAH

Curtesy and Dower

There is no doctrine of curtesy in Utah. There are no dower rights.

Divorce

The equitable distribution theory applies. The court may make orders in relation to property "as may be equitable."

Husband and Wife

All disabilities of married women have been removed. Property acquired by a wife before marriage or acquired thereafter by purchase, gift, grant, inheritance, or devise remains her separate property, and she may deal with the same as though unmarried. A married woman is not liable for her husband's debts but is jointly liable with her husband for family expenses.

Marriage

A common-law marriage is an "unsolemnized" marriage arising out of contract if a court finds the two parties are: "(1) Capable of consent; (2) legally capable of solemnized marriage; (3) have cohabited; (4) mutually assume marital rights, duties and obligations; and (5) contend and are believed to be husband and wife."

Personal Property

There is no statutory provision as to whether tenancy by the entirety is recognized in personal property.

Real Property

Tenancy by the entirety is not recognized. Every interest in real estate conveyed to two or more persons is deemed a tenancy in common unless expressly declared in the instrument to be otherwise. Joint tenancies (with survivorship right) may be created by express declaration.

Taxation

There is no inheritance tax.

There is an estate tax imposed on the transfer of property at death. It is based on the maximum amount of credit for estate state death taxes allowed on a federal return.

There is no gift tax, but the estate tax applies to gifts in contemplation of death or intended to take effect after the death of the donor.

Wills

Utah has adopted the Uniform Probate Code with modifications. There is a provision for an elective share for a surviving spouse who renounces a will. There is a provision for property to be applied first to satisfy such elective share before contributions due from other recipients or transferees are applied.

VERMONT

Antenuptial Contracts

Antenuptial contracts can be enforced in a court of equity. To remove such a contract from being in violation of the statute of frauds, there should be a *written* agreement after the marriage.

Curtesy

A widower is entitled to one-third of all the real estate owned by his wife at death. If the wife left only one heir, who is the natural issue of that husband (or adopted child of both), the husband is entitled to half in value of such real estate.

Divorce

The court is to decree such disposition of property owned by the parties separately, jointly, or by the entirety, as is "just and equitable." The court is to consider the respective merits of the parties, the condition in which they will be left by such divorce, and the party through whom the property was acquired.

Dower

A widow is entitled to one-third in value of all the real estate owned by her husband at his death. If the husband left only one heir, who is the natural issue of the widow (or adopted child of both), she is entitled to half the value of the real estate. Dower has preference over the claims of unsecured creditors of a deceased husband. Dower may be barred as follows: by jointure (roughly means "widow's portion") settled on a wife by her husband or another person, or some monetary provision made for her before marriage (with or without her consent), or after marriage with her consent which is expressed to be in lieu of dower; by testamentary provision intended to be in lieu of dower (unless she elects to relinquish such provision); or by election (if the husband left no children) to take the intestate share (as provided by statute if the deceased left no will) instead of dower.

Husband and Wife

A married woman holds as her separate property all real property owned by her and all personal property acquired by her either before or after marriage (excluding gifts from her husband). Her separate property and the earnings of her separate property are not liable for debts of the husband. A married woman may make contracts regarding her separate property, as though unmarried.

Personal Property

Tenancy by the entirety exists in personal property.

Real Property

Tenancy by the entirety is recognized in real property. Unless specifically stated to convey a joint tenancy, all property conveyed by a grant or deed to two or more persons (except to a husband and wife or in trust) is deemed to be owned by them as tenants in common.

Taxation

There is a tax imposed on Vermont estates of residents and nonresidents dying after December 31, 1979. The gift tax with respect to Vermont gifts after December 31, 1979, was repealed effective January 1, 1980.

Wills

Where a testamentary provision is made for a surviving spouse in lieu of dower or curtesy, the surviving spouse may elect to relinquish such provision and take dower or curtesy. A surviving spouse may take curtesy or dower in lieu of the statutory distributive share of an estate (where there was no will).

VIRGINIA

Curtesy

A surviving husband was entitled to curtesy, in fee simple, in one-third of the real estate owned by his wife during their marriage. This applied whether or not a child was born. A husband's joining in his wife's conveyance would bar curtesy. This law changed in 1991. See "Dower and Curtesy" topic.

Divorce

Division of property is by process of equitable distribution. The court may grant a monetary award, payable as lump sum or in installment. In determining the amount of award, the court is to consider both parties as having an interest in marital property. Marital property includes real, personal, tangible, or intangible property acquired during the marriage. Marital property is presumed to be jointly owned unless shown otherwise. Contingent rights of either spouse in property of the other are extinguished by divorce. Tenancy with right of survivorship is terminated and becomes a tenancy in common.

Dower and Curtesy

A surviving wife was entitled to one-third of the real estate owned by her husband during the marriage. When a wife joined in a conveyance with her husband, this released her dower right.

In 1990, the Virginia legislature repealed the historic concepts of dower and curtesy. **This creates a very important change in Virginia property law.** Dower and curtesy interests which vested before January 1, 1991 and vested rights of creditors or others who might be affected by this law will find those interests (established prior to January 1, 1991) follow the law in effect prior to that date.

Under the new rules, a surviving spouse may claim an elective one-third share of the decedent's "augmented estate." This is in accordance with Virginia's' adoption of the augmented estate concept from the Uniform Probate Code. This concept involves assets that become part of the decedent's estate despite certain types of attempted or incomplete pre-death transfers. The provision is very technical, and any surviving spouse who might be affected by this provision should act quickly, because there is a six-month time period in which to make an election. This is clearly a situation calling for experienced professional help.

Husband and Wife

A married woman may hold, use, and dispose of property as though unmarried (formerly subject to the right of curtesy) free from control of her husband and free from liability for his debts. She may contract as though unmarried. No judgment lien is viable against the principal residence of a husband or wife if that realty is held by them as tenants by the entireties.

Marriage

Common-law marriages are void if contracted in Virginia but are recognized if contracted in a state where such marriages are valid.

Personal Property

Personal property may be held by a husband and wife as tenants by the entireties.

Premarital Agreement

A Premarital Agreement Act was enacted to govern agreement entered into after July 1, 1986. Prospective spouses may enter into premarital agreements regarding support, disposition of property, etc., upon marital separation or dissolution, death, or other event. Married people also have the same right to enter into *marital* agreements with each other. Such an agreement must be in writing and signed by both parties.

Real Property

Common law estates are recognized. Tenancy by the entirety is recognized. There is no survivorship between joint tenants (other than tenants by the entireties) except where they hold as executors or trustees, or the instrument creating a joint tenancy clearly shows the intent that there shall be survivorship.

Taxation

There are no statutory provisions for inheritance or gift taxes. An estate tax is imposed on Virginia residents in the amount of the federal credit for state death taxes allowable by Internal Revenue Code S 2011, with certain adjustments. Specific provisions cover the estate of a U.S. citizen who is not a resident of Virginia but had real property located in Virginia and/or tangible personal property having a situs in Virginia. Stock in a corporation organized under the laws of Virginia is deemed to be physically present within the state.

Wills

Whether or not provision is made for a husband or wife by will, a survivor may renounce and demand distributive rights. Under the new rules, a surviving spouse may claim an elective one-third share of the decedent's "augmented estate" (one-half if there are no surviving children). See "Dower and Curtesy."

VIRGIN ISLANDS

Curtesy and Dower

Abolished in 1957.

Divorce

There are no statutory provisions as to division of property except that the court may divide the marital estate by making a monetary award of alimony. Either party may institute a separate action for partition of property held as tenants in common. If one spouse has a particular equitable interest in property, a separate equity action may be maintained to realize that interest. A separation agreement between the parties may be helpful to a court in arriving at appropriate terms for alimony, but the court is not bound to accept the judgment or agreement of the parties on this issue.

Husband and Wife

Neither husband nor wife has an interest in the property of the other. Neither spouse is liable for debts or liabilities of the other incurred before marriage and neither is liable for separate debts of the other during marriage, nor is the rent or property income of either liable for separate debts of the other. A conveyance, transfer, or lien executed by either husband or wife to or in favor of the other is valid to the same extent as between other persons.

Marriage

Common-law marriages are not recognized, but if valid in other jurisdictions, they will be recognized in the Virgin Islands.

Personal Property

There are no statutory provisions as to whether a tenancy by the entirety exists in personal property.

Real Property

A conveyance or devise to husband and wife creates an estate by the entirety unless otherwise provided in the deed or will. Upon divorce or annulment of a marriage, former spouses become tenants in common. A conveyance or devise of lands made to two or more persons (other than to executors and trustees or to husband and wife) creates a tenancy in common unless the instrument expressly declares that the grantees take as joint tenants.

Taxation

There is an inheritance tax, including a tax on inheritances between spouses (although the percentage is smaller than on inheritances received by more distant relatives).

A gift tax is imposed on transfers during a calendar year by a resident or nonresident of property located in the Virgin Islands.

The federal estate tax law is applicable.

Wills

There is a personal right of election given to a surviving spouse to take the share of the estate as in intestacy (as if there were no will), but this is limited to one-half of the net estate of the decedent after the deduction of debts and administration expenses. A husband or wife may waive or release the right of election to take against a particular will.

WASHINGTON

Antenuptial Contracts

An antenuptial agreement must reasonably and fairly provide for the party in question, and there must be full disclosure of property involved. The agreement should be entered into voluntarily and with full knowledge of the legal ramifications.

Curtesy and Dower

Curtesy and dower have been abolished. Property rights of husband and wife are fixed by community property law.

Dissolution of Marriage

A court presiding over the dissolution of a marriage may make disposition of property as "just and equitable" without regard to marital misconduct. Relevant factors to consider are: the nature and extent of community and separate property; the duration of the marriage; the economic circumstances of each spouse at the time the division of property is effective.

Husband and Wife

All property, real and personal, owned by the wife or husband before marriage or afterward acquired by gift, bequest, devise, or descent, or from the income and profits of such, is her or his separate property. Separate property of either is not subject to the separate debts of the other spouse. Either spouse may convey or encumber his or her separate real or personal property (other than the homestead) without the consent or joinder of the other spouse.

The community property law is in effect in the state of Washington. Property acquired after marriage by either husband or wife or both is community property. Excepted from this is property acquired by gift or inheritance, or from the sale or profits of separate property. Property acquired by a couple living together but unmarried is not community property (see "Property of Cohabitants"). Community property is not owned by the community as a separate entity. Each spouse owns an equal half interest in the whole. However, either spouse acting alone may manage and control all community property with the same power of disposition as a spouse has over his or her separate property. Neither spouse may devise or bequeath by will more than one-half of their community property; neither spouse may give community property without the consent of the other; neither spouse may sell, convey, or encumber community real property without the other spouse joining in the execution of the deed; any such deed must be acknowledged by both spouses; neither spouse may purchase or contract to purchase community real property without the other spouse joining in the transaction of purchase; neither spouse may acquire or sell assets, including real estate or the goodwill of a business where both spouses participate in its management, without the consent of the other (unless only one spouse manages the business); neither spouse may sell community household goods without the other spouse joining in the action.

On the death of one spouse, the surviving spouse is entitled to all of the decedent's share of net community property and one-half of "quasi-community property." (This is property that might have been acquired elsewhere but would have been community if the owner had been domiciled in Washington at the time of acquisition.) The other half of quasi-community property is subject to the decedent's will or the laws of intestate succession.

Marriage

Common-law marriage cannot be contracted in Washington, but common-law marriages consummated in a state that recognizes such marriages are valid.

Property of Cohabitants

Based on case law, the following statement is made in the Washington law section of Martindale-Hubbell's digest of state laws: "Property accumulated by unmarried persons living together [is] not community property. In dividing property of cohabitants, court[s] must examine relationship and property accumulations and, by analogy to community property laws, divide property justly and equitably."

Personal Property

Tenancy by the entirety may be permitted in personal property, but there is no right of survivorship.

Real Property

Washington has a "community property" system of property. Estates are recognized substantially as at common law. There are exceptions: estates in dower and curtesy are abolished; the right of survivorship as an incident of tenancy by the entirety is abolished. Joint tenancies with incidents of survivorship and severability as at common law may be created only by express provision in a written instrument.

Taxation

Both inheritance and gift taxes have been repealed.

There is an estate tax. The tax is in an amount equal to the federal credit imposed on the transfer of a net estate of every resident. There is a tax imposed on the transfer of a nonresident's net estate located in Washington, also computed to absorb the federal tax credit for state death taxes.

Wills

There is no statute giving a surviving spouse a right to elect against a will. However, if a deceased spouse attempted to dispose of a surviving spouse's share of community property, the surviving spouse may take under the will or renounce it, taking instead his or her one-half community interest.

WEST VIRGINIA

Curtesy

Curtesy is abolished, but a surviving husband has a dower interest in his wife's estate.

Divorce

In the absence of a valid separation agreement, a court is to divide marital property of the parties equally between the parties, but may alter such distribution on consideration of: the extent to which each party has contributed to the acquisition, preservation and maintenance, or increase in value of marital property by monetary contributions and by nonmonetary contributions, including childcare services and homemaker services; the extent to which each party expended his or her efforts during the marriage in a way that limited the party's earning ability or enhanced the income-earning ability of the other party (such as by direct contributions to education, forgoing employment, etc.); the extent to which each party, during the marriage, acted in a manner that dissipated or depreciated the value of marital property. Except for economic considerations of the enumerated conduct, fault is not to be considered by the court in determining proper distribution of marital property. All rights of either party to dower are barred by a divorce order, but the court may compel a guilty party to compensate an innocent party for an inchoate right of dower (presumably "guilt" is defined within these guidelines). The court may restore to a spouse property in control of the other spouse.

Dower

A surviving husband or wife is entitled to dower, which consists of a life estate in one-third of all the real estate the deceased spouse owned during the marriage. A court may award cash in lieu of dower in kind. Dower right is in addition to the right of inheritance. Dower may be barred by either spouse joining with the other spouse in a conveyance, by a contract to convey or by a subsequent separate instrument executed by the spouse who is contingent dower owner. The concept of jointure exists in West Virginia. Real or personal property, intended to be in lieu of dower, conveyed or devised (by will) for the jointure (estate limited for the life of the holder) of the wife or husband bars dower. In some circumstances, the surviving spouse may waive jointure and demand dower.

Husband and Wife

A married woman's rights with respect to property are the same as if she were single. Her separate property is not subject to disposal by the husband nor is it liable for his debts. It is not necessary that either spouse consent or join in a conveyance or encumbrance by the other spouse of his or her real estate, except to bar dower. Consent to dower may be given separately after, but not before, a sale, conveyance, or agreement to convey by the other spouse. A husband or wife may convey real estate by deed directly to the other.

Marriage

Common-law marriage is not valid if contracted in West Virginia, but children of such a marriage are legitimate. A common-law marriage contracted in a state where it is valid will be recognized in West Virginia.

Personal Property

Tenancy in personal property is presumed to be a tenancy in common unless there are words in the instrument indicating that survivorship was intended or unless the instrument by use of the word "or" with regard to multiple owners indicates that joint tenancy is intended and not a tenancy in common.

Real Property

Common law estates generally are recognized, unless modified by statute. Joint tenancies and estates by entirety are abolished, with this exception: where the instrument shows intention of conveying a survivorship interest among multiple owners, such as by use of the word "or," then ownership is as joint tenants with right of survivorship, unless expressly stated otherwise.

Taxation

The inheritance tax is repealed for estates of those dying after July 1, 1985. The provisions applicable prior to that date are in effect until any tax matters affecting those inheritances have been settled.

Whenever a federal estate tax is due to the United States, West Virginia imposes an estate tax in the amount of the federal credit for state death taxes.

Wills

A surviving spouse may renounce a provision in a will in lieu of dower. A provision in a will for a surviving wife or husband is in lieu of dower unless it clearly appears that the deceased intended otherwise. If there is no renunciation, the survivor takes real and personal property under the will. If there is not provision by will, or the surviving spouse renounces it, the survivor takes real and personal property of the deceased as if the deceased spouse had died intestate (without a will) leaving children.

WISCONSIN

Curtesy

No curtesy rights.

Divorce

Wisconsin is a marital property jurisdiction. Property shown to have been acquired by either party by gift, bequest, devise, or inheritance, or from funds so acquired, remains the property of such party unless the court finds it would create hardship. Other property is presumed to be divided equally, but the court may alter this distribution after considering various specified factors, but not marital misconduct.

Dower

Effective January 1, 1986, the Marital Property Act eliminates dower.

Husband and Wife

Effective January 1, 1986, Wisconsin adopted a community property system based on the Uniform Marital Property Act with variations. All property of spouses is presumed to be marital (community) property except property that is classified "separate" by statute. Under this system, each spouse has a present one-half interest in marital property. Income accrued during the marriage is marital property. The Martindale-Hubbell Law Digest on this subject includes this statement: "Mixing marital property with property having any other classification reclassifies other property to marital unless other property can be traced."

Property that was owned by a person who married after December 31, 1985 remains that person's separate property. Property acquired after that date is separate if it was acquired as a gift or inheritance; or with proceeds of separate property; by appreciation (unless the appreciation was due to "marital" efforts); by agreement of the parties; or personal injury damage payment.

Marital property agreements may be entered into and may cover any matter affecting either or both parties' property.

Spouses need not join in conveyance of separate real estate, unless it is the homestead.

A spouse acting alone may manage and control that spouse's nonmarital property and, in some circumstances, marital property as well. They may manage and control marital property as alternate managers or acting together.

Marriage

Common-law marriages are not recognized in Wisconsin. There is no authority as to the validity of common-law marriages contracted out of the state.

Personal Property

Tenancy by the entirety is not recognized. Personal property owned by married couples is governed by Wisconsin's modified form of community property known as marital property.

Real Property

There is a general rule that all transfers to two or more persons are construed to create a tenancy in common and not a joint tenancy. Transfer to married people is governed by the marital property system.

Taxation

The inheritance tax is repealed fully beginning in 1992. Up to that time it is imposed on the transfer of all property within the jurisdiction of the state at prescribed rates. The "phase-out" is as follows: inheritance tax otherwise payable was reduced by 20 percent in 1988; 40 percent in 1989; 60 percent in 1990; 80 percent in 1991; and 100 percent in 1992.

The estate tax is in an amount equal to the federal credit allowed for state death taxes.

The gift tax is being phased out along the lines of the inheritance tax.

Wills

A surviving spouse has no elective rights against the decedent spouse's individual property or one-half interest in marital property. The spouse may elect not more than one-half of the "augmented" marital property estate. The Wisconsin rules reflect the transition to the marital property system established by the law that became effective January 1, 1986.

WYOMING

Curtesy and Dower

Abolished.

Divorce

In granting a divorce, the court shall make such disposition of the property of the parties as appears just and equitable, having regard for: the respective merits of the parties and the condition in which they will be left by the divorce; the party through whom the property was acquired; and burdens imposed on the property for the benefit of either party or the children. "Just and equitable" disposition is not always equated with quantitative equality. Broad authority has been granted to the divorce court in determining "just and equitable" disposition of property. The court may decree to either party reasonable alimony out of the estate of the other, having regard for the ability of the party. The court may order so much out of the real estate or rents and profits as is necessary to be assigned to either party for life, or may decree a specific sum to be paid by either party. The court may, on petition of either party, revise the decree with respect to the amount of alimony. There are no statutory provisions regarding separation agreements, but such agreements are recognized and enforced if they are incorporated in a divorce decree.

Husband and Wife

Husband and wife may own property, contract, and sue or be sued in general as though they were unmarried.

All property belonging to a married person as separate property owned at the time of marriage or acquired separately by inheritance or otherwise, together with the profits and increase during marriage, is that person's sole and separate property and may be owned and enjoyed by that spouse as though he or she were single. Such property is not subject to disposal, control, or interference of his spouse and is exempt from execution or attachment for debts of his spouse (provided the property was not conveyed to him by his spouse in fraud of his creditors). Any married person may transfer his separate property in the same manner and to the same extent as if he were unmarried. [Note: The Wyoming statute uses the pronoun "he," but it is presumed the language means "he or she" or "his or her."]

All disabilities of married women have been removed.

Marriage

If entered into in Wyoming, common-law marriages are invalid, but if valid in the state where they are created, they are valid in Wyoming.

Personal Property

Tenancy by the entirety in personal property is recognized and may be established without the necessity of transfer to or through a third person.

Real Property

Common law estates are recognized, including joint tenancies, tenancy in common, and tenancies by the entirety. Joint tenancy or tenancy by the entirety may be created by the owner of property simply by designating in the instrument of conveyance or transfer the names of such tenants, including his own, without the necessity of conveyance to or through third persons.

Joint tenancies are *not* abolished, nor is any presumption established by statute or decision in favor of tenancy in common, even where the intent to create a joint tenancy is not clear. A joint tenancy can be created in a husband and wife, and may be terminated by one joint tenant's conveyance of his interest. Tenancies by the entirety for married persons are recognized. Tenancies by the entireties or joint tenancies may be terminated on the death of a joint tenant or of one spouse, by court procedure, or by simplified procedure by affidavit.

The common law tendency to favor joint tenancies has been modified by statute. However, joint tenancies are not abolished, nor is there any presumption established to favor a tenancy in common designation in the absence of clear intent to establish a joint tenancy.

Taxation

Previous inheritance tax legislation is repealed (effective January 1, 1983). New statutory enactments are intended to take full advantage for Wyoming of the credit allowed as a deduction from federal estate tax liability for state death taxes. There is no gift tax.

Wills

A surviving spouse of a decedent domiciled in the state has the right to take against the net estate one-half if there are no surviving children of a previous marriage; percentages differ depending on other heirs. If a married decedent was not domiciled in Wyoming, the surviving spouse's right to election is governed by the state of the decedent's domicile. The contribution of the portion of other heirs is based on rules of equity and justice. Adjustment is made between a decedent's power to make a will and a spouse's right to elect against the will. Provisions of the will are to be disturbed as little as possible, and a loss caused by a spouse's election is to fall on all equally.

Appendix 2

Samples of Documents

Introduction

There are included in this appendix samples of the following types of documents:

- ❖ Outline of possible agreement for Tenants in Common to own and occupy real estate together
- ❖ Nonmarital Partnership Agreement
- ❖ Antenuptial Agreement
- ❖ General Power of Attorney (also with language making the document a "Durable Power of Attorney")
- ❖ Revocable Living Trust (for a married person)
- ❖ Revocable Living Trust (for a single person)
- ❖ A simple Will
- ❖ A Will with provision for a Unified Credit Trust.

You are strongly cautioned against using any of these sample documents without first seeking professional guidance. The material furnished here is merely to give you A LOOK at what these agreements, wills, trusts, etc., might cover. They are **not** intended to be taken from the text and used directly. There are countless variations and any document relevant to your own situation must be tailored specifically by your own lawyer.

Outline of Possible Agreement for Tenants in Common to Own and Occupy Real Estate Together

This agreement is made by and between A and B.

A and B intend to purchase Unit 500 in the condominium at 100 South Street in the City of Northside. The price is $_____.

It is intended that A and B will pay the cash down payment as follows:

Share of A = $ Share of B = $

Mortgage payments will be paid monthly in accordance with the same proportion. Therefore,

A will own _____% share, and
B will own _____% share.

All other monthly payments will be paid equally, including home-owners insurance, condominium fees, and expenses of upkeep, repairs, and maintenance.

Real estate taxes will be paid in proportion to ownership.

If A or B desires to sell his (her) share, it shall first be offered to the other co-owner. [Establish terms for agreement on price, such as appraisal.]

No party shall have the right to assign any or all of the rights under this agreement.

This agreement shall be binding upon the heirs and personal representatives of the parties.

Witnesses:

_____   _____
                                                                              A

_____   _____
                                                                              B

Date of agreement: _____

Sample Agreement—Nonmarital Partnership

The following is a sample of a nonmarital partnership agreement from the author's files. It is not intended to be used per se. It is provided for information only. No agreement of this type has yet stood the test of time, and such agreements may be totally unacceptable in your state. The sample will show you some of the perhaps negative aspects of entering into such a written-down formality. Nothing of this sort should be entered into without the advice and assistance of your lawyer *before* anything is signed.

NONMARITAL AGREEMENT

Date _____

THIS AGREEMENT, made between the following persons, on the terms and conditions set forth below, is for the purpose of defining their property rights, both now and in the future, and various other terms relating to their agreed-upon life together.

_____(John)_____   _____
Name of Partner   Present Occupation

_____(Helen)_____   _____
Name of Partner   Present Occupation

(1) The life-together began (will begin) on _____.
This Agreement shall be effective as of _____
and shall continue until terminated by one of the following events:
   (a) Death of either partner.
   (b) Marriage of John and Helen or marriage of either of them to another.
   (c) An agreement in writing to terminate their life-together.

(2) A reasonably accurate and complete list of the capital and assets of each partner is listed below:
    John: Helen:

(3) The property listed as belonging to each of the partners in Clause (2) above is to remain the separate property of each. Any income earned from separate property is to remain the income of the owner of that property. Each partner is responsible for maintaining records relating to his/her own property.

(4) Any debts outstanding, credit card balances, and other liabilities owed by each partner individually shall remain the obligation of that individual.

(5) Any property acquired by either partner by gift or inheritance, and income from such property, as well as appreciation in value, shall remain the separate property of that partner.

(6) For purposes of providing funds for living expenses, rent, food, entertainment, and the like, each partner shall contribute a proportionate percentage of his/her income from work (but not from investments) to a common fund.

(7) If a home or condominium is purchased by one of the partners and that partner is obligated on the mortgage, the other partner shall pay a reasonable amount of rent. [This would apply also if one partner is already an owner.]

(8) If a home or condominium is purchased jointly by John and Helen, they shall take title as Tenants in Common. [Note to reader: See sample agreement for tenants in common.]

(9) All investments made by either partner from his/her own earnings or profits shall remain the property of that partner.

(10) Any investment properties acquired after the date of this agreement which are impractical to acquire separately shall be owned by John and Helen as tenants in common. The share of each shall bear the same proportion to the whole as the contribution of that partner bears to the total cost of the property. For tax and accounting purposes, the income or tax advantages of the investment property shall be similarly distributed.

(11) Either partner may make gifts to the other, which gifts are agreed to be permanent.

(12) Neither partner looks to the other for inheritances. Each partner is free to transfer assets owned by that partner either *inter vivos* or by will to other family objects of his/her bounty, or, if he/she desires, to the other partner.

(13) Both partners acknowledge that a life-together arrangement based on the terms of this agreement does not constitute a common-law marriage, and if such marriage were valid according to the laws of any state where the partners reside or might in the future reside, they agree not to claim marital status based on this agreement (provided this clause does not contravene the state law).

(14) The consideration for this agreement is the promise of each partner to contribute homemaking services and companionship for their common good.

(15) Each partner acknowledges that he/she has consulted with his/her own attorney prior to signing this agreement and that the legal significance of the provisions herein have been fully explained in accordance with the laws of the state where the partners reside.

(16) If any controversy arises with regard to the terms of this agreement, the partners agree to first seek the assistance of a mediator to resolve such conflict.

(17) Recognizing that tasks, responsibilities of daily living, personal habits, and the like are impossible to regiment by agreement, all reference to such minutiae are deliberately eliminated from this agreement.

IN WITNESS WHEREOF, this Agreement is signed on the date of _____ in the State of _____.

_____
JOHN

_____
HELEN

(Notarization)

Attorney's Certification: Words to the effect that the above agreement has been executed in his (her) presence and that the terms and significance have been explained by him (her) to the above partners to the agreement and that they have indicated full understanding.

Sample of an Antenuptial Agreement

WHEREAS MARY _____ and BILL _____ intend to be married within a short time, and

WHEREAS BILL and MARY have disclosed to each other the nature and extent of their various property interests, sources of income, and general financial condition, and

WHEREAS BILL desires to make a reasonable and sufficient provision for MARY in release of and in full satisfaction of all rights which after their marriage MARY might or could have, by reason of the marriage, in the property which BILL now has or may hereafter acquire, or in his estate upon his death, and

WHEREAS MARY desires to accept this provision in lieu of all rights which she would otherwise acquire, by reason of the marriage, in the property or estate of BILL,

IT IS THEREFORE AGREED:

(1) RELEASE OF MARITAL RIGHTS. MARY hereby waives and releases all rights including, but not limited to, dower, statutory allowance in lieu of dower, distributive share, right of election against a will, widow's allowances, or otherwise, which she may acquire by reason of her marriage to BILL in any property owned by him at any time or by his estate upon his death. This release is executed in consideration of the payment expressed in (2) below.

(2) PAYMENT FROM ESTATE. If MARY survives BILL as his lawful widow, there shall be paid to her from the estate of BILL outright, free of any estate or inheritance taxes, the greater of $_____ or_____ percent of the "net estate" of BILL. Such sum shall be paid to MARY as soon as may be practicable. Until so paid, such sum shall constitute a charge upon the sum in lieu of all other claims, statutory or otherwise, that she may have against the estate of BILL by reason of their marriage. For the purpose of this agreement, "net estate" shall mean the residue remaining in the estate after the deduction of all valid other debts and funeral and administration expenses, but not any liability for estate or inheritance taxes.

(3) NECESSARY DOCUMENTS. Each party shall execute and deliver whatever additional instruments may be required in order to carry out the intention of this agreement, and shall execute and deliver any deeds or other documents in order that good title to any property can be conveyed by BILL free from any claim of MARY acquired by reason of this marriage. BILL shall execute a will, or a codicil to an existing will, embodying the obligations contained in this agreement.

(4) TRANSFERS BETWEEN THE PARTIES. Notwithstanding the provisions of this agreement, any other rights acquired by MARY by virtue of any transfer or conveyance of property by BILL to her during his

lifetime, or by will upon his death, shall not be limited or restricted in any way.

(5) SEPARATE PROPERTY. Except as herein provided, each party shall have complete control of his or her separate property, and may enjoy and dispose of such property in the same manner as if the marriage had not taken place. This provision shall apply to all property now owned by either of the parties and to all property which either of them may hereafter acquire in an individual capacity; provided that BILL shall not, in the absence of a written consent by MARY, transfer any property for less than full consideration in money or money's worth if at the time of such transfer, or imminent thereto, his net worth is less than $_____.

(6) RELEASE OF PROPERTY RIGHTS BY HUSBAND. BILL releases all rights in the property or estate of MARY which he might have by reason of their marriage, whether by way of curtesy, statutory allowance, intestate share, or election to take against her will, under the laws of any jurisdiction that may be applicable.

(7) DISCLOSURE OF FACTS. BILL acknowledges that he has disclosed his full net worth to MARY and that such net worth is in excess of $_____. BILL acknowledges that the present approximate net worth of MARY has been disclosed to him and that such net worth is in the approximate amount of $_____. MARY and BILL acknowledge that they have had the advice of independent counsel and that they are entering into this agreement freely and with a full understanding of its provisions.

(8) EFFECTIVE PERIOD. This agreement shall become effective upon the marriage of the parties and shall bind the parties and their respective heirs, executors, and administrators, unless the marriage is legally dissolved. For the purpose of this agreement, in the event of a common disaster MARY shall be presumed to have predeceased BILL.

(9) ENTIRE UNDERSTANDING. This agreement contains the entire understanding of the parties, no representations or promises having been made except those set forth herein.

IN WITNESS WHEREOF, the parties have signed, sealed, and acknowledged this agreement on the day and year first above written.

BILL	(SEAL)

MARY	(SEAL)

Please note: This document contains provisions protecting Mary. Bill's lawyer will draft clauses to protect his interests.

Sample of a General Power of Attorney

Here is a sample of a power of attorney so that you can see just how inclusive such a document can be, provided it is in accord with state law.

GENERAL POWER OF ATTORNEY

KNOW ALL BY THESE PRESENTS: That I, _____, of the City of _____, State of _____, do hereby make, constitute, and appoint and have made, constituted, and appointed _____, of the City of _____, State of _____, my true and lawful attorney in fact for me and in my name, place, and stead, and on my behalf, effective from the date hereof:

1. To exercise or perform any act, power, duty, right, or obligation whatsoever that I now have, or may hereafter acquire the legal right, power, or capacity to exercise or perform, in connection with, arising from, or relating to any person, item, transaction, thing, business property, real or personal, tangible or intangible, or matter whatsoever;

2. To request, ask, demand, sue for, recover, collect, receive, and hold and possess all such sums of money, debts, dues, commercial paper, checks, drafts, accounts, deposits, legacies, bequests, devises, notes, interests, stock certificates, bonds, dividends, certificates of deposit, annuities, pension and retirement benefits, insurance benefits and proceeds, any and all documents of title, choses in action, personal and real property, intangible and tangible property, and property rights and demands whatsoever, liquidated or unliquidated, as now are, or shall hereafter become owned by me, or due, owing, payable, or belonging to me, or in which I have or may hereafter acquire interest; to take all lawful means and equitable and legal remedies in my name for the collection and recovery thereof, and to adjust or compromise and agree for the same; and to make, execute, and deliver for me, on my behalf, and in my name, all endorsements, acquittances, releases, receipts, or other sufficient discharges for the same;

3. To receive and receipt for any and all sums of money or payments due or to become due to me; to continue, to modify, and to terminate any deposit account or other banking arrangement made by me or on my behalf prior to the creation of this instrument; to open deposit accounts of any type with any banking institutions, wherever located, and to make such other contracts for the procuring of services by any banking institution as my attorney in fact deems to be desirable; to make, to sign, and to deliver checks or drafts for any purpose, to withdraw by check, order, or otherwise any funds or property of mine deposited

with, or left in the custody of, any person or banking institution, wherever located, either before or after the creation of this instrument, to receive statements, vouchers, notices, or other documents from any person or banking institution and to act as may be deemed appropriate with respect thereto; to have free access at any time or times to any safe-deposit boxes or vaults to which I might have access, if personally present;

4. To deal in, sell, assign, transfer, and purchase any and all securities, capital stocks, bonds, or indentures on my behalf and in my place, stead, and name;

5. To make, receive, sign, endorse, execute, acknowledge, deliver, and possess such contracts, agreements, options, conveyances, security agreements, leases, mortgages, assignments, insurance policies, documents of title, bonds, debentures, checks, stock certificates, proxies, warrants, receipts, withdrawal receipts, and deposit instruments relating to accounts or deposits in, or certificates of deposit of, banks, savings and loan, or other institutions or associations and such other instruments in writing of whatsoever kind and nature as may be necessary or proper in the exercise of the rights and powers herein granted;

6. To conduct, engage in, and transact any and all lawful business of whatever nature or kind for me, on my behalf, and in my name; to act for me in any business, corporation, partnership, limited partnership, joint venture, or any other enterprise in which I am or have been engaged or interested or have any investment, rights, or participation, hereby giving to my attorney full power and authority to exercise any and all rights, privileges, and/or decisions, including the right to vote with respect thereto to the same extent that I am possessed; and to execute any and all instruments required in connection with or incident to my interest therein;

7. To pay, to compromise, or to contest taxes or assessments of all kinds and to apply for refunds in connection therewith;

8. To execute, acknowledge, and deliver in my name any and all deeds, deeds of trust, notes, including promissory notes, necessary or desirable, to convey, encumber, or otherwise, affecting any real estate, or interest therein, now or hereafter owned or held by me, including the right, power, and authority to execute, acknowledge, and deliver assignments, sales agreements, leases, and other agreements relating to real estate or interests therein as aforesaid;

9. I grant to said attorney in fact full power and authority to do, take, and perform all and every act and thing whatsoever requisite, proper, or necessary to be done, in the exercise of any of the rights and powers herein granted, as fully to all intents and purposes as I might or could do if personally present, with full power of substitution or revocation, hereby ratifying and confirming all that said attorney in fact, or his substitute or substitutes, shall lawfully do or cause to be done by virtue of this power of attorney and the rights and powers herein granted.

10. This instrument is to be construed and interpreted as a general power of attorney. The enumeration of specific items, rights, acts, or powers herein is not intended to, nor does it, limit or restrict, and is not to be construed or interpreted as limiting or restricting, the general powers herein granted to said attorney in fact.

The rights, powers, and authority of said attorney in fact herein granted shall commence and be in full force and effect on _____, 19____, and such rights, powers, and authority shall remain in full force and effect until terminated by me in writing.

IN TESTIMONY WHEREOF, I have hereunto set my hand and seal this _____ day of _____, 19____.

WITNESSES:

_____   _____

_____   (SEAL)
(Notarization)

Formerly, a curious anomaly existed with regard to a power of attorney, depending on state law. Normally, a power of attorney is automatically revoked on the mental incapacity of the principal inasmuch as a power of attorney is an agency designation and an agency presumes a principal with capacity to appoint an agent. If this rule applies, the agency contract is revoked just at the point when the principal may most need an agent to act in his behalf. Consequently, all states and the District of Columbia have enacted provisions for a "durable power of attorney." This means that the agency transcends the incapacity of the one who appointed the agent. There are variations in the state statutes, but there is usually language providing that a durable power of attorney contain a phrase such as *"this power of attorney shall not be affected by my subsequent disability or incapacity."* The purpose of the wording is to show the principal's intent that the authority conferred be exercisable notwithstanding the principal's subsequent disability or incapacity.

Sample of a Revocable Living Trust (For a Married Person)

REVOCABLE TRUST AGREEMENT

THIS TRUST AGREEMENT made this _____ day of _____, 19____, by and between the undersigned Grantor of this Trust, ___JOHN OWNER___ and _____, Bank, a national banking association, and its successor or successors, hereinafter referred to as my "Trustee," WITNESSETH:

ONE: I hereby transfer to the Trustee the property described in Schedule A, attached hereto and made a part hereof, and I may from time to time transfer additional property acceptable to the Trustee.

TWO: My Trustee may receive any other property (provided said property is acceptable to my Trustee), real or personal, transferred, assigned or conveyed to the Trustee by me, my personal representative, or by any other person to constitute a part of the trust principal or trust fund hereby created, to be held, invested, managed and distributed by my Trustee in accordance with the provisions set forth below.

THREE: My Trustee shall pay the net income of the trust (and so much of the principal as I may from time to time in writing direct), at least quarterly, to me or for my benefit during my life. In the event that I should become unable to manage my own affairs (whether or not legally adjudicated an incapacitated or incompetent adult) and be certified to that effect by a physician, my Trustee shall be authorized to continue to pay such income to me or for my benefit and to invade periodically the principal of this trust for the payment of any and all expenses to provide for my comfortable support, maintenance and care, including but not limited to medical and hospitalization expenses and private nursing care. Should I become unable to manage my own affairs, as described above, my Trustee shall also be authorized to pay such portion of the income or principal (or both) of this trust as may be necessary, in the discretion of my Trustee, for the comfortable support, maintenance and care of my wife, JANE OWNER, in her accustomed manner of living, taking into account and considering any other means of support she may have to the knowledge of my Trustee.

FOUR: I hereby reserve the right at any time and from time to time to revoke, alter or amend this trust in whole or in part, in any particular, including but not limited to the power to change or add beneficiaries, by an instrument in writing delivered to my Trustee; except that the duties and compensation of the Trustee shall not be materially changed by any amendment without the Trustee's written approval. Any revocation, alteration or amendment shall take effect upon the delivery of the written instrument to my Trustee. If the trust is revoked in its entirety, my Trustee shall deliver all the trust assets to me as soon thereafter as may be reasonably possible.

FIVE: In the administration of this trust, my Trustee shall advise me of any proposed sales or purchases of investment property, and if I give my Trustee in writing any directions as to such changes in investments, my Trustee shall follow my instructions, in which case my Trustee shall have no liability in respect thereto, as I take full responsibility for any such changes in investments specified by me. If I give my Trustee no written investment directions within a period of time that I will specify from time to time or if I should become unable to manage my own affairs as described in Clause THREE above, then my Trustee may make any such sales or purchases of investments, in its sole discretion, without any written directions from me.

OR (Alternate Clause):

FIVE: In the administration of this trust, my Trustee may make such sales or purchases of investment property as it may deem advisable in its sole discretion; provided, however, that if I give my Trustee in writing any directions as to such sales or purchases of investments, my Trustee shall follow my instructions. If my Trustee follows my written directions, it shall have no liability in respect thereto, as I take full responsibility for any such changes in investments specified by me. In the event I am certified by a physician to be unable to manage my own affairs, as described in Clause THREE above, all investment discretion shall be in my Trustee.

SIX: Upon my death, if my wife survives me, the property in this trust, both principal and undistributed income, shall be transferred to my wife, and the trust continued upon her written instructions, or, on her instructions the trust shall end.

> (OR: Specific provisions may be inserted here, directing the Trustee to distribute the property to certain beneficiaries either outright or in continued trust for a specified period or until a specified event.)

SEVEN: My Trustee (and any successors) shall have the following powers, and any others that may be granted by law, but without necessity of order of any court, all within the terms and conditions as set forth in this trust:

(a) To retain any property or undivided interests in property received from me or from any other source, including residential property, regardless of any lack of diversification, risk, or non-productivity;

(b) To invest and reinvest the trust estate in any property or undivided interests in property, wherever located, including bonds, notes secured or unsecured, stocks of corporations regardless of class, including the stock of the Corporate Trustee [Note: A corporate trustee, as a bank, will certainly want that phrase inserted.], and to keep and maintain funds in savings accounts including the bank or banks of the Corporate Trustee, without being limited by any statute or rule of law concerning investments by trustees;

(c) To sell any trust property, for cash or on credit, at public or private sales; to exchange any trust property for other property; to grant options to purchase or acquire any trust property; and to determine the prices and terms of sales, exchanges, and options;

(d) To improve or repair or lease (as lessor or lessee) any real estate and to grant or receive options to purchase property; including a lease or option that may be made for a term that may extend beyond the period of the trust;

(e) To borrow money for any purpose, either from the banking department of the Trustee, or from others, and to mortgage or pledge any trust property;

(f) To employ real estate brokers, appraisers, attorneys, accountants or other expert assistants and to pay reasonable compensation from trust funds for their services;

(g) To make division or distribution in kind or in money, or partly in kind and partly in money; and if in kind not necessarily pro rata or in fractional shares among beneficiaries;

(h) To vote any stock by itself or by proxy; to enter into any plan or agreement for the sale, merger, consolidation, liquidation, recapitalization or other disposition of any trust property or of any public corporation issuing securities held as part of the trust, and to accept in such transaction any cash, securities or property that the Trustee deems proper.

(i) To determine the allocation of dividends, distributions, profits resulting from the maturity or sale of any asset, and any other receipts and the allocation of payments and expenses as between income and principal; provide (or not provide) reserves from income otherwise distributable for depreciation, obsolescence, or other prospective loss, reduction in value, or casualty; amortize (or not amortize) premiums, and accumulate (or not accumulate) discounts, at which securities or other assets were acquired; provided that all such determinations, allocations and other actions are reasonable;

(j) To exercise any and all options, whether such be options to purchase stock (qualified, nonqualified, restricted or other), or whether such shall be options to purchase other types or kinds of property;

(k) Operate and continue any and all businesses, including proprietorships and partnerships in which I may have an interest or which I may be operating; to liquidate or join in the liquidation of any such businesses, to sell or otherwise dispose of the same as going concerns, to incorporate or cause to be incorporated such businesses, to invest in any such businesses so incorporated as it shall see fit and to retain stock in any such businesses so incorporated without liability for depreciation in value, to become or remain a general or limited partner in any new or continuing partnership and to take such other action (including any election under Subchapter S of the Internal Revenue Code) as it may deem necessary or proper for beginning, continuing or liquidating such business; and to employ agents and advisers as necessary.

EIGHT: To the extent that such requirements can legally be waived, no Trustee or successor Trustee shall ever be required to give any bond as Trustee; to qualify before, be appointed by or account to any court, in the absence of breach of trust; or required to obtain the order or approval of any court in the exercise of any power or discretion hereunder.

NINE: Any Trustee or successor Trustee hereunder shall render semi-annually a statement to me and any other income beneficiaries showing the condition of the trust and the receipts and disbursements during the preceding six (6) months.

TEN: As compensation for its services my Trustee shall receive annually those fees set out and published in that fee schedule of my Trustee in respect to this type of trust which is current at the time or times such compensation is payable. If the compensation of my Trustee is not legally and effectively specified by any such fee schedule or by agreement, then my Trustee shall receive the compensation specified in that fee schedule respecting this type trust which is now currently in use and of which I am aware.

The construction of this instrument, the validity of the interests created hereby and the administration of the trust shall be governed by the laws of the State of _____.

IN WITNESS WHEREOF, I have hereunto set my hand and affixed my seal, the day and year first above written.

Witnesses:

_____(Seal)
JOHN OWNER

In token of the acceptance of this trust and to acknowledge receipt of the property described in Schedule A attached hereto, _____ _____ BANK has caused its corporate name to be hereunto signed and its corporate seal to be hereunto affixed by its duly authorized officer, this _____ day of _____, 19____.

BANK   (SEAL)

Witnesses:

By: _____
Trust Officer
TRUSTEE

(Notarization)

[and on next pages: SCHEDULE A]

Sample of Revocable Trust for a Single Person (Courtesy of Stanley H. Kamerow, Attorney at Law, Washington, D.C.)

TRUST AGREEMENT

TRUST AGREEMENT made and executed this _____ day of _____, 19__, by and between _____, hereinafter called the "**SETTLOR**" and _____, Trustee, hereinafter called the "**TRUSTEE**".

1. **TRUST ESTATE.** The SETTLOR does hereby transfer, assign, convey and quit claim to the TRUSTEE, in trust, the property described in Schedule A, hereto attached, to have and to hold such property and any other property of any kind which the TRUSTEE may at any time hereafter hold or acquire pursuant to any of the provisions hereof (all of which property is hereinafter collectively referred to as the _____ **TRUST** and sometimes as the Trust Estate or the Trust), subject to the trusts, purposes and conditions hereinafter set forth.

2. **LIFE INCOME TO SETTLOR.** During the lifetime of the SETTLOR, the TRUSTEE shall pay the entire net income from the Trust Estate in convenient installments to the SETTLOR, or otherwise as SETTLOR may from time to time direct in writing, and the TRUSTEE shall also pay to SETTLOR, such part or all of the principal of the Trust as SETTLOR, shall request in writing from time to time.

3. **TAX PROVISION.** If upon the death of the SETTLOR, any inheritance, estate, transfer or succession taxes are assessed by reason of the assets of this Trust or any other assets of the SETTLOR, or the interest of any beneficiaries thereof, the Successor Trustees shall pay such taxes, including any interest and penalties thereon, out of the principal of the Trust Estate as a whole, or make provision for such payment, without charging them against the interest of the several beneficiaries.

4. **DIVISION ON DEATH OF SETTLOR**. Upon the death of the SETTLOR, and the receipt by the Trust of all sums due it, the Trust created herein shall terminate and any amount remaining therein, either of principal or interest, shall go to

_____ .

5. **SPENDTHRIFT PROVISION**. The interests of beneficiaries (other than the SETTLOR) in principal or income of any of the trusts created herein shall not in any way be subject to the claims of their creditors or others, nor to legal process, and may not be voluntarily or involuntarily assigned, alienated or encumbered.

6. **UNDISTRIBUTED INCOME**. Any income accrued or undistributed at the termination of any estate or interest shall be paid by the TRUSTEE as income to the persons entitled to the next successive interest in the proportions in which they take such interest.

7. **PAYMENT OF FUNERAL BILLS, FINAL EXPENSES, ETC**. Upon the death of the SETTLOR, the Successor Trustees shall pay all debts of the SETTLOR and all expenses of ___ final illness, and shall pay all funeral expenses, even though same may exceed the statutory limitation, including purchase of a burial lot, if necessary, and erection of a tombstone, or any expenses incidental to any of the foregoing.

8. **GENERAL POWERS OF TRUSTEES**. In the administration of the Trust established hereunder, the TRUSTEE and the Successor Trustees shall have the following powers:

(a) To retain, in their absolute discretion and for such period as to them shall seem advisable, any and all investments and other properties, without liability for any loss incurred by reason of the retention of such investments or properties.

(b) To change investments and properties, and to invest and reinvest all or any part of the corpus of the Trust hereby established, in such securities, investments, or other properties to them seem advisable and proper including but not limited to marginal stock accounts.

(c) To sell all or any part of the property comprising the Trust, of whatsoever kind, at such time, upon such terms, for cash or on credit, with or without security, in such manner and at such prices, either at public or private sale, as to them shall deem advisable and proper, and to execute good and sufficient deeds and bills of sale thereof.

(d) To lease any property held by them hereunder and fix the duration of the term, irrespective of the provisions of any·statute or of the termination of any trusts; and to mortgage, pledge, collect, convert, redeem, exchange, or otherwise dispose of any securities or other property at any time held by them.

(e) To borrow money, whether to pay taxes, exercise subscriptions, rights, or options, to pay assessments or to accomplish any other purpose of any nature incidental to the administration of the Trust hereby established, and to pledge any securities or other property held by them as security therefore.

(f) To enforce any bonds, mortgages, security agreements, or other obligations or liens held by them hereunder; to enter upon such contracts and agreements and to make such compromises or settlements of debts, claims or controversies as they may deem necessary or advisable; to submit to arbitration any matter or difference; to vote personally or by proxy any shares of stock which may at any time be held by them, and similarly, to exercise by attorney, any rights appurtenant to any other securities or other property at any time held by them.

(g) To consent to the reorganization, consolidation, merger, liquidation, readjustment of or other change in any corporation, company, or association, or to the sale or lease of the property thereof or any part thereof, any of the securities or other property of which may at the time be held by them hereunder, and to do any act or exercise any power with reference thereto that may be, legally exercised by any person owning similar property in his own right, including the exercise of conversion, subscription, purchase, or other options, the deposit or exchange of securities, the entrance into voting trusts, and the making or agreements or subscriptions which they may deem necessary or advisable in connection therewith, all without applying to any court for permission so to do, and to hold and redeem or sell or otherwise dispose of any securities or other property which they may so acquire, irrespective of whether the same be authorized for the investment of trust funds by the Laws of the State of _____ .

(h) To cause to be registered in their names as trustees hereunder, or in the names of their nominee or nominees, without qualification or description, any securities at any time held in the Trust hereby established.

(i) To determine the manner in which the expense incidental to or connected with the administration of the Trust hereby established shall be apportioned as between income and principal

(j) To carry out agreements made by SETTLOR prior to the creation of the Trust, including the consumption of any agreements, relating to the capital stock of corporations owned at the time of the creation of the Trust, and including the continuation of any partnership at the time of the creation of the Trust, and to enter into agreements for the rearrangement or alteration of interests or rights or obligations under any such agreements in effect at the time of the creation of the Trust.

(k) To apportion extraordinary and stock dividends received by them between income and principal in such manner as they may see fit; provided, however, that all rights to subscribe to new or additional stock or securities, and all liquidating dividends shall be deemed to be principal.

(l) Except as otherwise may be specifically directed, to make any division or distribution required under the terms of this Trust in kind or in money, or partly in kind and partly in money, and to that end to allot to any part or share of such stock, securities, or other property, real or personal, as to them seems proper; provided, however, that the TRUSTEE shall not be required to make physical division of the funds except when necessary for distribution of the principal, but may, in h___ discretion, keep the Trust Estate in one or more consolidated funds; nor shall the TRUSTEE be required to make any provision on account of the diminution or increase in value of any securities or investments at any time constituting a part of the Trust hereby established, or for depreciation in respect of any tangible property, or for the purpose of amortizing or making good any amounts paid in premiums on the purchase of securities or of any other property.

The Trustees may freely act under all or any of the powers by this Trust given to them in all matters concerning the Trust hereby established, after forming their judgment based upon all the circumstances of any particular situation as to the wisest and best course to pursue, without the necessity of obtaining the consent or permission of any person interested therein, or the consent or approval of any court, and notwithstanding, that they may also be acting as individuals, or as trustees of other trusts, or as agents for other persons or corporations interested in the same matters, or may be interested in connection with the same matters as stockholders, directors or otherwise.

The powers herein granted to the Trustees may be exercised in whole or in part, from time to time, and shall be deemed to be supplementary to and not exclusive of the general powers of trustees pursuant to the law, and shall include all powers necessary to carry the same in effect. The enumeration of specific powers herein shall not be construed in any way to limit or affect the general powers herein granted.

9. **DEALING WITH TRUSTEES.** No person dealing with the Trustees shall be obligated to see to the application of any monies, securities or other property paid or delivered to them, or to inquire into the expediency or propriety of any transaction or the authority of said Trustees to enter into and consummate the same such terms as they may deem advisable. If there be more than one TRUSTEE, then the signature of only one TRUSTEE shall be needed to sign any checks or other documents.

10. **SUCCESSOR TRUSTEES.** At the death of the SETTLOR, or if at any time or times the SETTLOR is under a legal disability, or if by reason of illness or mental or physical disability is, in the sole opinion of the next Successor Trustee, unable properly to manage SETTLOR's affairs, the said Successor Trustee shall become the active Trustee subject to all of the provisions of this Trust, and with all of the rights and duties of the original TRUSTEE. The Successor Trustee shall be _____. In the event of ____ inability or refusal to serve, the next Successor Trustee shall be _____.

11. **ADDITIONAL PROPERTY.** The SETTLOR, or any person, shall have the right at any time and from time to time with the consent of the TRUSTEE to transfer, assign, convey, devise and bequeath any additional securities or property to the TRUSTEE to be held by h__ under this Agreement.

12. <u>**POWER OF AMENDMENT AND REVOCATION**</u>. The SETTLOR shall have the right, at any time and from time to time during h__ lifetime by instrument in writing delivered to the TRUSTEE, to alter, amend, or revoke this Agreement, either in whole or in part, provided, however, that if this Agreement is so altered or amended, the duties, power and responsibilities of the TRUSTEE shall not be substantially changed without h___ consent. In case of revocation, the Trust Estate, or that part thereof as to which this Agreement may be revoked, shall be conveyed by the TRUSTEE to the SETTLOR, or in accordance with h__ written directions.

13. The Successor Trustees named herein shall act as Trustees for all trusts created herein and shall have all of the powers and duties of the original TRUSTEE.

IN WITNESS WHEREOF, in multiple xerox copies, the SETTLOR has hereunto set h__ hand and seal, and the TRUSTEE, to evidence h__ acceptance of this Trust, have placed h__ hand and seal the day and year first above written.

_____ (SEAL)
_____, **Settlor**

_____ (SEAL)
_____, **Trustee**

STATE OF   )
) **ss:**
COUNTY OF   )

On this _____ day of _____, 1989, before me, a Notary Public in and for _____, personally appeared _____, known to be (or satisfactorily proven) to be the person whose name is subscribed to the within instrument and acknowledged that h__ executed the same for the purposes therein contained.

IN WITNESS WHEREOF, I hereunto set my hand and seal.

_____
                    NOTARY PUBLIC

My Commission Expires:

SCHEDULE A

TRUST AGREEMENT

All of the personal property and possessions of the SETTLOR, including, but not limited to all furniture, furnishings, objects of art, clothing, jewelry, silverware, etc., and all other articles of personal or household use.

All bank accounts and certificates of deposit or other securities owned by the SETTLOR.

Any and all real property, including any real property which may vest in SETTLOR prior to the death of the SETTLOR.

_____, **Settlor**

Sample of Simple Will (Courtesy of Stanley H. Kamerow, Esq., Washington, D.C.)

LAST WILL AND TESTAMENT

OF

KNOW ALL MEN BY THESE PRESENTS, that I,_____,
of the _____, being of sound and
disposing mind, do make and publish this my Last Will and Testament,
hereby revoking all former Wills and Codicils by me at any time
heretofore made.

All of my property, real, personal or mixed, of which I shall die
seized or possessed, or to which I shall be entitled at the time of
my decease, I give, devise, bequeath and dispose of in the following
manner, to wit:

ONE: I direct that my Executors hereinafter named pay all of my
just debts and funeral expenses as soon as it shall by them be found
convenient, including the erection of a suitable monument upon my
grave, and also for the purchase of perpetual care of said gravesite,
with the exclusion of any mortgages or deeds of trust which may exist
on any of my real estate. I further direct that my aforesaid funeral
expenses shall be paid out of my estate notwithstanding that the
amount thereof my exceed the statutory limitation.

TWO: All estate, inheritance and other death taxes by whatever
name called, including interest and penalties thereon, if any, payable
by reason of my death in respect of property included in my gross
estate for death tax purposes, whether or not such property shall pass
under this Will, shall be paid out of my general testamentary estate
as an expense of administration.

THREE: I hereby confirm my intention that the beneficial interest in all property, real or personal, tangible or intangible (including without limitation stocks, bonds, or other securities and checking or savings accounts in any bank, savings and loan association or similar institution), which is registered or held at the time of my death jointly (other than as tenants in common) in the names of myself and any other person, shall pass by right of survivorship or operation of law and outside of the terms and provisions of this Will to such other joint owner if such other joint owner survives me. In the event that my intention may be defeated by any rule of law with respect to any such jointly-held property, I give, devise and bequeath such jointly-held property to such other joint owner if such other joint owner survives me.

FOUR: All of the rest, residue and remainder of my estate shall go, in equal shares, to the following persons, if they survive me:

_____

_____.

FIVE: I direct that all estate, inheritance, succession, transfer or other taxes, by whatever name called, levied against my estate as a whole, or against any legacies or devises, or against any legatees or devisees, whether levied by the Federal Government or any State Government, or political subdivision of any State, shall be paid by my Executors hereinafter named, out of my general estate, it being my intention that my legatees and beneficiaries shall receive the full amount devised and bequeathed to them under the provisions of this Will without any diminution on account of taxes.

SIX: I hereby nominate and appoint _____ _____, or the survivors, as Executors of this my Last Will and Testament. I request that my Executors be not required to give bond for their faithful performance as Executors, and I hereby expressly authorize and empower my said Executors to sell and dispose of my estate, real, personal or mixed, or any part thereof, without any obligation on the part of the purchaser to see to the application of the purchase money for the purpose of discharging any debts or claims against my estate or for the distribution thereof.

WITNESS my hand and seal this ____ day of _____, 19____ .

_____(SEAL)

Signed, sealed, published and declared by the above named as and for his Last Will and Testament, in the presence of us, and we in the presence of each other and of the Testator, who have hereunto subscribed our names as witnesses thereto at the request of the Testator.

_____ residing at _____

_____

_____ residing at _____

_____

Sample of Will with Provision for Unified Credit Trust (Courtesy of Stanley H. Kamerow, Esq., Washington, D.C.)

<u>LAST WILL AND TESTAMENT</u>

<u>OF</u>

_____

KNOW ALL MEN BY THESE PRESENTS, that I,_____ ,

of _____, do make and publish this my

Last Will and Testament, hereby revoking all Wills and codicils by me at

any time heretofore made.

All of my property, real, personal or mixed, of which I shall die

seized or possessed, or to which I shall be entitled at the time of my

decease, I give, devise, bequeath and dispose of in the following manner,

to wit:

    1.   <u>PAYMENT OF DEBTS AND PURCHASE OF GRAVESITE</u>.

I direct my Executor as soon as practicable after my death to

pay my enforceable debts, in accordance with their terms, and the expenses

of my last illness and funeral (in connection with which I authorize my

Executor to purchase a suitable monument or memorial, for such amount as

he may deem proper), without regard to any statutory limits on such

expenses and without the necessity of any court order. My Executor shall

not, however, be required to pay prior to maturity any debt secured by a

mortgage, pledge or similar encumbrance on property owned by me at my

death, or in which I have an interest as a tenant by the entirety, joint

tenant with the right of survivorship or tenant in common, and such

property shall pass subject to such mortgage, pledge or similar

encumbrance.

    2.   <u>TAXES</u>.

All estate, inheritance and other death taxes by whatever name

called, including interest and penalties thereon, if any, payable by reason of my death in respect of property included in my gross estate for death tax purposes, whether or not such property shall pass under this Will, shall be paid out of my general testamentary estate as an expense of administration.

3. **BEQUEST OF PERSONAL EFFECTS; CONFIRMATION OF SURVIVORS' RIGHTS IN JOINTLY OWNED PROPERTY; OWNERSHIP INTEREST IN LIFE INSURANCE AND SPECIFIC BEQUESTS**

(a) I give and bequeath all tangible personal property owned by me at my death, including but not limited to, household effects, (such as furniture, furnishings, silver and objects of art), clothing, jewelry, books, cameras, sporting equipment, automobiles and all other articles of personal or household use or ornament, together with any insurance thereon, to my Husband, _____, (herein referred to as "My Husband"), if my Husband survives me. If my Husband does not survive me, such tangible personal property shall be distributed (either in kind or after sale and conversion to cash, as my Alternate Executors, in their absolute discretion, shall determine) to such of my children as survive me, in such shares of substantially equal value as my Alternate Executors, in their absolute discretion, shall determine. All determinations by my Executor, or as to the property to which this paragraph is applicable, and as to any division thereof, shall be conclusive and binding upon all persons having or claiming any interest in such property or in my estate.

(b) I hereby confirm my intention that the beneficial interest in all property, real or personal, tangible or intangible (including without limitation, stocks, bonds or other securities and checking or savings accounts in any bank, savings and loan association or similar institution), which is registered or held at the time of my death jointly (other than as tenants in common) in the names of myself and my Husband or myself and any of my children or grandchildren, shall pass by right of survivorship or operation of law and outside of the terms and provisions of this Will to such other joint owner if such other joint owner survives me. In the event that my intention may be defeated by any rule of law with respect to any such jointly-held property, I give and bequeath such jointly-held property to such other joint owner if such other joint owner survives me.

    (c) In the event that my Husband survives me, any policies of insurance on his life that I may own at the time of my death, I give and bequeath, in equal shares, to such of my children as survive me.

    (d) I hereby make the following specific bequests:

4. TESTAMENTARY TRUST

A. (1) If my Husband shall survive me, it is my desire to eliminate all Federal Estate Tax payable on account of my death without needlessly increasing the size of my Husband's estate; accordingly, I give to my Trustees hereinafter named a portion of my estate equal in value to the deduction equivalent to the Unified Credit Against Estate Tax and the Credit for State Death Tax that is allowed under Sections 2010 and 2011, respectively, of the Code, reduced by the deduction equivalent, if any, of that portion of the Unified Credit Against Estate Tax that may have been applied or allocated to gifts made by me during my lifetime.

    (2) Notwithstanding anything in sub-paragraph A (1), to the contrary, if it is possible to reduce the Federal Estate Tax due from both my estate and my Husband's estate to zero by allocating less than the amount specified in sub-paragraph A (1) to my Testamentary Trust created in paragraph A (1) and more to my Residuary Estate, then I direct that the amount going to my Residuary Estate be funded in the maximum amount which will make my Husband's taxable estate not exceed the deduction equivalent of the Unified Credit Against Estate Tax allowed under Section 2010 of the Code, reduced by that portion of the Unified Credit Against Estate Tax that may have been applied or allocated to gifts made by my Husband during his lifetime. The balance of my estate, in such case, shall be allocated to my Testamentary Trust.

B. My Trustees shall hold, manage, invest and reinvest the property received by them pursuant to Paragraph A, collect the income therefrom, and after deducting all charges and expenses properly attributable thereto, at least as often as quarter annually, pay to apply all of such net income to or for the use and benefit of my Husband during the lifetime of my Husband.

C.   My Trustees are authorized to pay or apply to or for the use and benefit of my Husband so much (even to the extent of the whole) of the principal of the trust created hereunder as my Trustees, in their absolute discretion shall deem advisable in the best interest of my Husband.

D.   Upon the death of my Husband the Trust created under the provisions of this Paragraph 4 of my Will shall terminate and any balance of principal or interest remaining therein shall go in equal shares to my children. In the event that either of my children dies prior to becoming entitled to a share, the interest of said child shall cease; except that if said child is survived by children, there shall be paid to said children, in equal amounts, the share to which the deceased child would have been entitled.

5. RESIDUARY ESTATE.

A.   If my Husband survives me, I give, devise and bequeath to him all of the rest, residue and remainder of my estate of any kind, nature or description whatsoever.

B.   If my Husband predeceases me or dies in a common disaster with me, then the remainder of my entire Residuary Estate shall go, in equal shares, to my children. In the event that any of my children dies prior to becoming entitled to a share, the interest of said child shall cease; except that if said child is survived by children, there shall be paid to such children, in equal amounts, the share to which the deceased child would have been entitled.

6. INFANT'S SHARE.

Whenever all or any part of the corpus of a trust or of my residuary estate shall vest in absolute ownership in a minor, I authorize and empower my Trustees, in their discretion, to hold the property so vested in such minor, or any part thereof, in a separate fund for the benefit of such minor. The property so held may consist of investments not authorized by law for trust funds, and my Trustees are empowered to invest and reinvest the same, collect the income therefrom, and during the minority of such minor, to apply so much of the corpus and so much of the net income thereof to the support, education and maintenance of such minor, as my Trustees shall see fit, and to accumulate, invest and reinvest the balance of the income until such minor shall attain the age of Twenty-One (21) years, and thereupon to pay over the corpus, together with any accumulated and undistributed income, to such minor; if such minor shall die before attaining the age of Twenty-One (21) years, the corpus, together with any accumulated and distributed income, shall be paid over to the estate of such minor. The authority conferred upon my Trustees by this Paragraph shall be construed as a power only, and shall not operate to suspend the absolute ownership of such property by such minor or to prevent the absolute vesting thereof in such minor. With respect to the administration of any such property which shall vest in absolute ownership in a minor, and which shall be held by my Trustees as authorized in this Paragraph, my Trustees shall have all the powers vested in them under the provisions of this Will.

7. <u>POWERS OF FIDUCIARIES</u>.

In the administration of my estate and of the trusts established under this Will, my Executor and Trustees shall have the following powers, which shall be exercised primarily in the interests of the life beneficiaries:

(a) To retain, in their absolute discretion and for such period as to them seem advisable, any and all investments and other properties held by me at my death without liability for any loss incurred by reason of the retention of such investments or properties.

(b) To change investments and properties, and to invest and reinvest all or any party of the corpus of my estate, or of any of the trusts hereby established, in such securities, investments or other property as to them seem advisable and proper, irrespective of whether the same are authorized for the investment of trust funds by the Laws of the _____ or otherwise.

(c) To sell all or any part of the property of whatsoever kind of which I may die seized or possessed, or to or in which I may be or become in any way entitled or have any interest whatsoever, or over which I may have any power of appointment, or which at any time may constitute a part of my estate or of the trusts hereby established, at such time, upon such terms, for cash or on credit, with or without security, in such manner and at such prices, either at publish or private sale, as to them shall deem advisable and proper, and to execute good and sufficient deeds and bills of sale thereof.

(d) To lease any property held by them and fix the duration of the term, irrespective of the provisions of any statute or of the termination of any trusts; and to mortgage, pledge, collect, convert, redeem, exchange, or otherwise dispose of any securities or other property at any time held by them.

(e) To borrow money, whether to pay taxes, exercise subscriptions, rights, and options, pay assessments or to accomplish any other purpose of any nature incidental to the administration of my estate or of the trusts hereby established, and to pledge any securities or other property held by them as security therefore.

(f) To enforce any bonds, mortgages, security agreements, or other obligations or liens held hereunder; to enter upon such contracts and agreements and to make such compromises or settlements of debts, claims, or controversies as they may deem necessary or advisable; to submit to arbitration any matter or difference; to vote personally or by proxy any shares of stock which may at any time be held by them hereunder, and similarly to exercise by attorney any rights appurtenant to any other securities or other property at any time held by them hereunder.

(g) To consent to the reorganization, consolidation, merger, liquidation, readjustment of or other change in any corporation, company or association, or to the sale or lease of the property thereof or any part thereof, any of the securities or other property of which may at the time be held by them hereunder, and to do any act or exercise any power with reference thereto that may be legally exercised by any person owning similar property in his own right, including the exercise of conversion, subscription purchase, or other options, the deposit or exchange of securities, the entrance into voting trusts, and the making or agreements or subscriptions which they may deem necessary or advisable in connection therewith, all without applying to any court for permission so to do, and to hold and redeem or sell or otherwise dispose of any securities or other property which they may so acquire, irrespective of whether the same be authorized for the investment of trust funds by the Laws of the _____ .

(h) To cause to be registered in their own names, without qualification or description, or in their names as executors or trustees hereunder, or in the names of their nominee or nominees, without qualification or description any securities at any time held in my estate or in the trusts hereby established.

(i) To determine the manner in which the expense incidental to or connected with the administration of my estate and the trusts hereby established shall be apportioned as between income and principal.

(j) To carry out agreements made by me during my lifetime, including the consummation of any agreements, relating to the capital stock of corporations owned by me at the time of my death, and including the continuation of any partnership of which I may be a member at the time of my death whenever the terms of the partnership agreement obligate my estate or my personal representative to continue my interest therein, and to enter into agreements for the rearrangement or alteration of my interests or rights or obligations under any such agreements in effect at the time of my death.

(k) To apportion extraordinary and stock dividends received by them between income and principal in such manner as they may see fit; provided, however, that all rights to subscribe to new or additional stock or securities, and all liquidating dividends shall be deemed to be principal.

(1) Except as otherwise may be specifically directed in this Will, to make any division or distribution required under the terms of this will in kind or in money, or partly in kind and partly in money, and to that end, to allot to any part or share such stock, securities, or other property, real or personal as to them seems proper; provided, however, that the Trustees shall not be required to make physical division of the funds except when necessary for distribution of the principal, but may in their discretion keep the trusts in one or more consolidated funds; nor shall the trustees be required to make any provision on account of the diminution or increase in value of any securities or investments at any time constituting a part of my estate or of the trusts hereby established, or for depreciation in respect of any tangible property, or for the purpose of amortizing or making good any amounts paid in premiums on the purchase of securities or of any other property.

(m) My Executor shall have full discretionary power, without order or approval of any Court, to qualify any trust hereunder (which would otherwise qualify for the marital deduction under IRC Section 2056(b)(7) as a Qualified Terminable Interest Property Trust by making an election on the Federal estate tax return required to be filed for my estate. My Executor's decision as to whether or not an election should be made under this provision shall be in their sole discretion; shall be binding on all persons, whether adult, minor or not yet being, and organizations; and such election or omission to elect shall not render my Executor liable for any loss or increased tax liability sustained by any such person or organization by reason thereof.

My Executor and Trustees may freely act under all or any of the powers by this Will given to them in all matters concerning my estate and the trusts hereby established, after forming their judgment based upon all the circumstances of any particular situation as to the wisest and best course to pursue, without the necessity of obtaining the consent or permission of any person interested therein, or the consent or approval of any court, and notwithstanding that they may also be acting as individuals, or as trustees of other trusts, or as agents for other persons or corporations interested in the same matters, or may be interested in connection with the same matters as stockholders, directors or otherwise; and the devisees and bequests, in trust or otherwise, made in this Will have been so made in contemplation of such freedom of judgment and action.

The powers herein granted to my Executor and Trustees may be exercised in whole or in part, from time to time, and shall be deemed to be supplementary to and not exclusive of the general powers of executors and trustees pursuant to the law, and shall include all powers necessary to carry the same in effect. The enumeration of specific powers herein shall not be construed in any way to limit or affect the general powers herein granted. Notwithstanding any other provisions in this Will, my Executor and Trustees shall not exercise any power in a manner inconsistent with the right to the beneficial enjoyment of trust property accorded to a life beneficiary of a trust under the general principles of the law of trusts.

8. **DEALINGS WITH FIDUCIARIES.**

No person dealing with my Executor, Alternate Executors, Trustees, Alternate Trustees or Successor Trustees, shall be obligated to see to the application of any monies, securities, or other property paid or delivered to them, or to inquire into the expediency or propriety of any transaction or the authority of my Executor or Trustees to enter into and consummate the same upon such terms as they may deem advisable.

9. **SPENDTHRIFT CLAUSE.**

No interest of any beneficiary in the corpus or income of my estate or of any trust created hereunder shall be subject to assignment, alienation, pledge, attachment or claims of creditors of such beneficiary and may not otherwise be voluntarily or involuntarily alienated or encumbered by such beneficiary, except as may be otherwise expressly provided herein.

10. **RULE AGAINST PERPETUITIES.**

If any trust created hereunder shall violate any applicable rule against perpetuities, accumulations or any similar rule or law, my Trustees are hereby directed to terminate such trust on the date limited by such rule or law, and thereupon the property held in such trust shall be distributed to the persons then entitled to share the income therefrom in the proportions in which they are then entitled to share such income, notwithstanding any provision of this Will to the contrary. No power of appointment granted hereunder shall be so exercised as to violate any such applicable rule or law and any attempted exercise of any such power which violates such rule or law shall be void notwithstanding any provision of this Will to the contrary.

11. **APPOINTMENT OF FIDUCIARIES.**

I hereby nominate and appoint my beloved Husband, _____, as Executor of this my Last Will and Testament. In the event of his death or disability, then and in such event, I nominate and appoint _____ as my Alternate Executors. I nominate and appoint _____, or the survivor, as my Trustees under the trusts created herein. In the event that there be only one Trustee remaining, I authorize, empower and direct said Trustee to name one (1) or more Successor Trustees so that there shall at all times be at least two (2) Trustees. Alternate and Successor Trustees shall have all the power and authority of the original Trustees. I request that my Executor, Alternate Executors, Trustees, Alternate Trustees and Successor Trustees be not required to give bond for their faithful performance as Executors and Trustees, and I hereby expressly authorize and empower my said Executor, Alternate Executors, Trustees, Alternate Trustees and Successor Trustees to sell and dispose of my estate, real, personal and mixed, or any part thereof without any obligation on the part of the purchaser to the application of the purchase money for the purpose of discharging any debts or claims against my estate or for the distribution thereof.

WITNESS my hand and seal this _____ day of _____, 19__.

_____ (SEAL)
Name of Testatrix

The above instrument, consisting of ___ typewritten pages, including the page on which we, the undersigned, have subscribed our names as witnesses, was at the date thereof subscribed, sealed, published and declared by _____, the aforesaid Testatrix, as and for her Last Will and Testament, in the presence of us and each of us, who at her request, in her presence and in the presence of each other, have hereunto subscribed our names as witnesses thereof.

_____ residing at _____

_____

_____ residing at _____

_____

Glossary

(Note: The words are given their meaning as used in the preceding text which is not necessarily the usual dictionary meaning.)

Agent: One who acts for another, the principal, by authority of the principal and only with regard to those acts specified by the principal. *See* Power of Attorney.

Alimony: Usually fixed, periodic payments established in a decree of divorce or legal separation issued by a court, or in a written settlement agreement, requiring one spouse to make the payments to the other spouse. Also sometimes called spousal maintenance or support.

Alternate Valuation Date: A date (usually) six months after a decedent's death which an executor can elect in lieu of date of death for purposes of valuing the assets of the decedent's gross estate.

Annual Exclusion: The sum of $10,000 ($20,000 for a married couple) or assets amounting to that sum in value. This amount may be given annually to each and every donee free of federal gift tax, provided it is a gift of a *present* interest (as opposed to one which only becomes effective in the future).

Antenuptial Agreement: A contract or agreement made between a man and woman before marriage in contemplation and in consideration of marriage, in which the property rights of each party are fixed by the terms of the contract rather than by state law.

Basis: Usually the cost of an asset. *Adjusted basis* is generally original cost increased by capital improvements and decreased by capital writeoffs such as depreciation or depletion. On the sale of the asset, the amount of taxable gain or loss is determined by the difference between basis (original or adjusted) and amount realized.

Beneficiary: One entitled to gifts by will; one entitled to receive the benefit of property held in a trust; one named to receive life insurance proceeds or survivor benefits under a pension plan.

Capital Assets: In general, all property that you own. **Capital gain** or **loss** is generally the difference between the amount received on the sale of an asset and its cost basis or adjusted basis. There are special IRS rules for reporting capital gain or loss income.

Cohabitation: The act of living together engaged in by two persons without any pretensions of being married.

Common Law: The law that this country received from England based on juristic theory, court decisions, and some early English statutes. It designates that portion of the common law of England which had been adopted and was in force here at the time of the Revolution. It is recognized as an organic part of the law of a majority of American states.

Common-Law Marriage: A form of marriage not entered into in accordance with religious or civil requirements but with the intent to live together as husband and wife and a holding out to others of that relation. Elements required for a relation to be considered a common-law marriage vary among the states that recognize this status (many do not).

Community Property: A form of co-ownership of property by husband and wife in which each spouse owns an individual one-half interest in assets and earnings acquired during the marriage. The system prevails in: Arizona, California, Idaho, Louisiana, Nevada, New Mexico, Texas, Washington, Wisconsin, and Puerto Rico. Does not include property owned by a spouse before marriage or acquired during marriage by gift or inheritance or any property which the married person designates as "separate." *See* Separate Property.

Conservator: One appointed by a court to conserve and manage the affairs, particularly financial, of a person found by the court to be incompetent or incapable of managing his/her property.

Consideration: Anything of value (not necessarily money) that provides the inducement for entering into a contract.

Corpus: The property making up the principal of a trust, as distinguished from the income it produces.

Co-Tenancy: Co-ownership. *See* **joint tenancy, tenancy by the entireties,** and **tenancy in common** for definitions of various forms of co-ownership.

Curtesy: Estate allowed by common law to a surviving husband in the real property left by his wife, provided they had lawful issue. Now largely abolished or modified by state statutes.

Custodian: The term used in the Gifts to Minors Statutes to designate the one who receives the minor's property with fiduciary power to use it for the minor until majority.

Decedent: A deceased person, usually (but not always) referring to a person who has died recently.

Deed: A written conveyance of property transferring title from one to another. Should be distinguished from a Deed of Trust.

Deed of Trust: A document used in certain states in lieu of a mortgage. In a Deed of Trust, legal title to property (usually real estate) is placed in a trustee, or trustees, to hold while purchasers of the property make periodic payments. Similar to a mortgage securing payment for the property but differing in form.

Depreciable Property: A business or income-producing asset with a useful life determined according to specific IRS rules.

Depreciation: An accounting concept describing a deduction for income tax purposes in writing off the taxpayer's cost of depreciable property used in business, profession, rental or other income-producing activities, according to specific provisions of the tax law.

Devise: A testamentary gift of land or real property by the last will and testament of the donor.

Devisee: One who receives the gift by will.

Domicile: The place of one's permanent home. Estates are administered and wills probated in the state of decedent's legal home at time of death. It is also the state entitled to collect any estate or inheritance taxes due the state.

Donee: The one to whom a gift is given.

Donor: The one who makes a gift.

Dower: The interest in the real property of a husband which a wife has during the marriage unless she releases her dower right by signing a deed conveying the real property to another. If not released, it is an inchoate interest that becomes a claim against his estate upon the husband's death. Applies only in common law states, and in most of these, dower has been abolished or modified by statute. In some states where dower still exists, it can apply to either spouse.

Durable Power of Attorney: A written document confering authority on an agent to act on behalf of the principal which by the terms of the writing continues this authority beyond the incapacity of the principal. Sometimes a person will give such a power provided it only becomes exercisable upon the principal's disability or legal incompetence. *See* Power of Attorney.

Elective Share: Share of a decedent's estate which a surviving spouse may elect to take after renouncing or dissenting from the decedent spouse's will. It is usually the same share designated by statute as that to which a surviving spouse is entitled if the decedent spouse died intestate (without a will). Sometimes called "statutory share." Taking the elective or statutory share is also called "taking against the will."

Equitable Distribution: System of distribution of property by a court upon dissolution of a marriage based on fairness in consideration of certain factors, often specified by statute. State statutes define the court's authority and frequently provide guidelines for its action; these guidelines vary from state to state. Such statutes are in force in virtually all states.

Equitable Title: Beneficiaries of a trust are said to have "equitable title," while the trustee has "legal title." Equitable ownership is the interest of a person who has a beneficial right in property, such as in a trust, but the legal title is in the trustee. Business is conducted with the trustee having **legal** title. *See* **trust.**

Estate: Anything one owns is that person's "estate." It may vary all the way from "fee simple" (absolute) ownership of real property to a "life estate," which is only an interest for life. For example, a person who has a life estate may live on the property or receive income from property during his/her life. Estate designates the real or personal property in which one has a right of ownership or an interest.

Estate Tax: The death tax imposed by the federal government and some states on the estate of a decedent, taxing the transfer of property at the owner's death. At present (1991) and until changed by Congress, the federal tax is imposed if the value of a decedent's taxable estate (after allowable deductions) is greater than $600,000. Of course, a life interest (see above) would not be subject to estate taxation, because the value of such an interest ended with the holder's death.

Exemption Equivalent: The value of property that may be transferred during life by gift or at death by will or that descends at death by intestacy (where the decedent had no will) or by operation of law (as to a joint owner survivor) without incurring any federal gift or estate taxes. It is the figure arrived at by applying a unified estate and gift tax credit against the tax computed on a taxable gift or estate according to a federal rate schedule. (IRS Code Section 2001). The resulting amount is the **exemption** on which a tax will not apply. The present amount of this exemption is $600,000.

Fee Simple: The maximum ownership of property possible in law. It is the entire or whole ownership of real property with unconditional power of disposition during the owner's life or at death by will or, if undisposed of, descending by state laws of intestacy to the decedent's heirs.

Feme Sole: A single woman; could be married but designated to have certain property ownership rights as "though she were a feme sole."

To be contrasted with a "feme covert," meaning a married woman, who had certain legal disabilities at common law.

Generation-Skipping Tax: A tax imposed on any transfer skipping a generation (as, for example, a transfer from a grandparent to a grandchild). Congress intended that this tax would be substantially equal to the gift or estate tax that would have been due if the property had been transferred to each generation in turn. There is (according to present law) an exemption of $1 million for each person making a generation-skipping transfer.

Generation-Skipping Trust: A trust established to administer a generation-skipping transfer.

Gift Tax: A tax imposed by the federal government since 1932 (and by some states) on transfers of property by gift during the donor's lifetime. Gifts of assets or money in an amount greater than the $10,000 per donee annual exclusion currently in effect are subject to the federal gift tax but may be offset by the unified gift and estate tax credit (*see* Unified Credit). The unified credit provisions are intended to equalize the tax effect of gifts made during life or from an estate at death.

Grantor: The one who establishes a trust. Also sometimes called Settlor or Trustor.

Gross Estate: For purposes of federal estate tax, all property, including interests in property, owned at time of death. To be distinguished from **taxable estate**, which is the gross estate minus certain allowable deductions.

Heirs at Law: Those who are entitled to the property of one who has died intestate according to applicable state law. "Heir" often is used loosely to refer to one who inherits either by operation of law or by will.

Incidents of Ownership: The rights an owner has in a life insurance policy, such as the right to cash it in, to borrow against it, etc., or other evidences of ownership such as paying the premiums directly. If the insured retains such incidents of ownership the proceeds, of the policy become an asset of that person's estate and subject to tax in a taxable estate.

Inheritance Tax: A tax imposed in some states on receipt of an inheritance. The rate applicable varies with the degree of the heir's relationship to the deceased.

Inter Vivos: During life.

Intestacy: The state of dying without a valid will. State laws of descent and distribution then determine who will inherit the decedent's property.

Intestate: Description of a decedent who had not made a will. That decedent is said to have died "intestate." One who makes a will that fails to dispose of the entire estate dies partially intestate.

Irrevocable Trust: A trust which by its terms cannot be revoked or recalled by its creator.

Last Will and Testament: A legally enforceable statement of the maker's wishes (usually) regarding disposition of money and assets after death and not operative until the death of the will maker (called "Testator.") Until death it is revocable and amendable (by means of a codicil).

Joint Tenancy: Co-ownership between two or more people with right of survivorship, meaning a survivor takes the decedent's interest by operation of law. Abbreviated: "JTRS." Avoids probate.

Legacy: A gift of money by will. The one who takes is a "legatee."

Life Estate: The right to use or receive the income from property during life.

Living Trust: A trust established during a person's lifetime. Also called an inter vivos trust. *See* **trust.**

Marital Deduction: A deduction that applies to transfers between spouses allowed in computing federal gift tax or estate tax liability. It is available for lifetime gifts to a spouse and for transfers at death to a surviving spouse. The transfer must be in one of several possible forms that "qualify" for the deduction. Since 1981, there has been no ceiling on the amount of this deduction, resulting in transferability between spouses free of federal gift tax or estate tax.

Marital Property: Property acquired by married individuals during the marriage except that acquired by either spouse by gift or inheritance or traceable to such separate property.

Partition: A court proceeding established by law in most states allowing a co-owner of property to petition for a separation of the co-ownership interests. Not available where property is held as tenants by entireties, except upon divorce.

Personal Property: Tangible or intangible "movable" property; chattels; things; certain rights.

Power of Attorney: A document granting authority to an agent (not necessarily an attorney) to act on behalf of the principal (the one who appoints the agent). It may be general (giving broad authority) or special (limited to particular specified acts). Actions by an agent authorized under the terms of the power of attorney are legally binding on the principal. Sometimes the agent is called "attorney in fact." *See also* **Durable Power of Attorney.**

Probate: The administration of a decedent's estate under supervision by a state court. Probate estate refers to the property subject to that administration, i.e., that owned outright by the decedent. Joint property that passes by right of survivorship is not administered by the probate court. The potentially taxable estate of a decedent might include everything the decedent owned, including nonprobatable assets.

Probate Court: A court that has jurisdiction over administration of decedents' estates, whether transfers are made by will or the state law of descent and distribution (intestacy). The same court usually also has jurisdiction over conservatorships and guardianships.

Qualified Terminable Interest Property ("QTIP"): One of the several forms of transfer that will qualify for the marital deduction under the federal estate tax law. The deceased spouse's executor must elect to claim the property on the decedent's estate tax return; the surviving spouse must be entitled to all of the income from the qualifying property for life; the deceased spouse's will may designate the recipient of the property after the surviving spouse's death; and the value of the property will be treated as transferred by the surviving

surviving spouse and taxed accordingly. Such terminable interest property "qualifies" for the 100 percent marital deduction.

Revocable Living Trust: A trust that by its terms may be changed or revoked. Usually established as a means of providing management during life and transfer of assets at death without the necessity of probate as to the assets in the trust. Does not provide protection from income or estate taxes. Often used as a will substitute.

Real Property: Land, including buildings and structures on the land with items permanently affixed to them. Ownership of real estate is transferred by deed signed by the transferor and identifying the transferee. Some states require a deed to be recorded in order to take effect.

Separate Property: Property owned by a married person in a community property state which is not community property. It includes property acquired before the marriage, property acquired during the marriage by gift or inheritance, and property acquired during the marriage traceable to proceeds of the sale of other separate property. It can also be used to describe similar property of married persons not residing in a community property state. State laws vary as to whether title alone determines ownership between spouses when the property was acquired during the marriage.

Settlor: One who establishes a trust. Also called trustor or grantor.

Statutory Share: Shares of an estate taken by heirs of a decedent who died without having made a will. State laws establish the proportion of the estate taken by certain heirs, based on family relationship to the decedent. Also used to refer to the share a surviving spouse may elect to take (in some cases as specified in state law) when renouncing the share designated in the will of the decedent spouse. *See* **elective share.**

Stepped-Up Basis: Basis assigned to assets transferred at death. It is the date of death value (or value on a date six months thereafter, if elected by the executor). It is said to be "stepped up," but the term merely reflects the expected effect of inflation on assets in an estate. This may benefit an heir because the "stepped-up basis" becomes the heir's basis for income tax purposes on a sale of the inherited property.

Taxable Estate: The dollar value of a gross estate less all allowable deductions to which the rate structure is then applied to fix the federal estate tax due (before subtracting credits). Gross estate is the total inventory of property that can be taxed by an estate tax, as established in the Internal Revenue code.

Tenants by the Entireties: A co-tenancy with right of survivorship, but the co-tenants must be husband and wife. Unlike the joint tenancy, one tenant cannot sever the co-tenancy alone. It will be changed only if both spouses act in concert or if there is a divorce. A divorce severs the "entirety."

Tenancy in Common: Co-ownership between two or more parties in which each co-owner holds a defined percentage of the whole and there is no right of survivorship between the co-owners, so that a deceased co-tenant's share passes through his or her estate.

Tentative Tax: Federal transfer tax on a gift or estate before the unified credit is applied. *See* **Unified Credit.**

Testamentary: Pertaining to transfer effective at death of the transferor. Testamentary gift is one made by terms of a will. A testamentary trust is one created in a will.

Title: Evidence of right of ownership, usually (but not exclusively), as to real estate. Title deed is a document that establishes title to property.

Transfer Tax on a Gift: A tax levied by the federal government or a state on gratuitous transfers of property during life (inter vivos gift) or at death (testamentary gift).

Trust: A form of property holding in which ownership is divided between a trustee or trustees holding legal title and one or more beneficiaries who hold equitable title. The trustees have a fiduciary duty to manage and distribute the property or its earnings to or for the benefit of the beneficiaries.

Trustee: A person, persons, or institution appointed to carry out the terms of a document establishing a trust.

Unified Credit: A credit against the federal transfer taxes that otherwise would be payable on inter vivos gifts or death transfers. The unified estate and gift tax credit is $192,800 for decedents dying in 1987 and thereafter (unless the law is changed). The credit must be applied to reduce any gift taxes on lifetime transfers, but to the extent it is so applied the amount of credit available for taxable transfers at death is reduced.

Uniform Gifts to Minors Acts: Statutory authority for making gifts to a minor by delivery to a custodian empowered by state statutes to hold and use the property for the benefit of the minor until the age of majority according to state law. *See* **custodian.**

Index